Intensive Culture

Theory, Culture & Society

Theory, Culture & Society caters for the resurgence of interest in culture within contemporary social science and the humanities. Building on the heritage of classical social theory, the book series examines ways in which this tradition has been reshaped by a new generation of theorists. It also publishes theoretically informed analyses of everyday life, popular culture and new intellectual movements.

EDITOR: Mike Featherstone, *Nottingham Trent University*

SERIES EDITORIAL BOARD
Roy Boyne, *University of Durham*
Nicholas Gane, *University of York*
Mike Hepworth, *University of Aberdeen*
Scott Lash, *Goldsmiths College, University of London*
Roland Robertson, *University of Aberdeen*
Couze Venn, *Nottingham Trent University*

THE TCS CENTRE
The *Theory, Culture & Society* book series, the journals *Theory, Culture & Society* and *Body & Society*, and related conference, seminar and postgraduate programmes operate from the TCS Centre at Nottingham Trent University. For further details of the TCS Centre's activities please contact:

The TCS Centre
School of Arts and Humanities
Nottingham Trent University
Nottingham Trent University
Clifton Lane, Nottingham, NG11 8NS, UK
e-mail: tcs@ntu.ac.uk
web: http://sagepub.net/tcs/

Recent volumes include:
Informalization: Manners and Emotions Since 1890
Cas Wouters

The Culture of Speed: The Coming of Immediacy
John Tomlinson

The Dressed Society: Clothing, the Body and Some Meanings of the World
Peter Corrigan

Advertising in Modern and Postmodern Times
Pamela Odih

The Saturated Society: Regulating Lifestyles in Consumer Capitalism
Pekka Sulkunen

Globalization and Football: A Critical Sociology
Richard Giulianotti & Roland Robertson

Peer to Peer and the Music Industry: The Criminalization of Sharing
Matthew David

Changing Bodies: Habit, Crisis and Creativity
Chris Shilling

Intensive Culture

Social Theory, Religion and Contemporary Capitalism

Scott Lash

Los Angeles | London | New Delhi
Singapore | Washington DC

Hm
621
.L37
2010

First published 2010

SAGE Publications Ltd
1 Oliver's Yard
55 City Road
London EC1Y 1SP

SAGE Publications Inc.
2455 Teller Road
Thousand Oaks, California 91320

SAGE Publications India Pvt Ltd
B 1/I 1 Mohan Cooperative Industrial Area
Mathura Road, Post Bag 7
New Delhi 110 044

SAGE Publications Asia-Pacific Pte Ltd
33 Pekin Street #02–01
Far East Square
Singapore 048763

Library of Congress Control Number: 2009935177

British Library Cataloguing in Publication data

A catalogue record for this book is available from
the British Library

ISBN 978-1-4129-4516-5
ISBN 978-1-4129-4517-2 (pbk)

Typeset by C&M Digitals (P) Ltd, Chennai, India
Printed in India at Replika Press Pvt Ltd
Printed on paper from sustainable resources

Contents

Acknowledgements

The material used in Chapters 2 and 6 was previously published in *Theory, Culture & Society*:

Chapter 5 uses some material from 'Capitalism and Metaphysics' © Scott Lash 2007 TCS 24(5), but 60 per cent of the material is entirely new, and the arguments on value and ontology are corrected and fundamentally, re-worked.

Chapter 6 adapted from 'Power after Hegemony: Cultural Studies in Mutation' © Scott Lash 2007 TCS 24(3).

1

Introduction

Culture: extensive and intensive

Contemporary culture, today's capitalism – our global information society – is ever expanding, is ever more *extensive*. There are Starbuck's and McDonald's – indeed many Starbucks and many McDonalds – in not just London, Paris and Berlin, but in seemingly every district of Shanghai and Beijing, Delhi and Bombay, Johannesburg and Lagos, Dubai and Abu Dhabi, Sao Paulo and Mexico City, and also increasingly in Chongqing and Wuhan, in Bangalore and Madras, in Nairobi and Cairo, Buenos Aires and Bogotá. Vodafone has subscribers in all continents, BP petrol stations are ubiquitous in the United States as much as England, Carrefour is everywhere in China and Latin America, Pepsi Cola and Nike are omnipresent in cityscapes around the world. Despite the meltdown of 2008–09, the general tendency is for finance to become ever more extensive. Capitalism, society, culture, politics are increasingly extensive. It is not only multinational corporations that are driving this increasing extensity of contemporary social relations. It is international intergovernmental organizations such as the International Monetary Fund, the World Bank, the World Trade Organization, the United Nations, the International Criminal Court, the International Labour Organization, and international non-governmental organizations such as Médecins sans Frontières, Amnesty International, Oxfam, CARE International and the Save the Children Alliance. This growing extensity is also 'regional'. Thus there are regional intergovernmental economic and political organizations such as the European Union, and extensive regional trade agreements such as NAFTA, ASEAN, Mercosul and SAFTA. Extensive also are intergovernmental military organizations like NATO, as is the worldwide distribution of US and NATO military bases. There are US Air Force bases in 15 countries, US Navy in 12, Marines in eight countries and army bases in four. All this documents the increasing extensity, the extensive universalization of contemporary social relations, of contemporary culture. This growing extensity has meant, first, a gain in geographical spread. It has at the same time brought homogenization. Thus the urban homogenization based in Corbusier's identical units of habitation and the city grid model has spread from New York and Chicago to Shanghai and Guangzhou, to India and Africa and Latin America. These homogeneous units of space have run parallel to an effective homogenization of (Newtonian) time and the spread of homogeneous units of value in the commodity. And commoditization has surely been the major driver of this growing extensity of social relations.

Given this growing extensification of contemporary culture, on another level and at the same time, we seem to be experiencing a parallel phenomenon whose colours are other; they come in a different register and can only be characterized as *intensive*. The drug experience, the sexual relations, the sheer pace of life in the streets of today's mega-city would seem somehow to be intensive. The pace and volume of capital market transactions – despite the end-of-noughties credit crunch – is intensive. There is a longer-term process of intensification of culture and media – with laptops, iPhones, iPods, WiFi, YouTube, Facebook and Twitter and platforms for downloading and streaming of just about everything. Work experience is becoming more intensive. We once had life-long employment in rule-bound and hierarchical bureaucratic organizations. Now we work increasingly in often precarious 'project-networks', in intensive close personal relations of work groups for shorter periods of time bound by the length of the project, which itself is often a one-off to be patented or copyrighted. Our closest friendships may now be at a great distance and abetted by air travel, thus intensive and compressed into the shortest time. Instead of watching television over the extensivity of a weekly TV series, we may download or buy the DVD of a series like *The Wire* and watch with one or two intensively significant others the 14 episodes of a season over just a few days. If a city like Paris is organized around an extensive and open framework of Baron Haussmann's grand boulevards, there is at the same time another Paris around fractal and intensive nodes, such as the medieval Hôpital Salpetrière of Charcot's infamous neurology experiments or, say, the interior of Oscar Niemeyer's Parti Communiste Français headquarters. The City of London may have financial tentacles all around the world yet the Square Mile has a density and intensity of people and work that makes even pedestrian traffic difficult and lends its pace and rhythm to the whole of

London. We may encounter a series of identical commodities rolled off Nike production lines, but the intensity of the brand Nike, compressed into the logo, is something we never see. If we encounter successions of extensive and metric figures on our laptop computer and mobile phone interfaces, there is another smaller group of intensive software codes or algorithms, which we may never see but yet generate these figures that we do encounter. This increasing global *extensity* has conquered not just space but also time – thus the spread of futures exchanges from the Chicago Board of Trade to China's Dalian Commodity Exchange and the United Arab Emirates' Dubai Mercantile Exchange. Indeed, the size of a global corporation is no longer measured in terms of its assets or its revenues but in terms of its market capitalization, its stock market value, which is its expected future profits. Despite the meltdown of neo-liberal banking, global capitalism over the long term will inexorably remain a still importantly financialized capitalism. And this financialization has brought an intensive economic temporality. In classical industrial capitalism you bought and sold commodities in a Newtonian temporality of the present, in which each moment is experienced as a succession of nows. But financial products and transactions have a longer-term temporality built in, in which past and especially the future are infolded into the present, in what amounts to an intensive time.

We live thus in a culture that is at the same time extensive and intensive. Indeed, the more globally stretched and extensive social relations become, the more they simultaneously seem to take on this intensity. This book is dedicated to the study of such *intensive culture*.

What is intensive culture?

1. Homogeneity versus difference

Extensive culture is a culture of the same: a culture of *equivalence*; while intensive culture is a culture of *difference*, of *inequivalence*. Things and beings in extensive culture are equivalent or consist of units of equivalence. The intensive, in contrast, consists of units of difference, of the one-off, of the singular. For example, the commodity – which is extensive – consists of equivalent, indeed identical units of value. The brand, in contradistinction, is intensive. Each brand constitutes itself as different from every other brand. The brand only has value, or adds value, in its difference from other brands. The commodity takes on value as it incorporates greater quantities of homogeneous labour power or homogeneous units of market exchange. The value of the brand is inherent instead in this difference, in its inequivalence. In extensive politics, we have notions of citizenship, or 'the people' (*le peuple* in Rousseau's *Social Contract*, 1999) or the proletariat: each of these presumes equivalence. There is an equivalence of human beings as citizens, *peuple* or proletarians. This is an equivalence before the law, in which each person is the same as every other; an equivalence in collective struggle; or an equivalence of individuals constituting a body (*le peuple*) that is a party to the social contract with the state (or government). In contrast, the 'multitudes' (Hardt and Negri 2000) give us an intensive politics of difference. Each member of the self-organizing 'multitudes' is different from every other. Radical social movements over several decades have incorporated such a politics of singularity: one based on inequivalence and individuality, in which organization comes no longer from the outside – as in the classical Leninist party – but instead from the inside as self-organization. The bureaucratic and hierarchical corporation is engaged in extensive production in that it may produce a very large number of the same identical object. This stands in contrast to the intensive economy of today's project-networks, which come together for short periods of time to make one-off goods or services, in each case a different product. So at the heart of extensity are homogeneity, equivalence and identity; at the heart of intensity is heterogeneity and inequivalence, difference.

2. Actual and virtual (potential)

We encounter commodities: they are thus actual. They are actualized. We do not encounter brands. We never see a brand itself. We see branded products. Brands (Lury 2004) actualize: they generate products or commodities that we do encounter. Brands in this sense are not actual but virtual. Brands are thus intensities that actualize into extensities. To be virtual is also to be in *potentia*, to be a potentiality. A potential has an inherent capacity for growth, development or coming into being. Potent means 'to be able to'. Its roots are in the Latin *potentia*, meaning power or force or, in a sense, potential energy. The point here is that extensities are actual. They are the things you encounter. Intensities are virtuals or potentialities. They generate what you encounter. Further, extensities are fixed, while intensities are always in process. They are always in movement. This is movement not through space but the movement of change and instability in the intensity itself. Extensities have the stability of a system in equilibrium. Extensities thus are 'beings' while intensities are 'becomings'. An algorithm, i.e. software coding, is an intensity. The algorithm then generates the extensive figures and data on your computer screen. The figures encountered are actual; the algorithm is virtual. This is also the difference between material and immaterial labour (Lazzarato 2004). Immaterial labour produces difference. It produces virtuals that can generate actuals. These can be intensive goods, singular prototypes from research and development. These intensive goods are often the product of a 'design process'. These prototypes are then produced in thousands of extensive copies, in what Marx called the 'labour process'. Often these intensive designed goods are things we never encounter that produce other things we do see and buy. Thus virtual things produce actual things. The virtual things have a value in *potentia*, and the actual things have what Marx called exchange-value. That is an actual value, a price we pay for these things in a market. Things that are actual possess a figure. They *ex*-tend towards the viewer as a figure, to the hearer as a sound. Intensities, for their part, do not ex-tend towards us. They *in*-tend into themselves. Because they in-tend, we encounter no figure. Ex*tension* and in*tension*: in in-tension there is compression and in ex-tension decompression.

3. Thing-for-us, thing-in-itself: against instrumental reason

There are two ways in which we can approach beings, whether human or non-human beings. Either we can approach them as extensities – that is in terms of how they ex-tend to us or how they are for us. Or we can approach them more as intensities, that is intrinsically: not ex-trinsically but in-trinsically. We can approach them as they in-tend or in-tense into themselves. As they ex-tend to us and thus are for us, we approach these things through our categories. As they in-tend into themselves, we approach the thing in its own terms. Take you, the reader, as an individual human being. Either someone else approaches you through general categories, such as ethnicity, gender, age, degree of beauty. Or he/she approaches you in your own singularity, as you are in yourself. You will say that the more he/she can know you the more he/she can approach you in your own singularity and not through these general categories. To be treated in your singularity is to be treated as an intensity: to be treated as different from every other being. To be approached through these general categories is to be treated like an 'atom': like any other of the tens of thousands of atoms that fit into these categories. Immanuel Kant called the extensive thing, as you approach it through your or general categories, the 'thing-for-us' or the 'thing-for-itself'. It is a thing for itself, if you can imagine the thing as external to itself and approaching itself through these general categories. The intensive thing that you approach as a singularity and through effectively its own categories is the thing-*in*-itself. It is how the thing *in*-tends. Kant (1929: 266ff.) called the for-itself or the extensive thing the 'phenomenon' and the thing intrinsically or intensively the 'noumenon'. He held that we can only know phenomena. This book, contra Kant, is about knowledge of things in themselves. Knowledge of the thing-in-itself is intensive knowledge. To know the thing, not in terms of our own, extrinsic categories but in terms of its own intrinsic categories, is such intensive knowledge. To know the thing extensively in terms of our categories is also to know the thing, for example nature, *instrumentally*: as an instrument we can use for our own purposes. To know nature in terms of its own categories, to know it intensively, means a fundamental break with such instrumental knowledge. Intensive culture is intrinsically a critique of such instrumental reason.

4. Life versus mechanism

Extensities – like the bodies in Newtonian physics – do not have their own energy. They need to be acted upon from without. They are in need of external force. Intensities, for their part, possess their own sources of energy. Extensities are mechanical while intensities incorporate 'life' and are vital. Thus intensive culture is not mechanistic but vitalist. The material body in Descartes, Galileo or Newton is mechanistic. The body for Friedrich Nietzsche, in contrast, is vital. Nietzsche spoke of power not primarily acting on bodies from the outside, but of bodies having their own 'will-to-power'. Against Newtonian mechanism, Nietzsche's (1966b) will to power was life itself. All beings – human, organic and inorganic – have such a will to power. Nietzsche's will to power, his vitalism, appear again as the notion of 'desire' in Gilles Deleuze and Felix Guattari. These authors (1984: 5–6) write about 'desiring machines' in which the intensive and the material come together, in which inorganic machines themselves become vital. For Michel Foucault (2008), power is not just something that is exercised externally from above. Power is not just repressive. For him, life and intensity become also a principle of domination, in what he calls 'bio-power'. Bio-power is not a mechanistic but vitalist mode of domination, which seizes subjects through the capillaries of the living body itself. If energy is internally generated, then causation itself is no longer external but instead internal. Systems are no longer caused or organized from the outside, but instead become self-organizing. Mechanistic systems are organized from elsewhere as cause or force or energy starts as external to the system. Once the force ends, these linear systems move back to equilibrium. Vitalist, intensive systems are self-organizing, the internally generated energy tending to drive the system to far-from-equilibrium states, hence change is the byword. To self-organize – whether for systems or for individuals or indeed communities – is to be *reflexive*. At stake in intensive politics, for example, is not just mechanistic domination, domination through the mechanistic commodity and resistance through non-linear intensity. Domination itself takes on non-linear colours. Domination itself comes about through difference. If extensive culture is painted in Cartesian colours, vitalist intensive culture is very much Nietzschean.

Ontology and religion

There is in these times a lot of talk about 'ontology'. People speak about an 'ontological turn' in, for example, sociology, anthropology, geography and politics. But there is an alarming looseness to the notion of ontology that is banded about. The concept is used to cover just about anything. If everything is ontological, then the concept has little analytic purchase: indeed, it has little value in any sense. This book takes ontology very seriously, and will take it seriously not just on the level of philosophy but on the level of social theory more generally, for all the social sciences. You hear a lot about an idea of 'realist ontology'. Scholars who say they subscribe to a realist ontology insist that there is a reality outside the observer and that the observer can know this reality. This book indeed holds that there is a reality outside us. The problem is that *ontology* is not a doctrine of reality but a question of *being*. 'Realism' speaks of knowledge of reality as comprised of actual things or beings that we encounter. Ontology looks beyond the actual beings or things we encounter to the *being* of those things, to the *being* of those beings. Realist 'ontology' looks at those actual things or beings through the categories of the observer. Ontology will look at the singular and even processual nature of those beings, i.e. the being of those beings, through those beings' own ontological structures. Realist ontology, in the above sense, is thus a question of what is described above in terms of the thing-for-us; it is a question of extensive knowledge. Ontology is at the heart of intensive knowledge and intensive culture. So we want to make a first analytic distinction in terms of what is not ontological. Here such a realist doctrine of knowledge, or any doctrine of knowledge in which an observer who is separated from the world of things that she studies and understands those things in terms of our world and our categories, is *epistemological*. Intensive knowledge, in which the observer is placed in the world with the things or beings that she studies, in terms of their own world, and through their own categories, is *ontological*.

Martin Heidegger is the lynchpin of modern ontology. He formulated this very much as a student against the dominant positivist and neo-Kantian (indeed 'realist') epistemology of his teachers. These neo-Kantians, like Kant, advocated notions of extensive and epistemological knowledge. Heidegger wanted to go beyond epistemology and the knowing of beings through the observer's categories to the study of being itself. For this the very young Heidegger (Sheehan 1988: 70–1) went back to Aristotle. Aristotle did speak of categorical knowledge. But one of Aristotle's categories, 'substance', was unlike all the others. The others could describe things in terms of their external characteristics, but substance went to the heart of the being, the intrinsic being of things. To look at substance is one very important way of understanding the being of things. Most modern philosophical ontologies break with the concept of substance. But all ontologies, ancient, modern and postmodern all inquire into the being of things (beings). Thus ontology normally harkens back to Aristotle's *Metaphysics* (Loux 2003: 166–7). Aristotle's ontology was based in a more or less linguistic ontology, formed in his re-reading of the grammar of classical rhetoricians. Here his idea of substance took the role of subject of an expression and the other categories were its predicates. Say the sentence 'Susan is middle aged, female, an architect, of oriental extraction and Chinese speaking'. Here Susan is the subject and all of her characteristics are her predicates. Susan's or the subject's intrinsic being is her substance, quite apart from her extrinsic categories. But other ancient Greek thinkers, like Plato, rejected the rhetoric formulations of the Sophists altogether and did not have such a linguistic mediation between the beings that we encounter and the ideas that are their truth. This too is an ontology, a doctrine of the truth of beings, of the being of beings. For Pythagoras even earlier, this truth lay in a doctrine of number. So we can have ancient and modern mathematical ontologies, for example in the work of Alain Badiou (2005: 31–2). Here I want to lay down another marker in terms of what is ontology. Ontology is in some sense fundamentally 'Greek'. We Westerners are in a very important sense fundamentally Greek. Greek thought and its successors have focused on the *truth* of the being of beings. Eastern thought, on the other hand, which gives priority to *conduct*, is not in this sense ontological. Chinese thought, for example, works in terms of abstraction, but it thematizes the way and conduct and not the truth of being (Lloyd and Sivin 2002: 158–9).

Ontology is not just a question for philosophers. It is a question for social science in the very broadest sense too. For social scientists, ontology comes to us through one of the various forms of phenomenology. Thus Heidegger's ontology emerged from the phenomenology of Edmund Husserl. Phenomenology broke with Kant's focus on things as they are for the objective observer and went to study the being of things as they were in themselves (Husserl 1993: 48–9). Social science positivism has its roots in such extensive knowledge and the epistemological knowledge of things as they are for us. Positivists will thus study the extrinsic categories of beings such as gender, income, ethnicity, social stratification, income, etc., and they will look at correlations and regressions of how these variables work. Phenomenology will, in contrast, look at the nature of social being, at the forms of life that are at the core of say certain working-class cultures. Positivism and epistemological knowledge presumes that the observer is objective: that he/she is outside of the world that he/she studies. In phenomenological or ontological knowledge, inquiry takes place as much as possible from being in the same social world as those whom we study. Or at least from situating ourselves within our world and establishing links of communication and interpretation between this and the world of those we study.

Religion is in a very important sense at the heart of critical theory. It is there not just as a break with epistemology, but also as a critique of ontology. Here I am referring to the *messianic* ethos of Judaism and important traditions in Christianity – in particular, the diasporic Christianity of, for example, Martin Luther King. In critical theory, Jacques Derrida (1967: 166–7) formulates his notions of deconstruction and difference as a critique of ontology partly from the point of view of Messianic Judaism. He criticizes Heidegger's 'Greek' ontology from the viewpoint of the unknowable Jewish and messianic 'to-come'. If Heidegger's Greek ontology, and for that matter mainstream Christianity, for whom the saviour and the good news has already come, are about the 'already-there', then messianic thought is about what is not already there but yet to come. Thus Derrida counterposes the 'Greek' of ontology with the 'Jew' of religion. Both of these are for us – unlike extensive epistemology and positivism – part and parcel of intensive culture. Critical theory begins with Kant's (1784) essay 'What is Enlightenment?' Here Kant speaks of the three dimensions of Enlightenment: of the 'What can I know?', the question of knowledge; of the 'What should I do?' which is the question of ethics; and of the 'What can I hope?' Critical theory is based neither primarily in matters of knowledge nor ethics, but in the question of the to-come, of the 'What can I hope'? This messianism of the what-can-I-hope is at the core of the critical theory of not just Derrida but Walter Benjamin, Giorgio Agamben, Emmanuel Levinas and of course Karl Marx. Marxism and critical theory are inevitably messianic.

Derrida (1967) says that we are ultimately condemned to be 'Jew-Greeks' and 'Greek-Jews'. That we must be epistemological in our need to express ourselves in categories and the subject–predicate logic of propositions. And we must, if we want to be critical thinkers, think in terms of a more or less messianic to-come. Indeed, in a more straightforward sense, the Western tradition is indissolubly a question of Jerusalem and Athens. Mainstream functionalist sociology of, say, Talcott Parsons has been explicit about this. So has Max Weber, for whom rationalization is about both Greek reason and (Christian) religion. Now, just as 'Greek' reason has two sides, one which is intensive – substance, the idea, Pythagorean number – and the other which is extensive – Aristotle's categories, Plato's material world – so does religion. The Christianity of Weber's Protestant ethic, which constitutes part of Weber's formal rationality, is extensive. It is based on rule-following deeds. These are general rules that the Protestant entrepreneur must follow if he is to achieve grace (Whimster 2007: 56–7). They also contribute to the extensive individualism of capitalism. This is possessive individualism of any capitalist in general; it is not the intensive individualism of the singularity of the artist or

Nietzsche's *Übermensch*. Weber's Protestant entrepreneur also shares the extensive Christianity of the first three Gospels. Matthew, Mark and Luke focus on Jesus' good works – the implication is that salvation comes through works. Salvation through rule-bound good works can apply to anyone. In St Paul, however, and in the Fourth Gospel John, salvation is based not on good works but instead on faith. It is outside the extensive rules of good works, and instead a question of the engagement of the singular soul with the singular Christ. The same is true for Judaism. In Judaism there is, on the one hand, the intensity of messianism and, on the other, the rule-bound extensity of Pharisaic Law.

Overview

Chapter 2 opens our explorations into intensive culture through Georg Simmel's vitalist sociology. Here we see Simmel in a critique of positivism through sociological notions of 'life' and vitalism. Simmel opens up a life-infused notion of sociality that he understands literally as metaphysical. He does so in an argument against neo-Kantian and positivist understandings of the social 'Das Soziale'. Here he endorses Nietzsche and a vitalist reading of Goethe against the a priori epistemology of the Kantian categories. The young Simmel was a neo-Kantian and positivist. It was only later in his writings that Simmel took on this sociological vitalism. The early Simmel drew on Kantian cognition to develop a (positivist) idea of the social. Kant's theory of cognition, as developed in his first critique, *The Critique of Pure Reason*, was importantly influenced by mechanistic assumptions drawn from Isaac Newton. Simmel transplants these into a Darwinian and functionalist idea of society. Kant asks the epistemological question of how is knowledge possible, and Simmel the sociological question of how is society possible. Thus Kant addresses the epistemological a priori, while Simmel addresses the social a priori. These turn out both to be questions of 'form'. Kant's a priori forms are the cognitive categories. Simmel asks the same question: what social forms are the condition of possibility of society? In the young Simmel's neo-Darwinian positivism, form takes on the colours of function. Standing in radical counterposition to form, for Simmel, is *substance*. Simmel understands such substance as life itself, as the flux, the *élan vital*, of life. We see how Simmel's life-substance is grounded in the assumptions of Leibniz's monad; the monad, we shall see, is simple substance. And every simple substance is different from every other. Hence the monad, or vitalist simple substance, is at the same time difference. Simmelian simple substance is self-organizing. It is conceived on the lines of not Cartesian *res extensa*, but the intensity of *res cogitans*. The monad as simple life-substance is possessed with memory as trace; it is comprised of relations of perception; it is reflexive. We consider the impetus from Nietzsche and Henri Bergson in Simmel's shift from Darwinian atomistic evolution to his substantialist 'creative evolution'. We compare Marx's labour theory of value with Simmel's 'life theory of value'. For Marx, labour is the content of (value) substance; for Simmel, it is life. We examine Simmel's core notion of life as *social* substance: as a primordial intersubjectivity of flux. We conclude with a contrast of such 'flux' and flow: of such a flux of 'becoming' and invention in contrast to the flows of domination of today's global capitalism.

Chapter 3 searches for a philosophical basis of such an intensive sociology in the work of Gottfried Wilhelm Leibniz. Leibniz's monad is, for this book, the fundamental unit of intensity. Each monad is different from every other monad because each monad has a different world. The monad is ontology's thing-in-itself. And this in-itself, the intrinsic nature of the monad, is the monad's world. That is, you are different from every other being because your world is different from each one of theirs. In other words, each monad is a different point of view of the world. In that your point of view is different from mine, so is your world, and so is your intensive being. Let us go back to knowledge. I can either know you positivistically or epistemologically though my categories or ontologically (intensively) through your world. We study Leibniz in this chapter to see how indeed your world is at the same time your categories. This is also Leibniz's philosophy of language. As for Aristotle, for Leibniz these categories are predicates. For Leibniz and Aristotle the only category that is not a predicate is substance. Substance is also the grammatical subject and the categories are the predicate modifiers of this subject (substance). I can regard you epistemologically in terms of a semantics I attach to you, such as very general notions of gender, ethnicity and class. In this case, these predicates are *external* to you as a subject. But I can also, and this is Leibniz's great innovation, look at you ontologically. If I do this, then I am understanding you in terms of the predicates that are *internal* to you as a subject. To study you in terms of these predicates that are internal to you as subject is a question of intensive knowledge. To engage with you intensively, in terms of your internal predicates, in terms of your world, is to engage with you as, not a generality, but a singularity. It is to engage with you in your being. This chapter deals with Leibniz's grammar and further looks at how this ontology of predication is also a basis for Leibniz's differential calculus. Here the subject is the function, $y = f(x)$. And any actual instantaneous point along the curve of $y = f(x)$ is the actual predicate of this (virtual) function. Thus the derivative dx/dy at any point on this curve, the instantaneous acceleration at any moment, is the predicate. Finally, we look at Leibniz's contrast of substance and mechanism. Leibniz understood such Galilean (and Newtonian) mechanism as 'system'. Such system works through collisions and mutual causation of equivalent atoms and their exchange – the exchange of equivalents. Substance, for its part, is far from equilibrium. It works not through cause but representation and predication: each substance is different from every other. In positivism, we understand society as system. As positivists we use our categories and our predications to analyse the mechanistic causes of social atoms. There is another choice though. It is to treat those social atoms as themselves doing the predicating, doing the representing. In doing their own predication, those social atoms take on difference, establish themselves as differences: the atoms become Leibniz's monads.

Chapter 4 is a study of Walter Benjamin on language. Whereas Leibniz gives us a theory of intensive language, Benjamin, we will see, gives us a realm that mediates between the intensive and extensive, between the transcendental and empirical. In Benjamin, language becomes a mediator, a partly autonomous linguistic sphere of mediation. This said, Benjamin distinguishes between two types of language. These are, first, a language as 'means' or extensive mediation. This is juxtaposed to intensive language, in which language is not an instrument but a medium, an end-in-itself. Further, he displaces intensive language from ontology on to religion, on to a messianic language. Here the Jew, Benjamin, shares a certain Kabbalism with the Christian, Leibniz. We study Benjamin's essay on 'Language in General and the Language of Man'. In this essay Benjamin understands intensive language, i.e. the language of difference and singularity, in terms of the language of 'the name'. Here we see extensive language as a classificatory language of the common noun, which for Benjamin is also a language of judgement and the law. The language of the name is, in contrast, an intensive language of the singular proper noun. God gave such intensive language to man in order to name things. God names man in his singularity so that man can name things in their singularity. This again is not ontological but religious. It is religious in the sense of the messianic to-come. Benjamin contrasts the language of man with the language of things. For him, things have their own proper language, the difference being that man's language takes place through *symbols* while things speak in *images*. Thus God bequeathed to man the symbolic and to things the imaginary. We then turn to Benjamin's most prominent methodological statement in the 'Epistemo-Critical Prologue' to his *Origin of German Tragic Drama* (1977b). Here Benjamin takes his distance from Nietzsche, in an effectively religious critique of Nietzschean ontology. Benjamin thus explicitly displaces Nietzsche's 'aesthetic theory' with his own religious theory of tragedy. In Nietzsche's *Birth of Tragedy* (1966a) an 'epistemological' Apollonian aesthetic of form is rejected for an ontological and Dionysian aesthetics of life. For Benjamin, after the Fall from Paradise, which is also modernity's fall into commoditization, life is drained from tragedy and other forms of art. Thus aesthetic value, and indeed life itself, must be displaced to a messianic to-come of the singular name. Here we find a double displacement of Nietzsche's *Übermensch*. First, there is the decidedly *untermenschlich* and messianic hope of the Jew, the Black, the displaced for the to-come. Secondly, we also see the *unterdinglich* from the language of things. This subordinate and indeed subterranean language of things will inform the 'street-life imaginary' in Benjamin's world of more popular culture.

For Benjamin, capitalism worked through the extensity of the commodity. Chapter 5 outlines a possible shift in the economy from an extensive to a contemporary intensive capitalism. Marxian exchange-value shares assumptions of extensity with Newtonian physics. For both there is a move from concrete things to abstract units of analysis. There are assumptions of equivalence in Marx's units of exchange and for Newton in the make-up of physical bodies. For both there are assumptions of external causation. In classical Marxist exchange-value, both the labour that goes into producing value and the politics are comprised of equivalents, of atom-like equivalents. What Chapter 5 understands as intensive capitalism is more closely connected with Aristotle's or Leibniz's metaphysics. This is a capitalism of difference, in which, like Aristotle's substance and Leibniz's monad, each thing is different from every other. This difference extends to the labour that goes into producing these things. Heidegger, in the 'Question Concerning Technology' (1954), rethought technology via the four Aristotelian (efficient, material, formal and final) causes. I draw on these causes to reflect on Marxian value in an attempt to develop a theoretical basis for intensive capitalism. The second part of the chapter attempts more empirically to understand intensive capitalism in terms of the 'externalities' generated from what might be today's terminal crisis of neo-liberalism. I do this through a critique of Ronald Coase's neo-liberal transaction costs economics. Intensive capitalism entails a dominant role for finance. I finish the chapter with an analysis of financialization and its crisis.

Chapter 6 on intensive politics argues that a new regime of intensive power is developing in contemporary capitalism. In this chapter we contrast a previous *extensive* regime of capitalist power that is based in a politics of hegemony with a contemporary regime of *intensive* politics. I will trace the shift from hegemony or extensive politics to such an intensive politics in terms of: (1) a transition to an ontological regime of power, from a regime that in important respects is 'epistemological'; (2) a shift in power from the hegemonic mode of 'power over' to an intensive notion of power from within (including domination from within) and power as generative force; (3) a shift from power and politics in terms of normativity to a regime of power much more based in what can be understood as a 'facticity'. This points to a general transition from norm to fact in politics, from hegemonic norm to what we will see are intensive facts. The fourth section of this chapter will look at this shift through a change from an extensive (and hegemonic) regime of representation to an intensive regime of communications, and the final section considers the implications for cultural studies.

Chapters 4, 7 and 8 are fundamentally about religion. Chapter 4, as we saw, addresses Judaism, Chapter 7 addresses early, tribal religion and Chapter 8's focus is on Christianity. More specifically, Chapter 4 is Benjamin's Judaism, Chapter 7 looks at Durkheim on the very earliest 'primitive' religion and Chapter 8 examines Philip K. Dick on Christianity. Yes, Philip K. Dick, the science fiction writer: author of *Blade Runner* and *Total Recall*. Dick's very last novels registered his apocalyptic conversion to Christianity. They are science fiction but at the same time fundamentally theological. They are also a theology of the distant future, indeed an *information theology*. These three thinkers bring religion into a very significant juxtaposition with ontology. For Benjamin, religion and the messianic, the language of man, are for all practical purposes a critique of ontology. Not so for Durkheim and Dick, for whom religion is quintessentially ontological. Durkheim's *Elementary*

Forms of Religious Life (1995) addresses 'elementary' religion as experienced in *totemism*. It is the totem that is at the heart of the birth of the sacred and indeed the origins of society for Durkheim. The totem is the symbolic basis of the clan, a given number of which comprise a tribe. For a tribe, the system of individual clan-totems is the basis of 'the sacred'. This sacred is born in ritual, in totem-based, often orgiastic rituals and rites. For Durkheim, the primary condition of possibility of society is the symbol. The totems are the original symbols. They also generate an energy, a vital energy that is the primal source of motivation for social life. Thus our theme of an intensive sociological vitalism is pursued from Simmel through Durkheim. This is neither natural energy nor even psychic energy (libido), as proposed by Durkheim's contemporary, Sigmund Freud. It is instead *social* energy. Whereas Freud's libido is produced in the unconscious mind (not brain), the fount of Durkheim's social energy is the sacred. Please note here that Freudian energy and Durkheimian energy are less material than spiritual. In each case at stake is less the physical than the metaphysical.

In the sacred, the totem works through a principle of difference – each totem is singular and different from every other totem. But once the orgiastic rites come to an end in the cold light of day, these same tribes enter the world of the profane. In the profane, those totems lose their energy and become the forms, the categories of classification of knowledge. Here they are no longer singular and based on difference, but generic and become common nouns or adjectives. Readers will have encountered notions of the symbolic and its counterpart, the imaginary, in the work of Jacques Lacan and Slavoj Zizek or Judith Butler. The origins of the symbolic trace a lineage in French thought from Lacan back through Lévi-Strauss to Marcel Mauss and in Durkheim's account of religion. The elementary form of religious life is the original symbol, the totem. Durkheim argues systematically against contemporaneous English empiricist anthropology, which would substitute empiricism's image in place of Durkheim's rationalist symbol. For Durkheim, before the birth of the sacred and the social, man, like animals, operated in the register of images and the imaginary. Only with the birth of religion does man move into the register of the symbol. For him, as for Benjamin, the symbol is what makes us humans distinctively human, while the images are very much the language of non-humans or, in the case of children, proto-humans. Chapter 7 further addresses the origins of Durkheim's notion of the 'social fact'. Though this idea is later taken up by positivism and empiricism, for Durkheim, again the original social fact is the totem: the totem in the realm of the sacred. This social fact is not static but processual and incorporates vital energy. We can straight away see the parallels with Aristotle and ontology. Durkheim's singular, different and processual, life-infused social facts are indeed ontological facts. Durkheim speaks of the totems in the sacred in terms of 'substance', and in the profane in terms of 'forms'. Durkheim's sacred becomes Aristotelian ontology, the profane the predicates of epistemology – the sacred intensity, the profane extensity.

For Philip K. Dick in his novels *The Transmigration of Timothy Archer* (1991) and *Valis* (2001), religion is again ontological. For him, the religious is not the to-come of messianic Judaism but the 'ontological' already-there of Christianity, in which, of course, salvation has already happened. Dick is a Pauline. Paul's Damascus saw him break with Pharisaic Jewish Law for the faith, the passion of an engagement with Christ. This is not the 'epistemological' Christ, of good deeds of the first three gospels and Max Weber's *Protestant Ethic*, but the death-and-resurrection Christ of John, the Fourth Gospel. This critique of, on the one hand, rule-bound, and in this sense legal, Christianity and, on the other, Pharasaic Law, is at the same time also a critique of Roman Law. Paul is not a rule follower, but attains grace through coming face-to-face with Jesus Christ. Dick's Christianity is also not one of rules but immediate and intensive communication. This communication, in an age of planetary time–space compression, comes through divine invasion by a laser beam from a distant planet. This McLuhanite beam of light carries to Dick a God who is Valis, a vast, active, living intelligence (information) system. Such an immaterial divine invasion apprises Dick (and his protagonist) that he was in an earlier incarnation a first-century Christian, locked in a Roman prison. Christ Himself is an incarnation of God as this Valis, this non-linear system of differences. Christ was invaded by Valis and so is Dick. What is at stake here is not Benjaminian or Leibniz's Kabbalism. Valis instead incorporates a Gnostic God, opposed to the mainstream Judaeo-Christian God of Creation, whom Dick and Gnosticism see as blind and mechanistic. The Creation God's blind mechanism is repeated in Pharasaic and Roman Law for St Paul and Dick. It is repeated again for Dick in the corrupt, commoditized, modern American society of the 1960s and 1970s. Valis is the antidote. Again we have the battle of extensity and intensity. And again intensity is profoundly spiritual. In Durkheim, it is the distant past of the totem; in Dick the distant future of an informational utopia. The debates around St Paul have been central to cultural and social theory in the past half-decade. They have counterposed Giorgio Agamben's (2006) messianic Paul and Badiou's (2003) more mainstream Christian Paul. Badiou's Paul is very much like Dick's, though Badiou does not take on Dick's Gnostic opposition to Law. There is another parallel between Dick and Badiou. Agamben and Benjamin's critique of ontology is fundamentally linguistic. It is a critique, as is Derrida's, of Aristotelian ontology. Badiou is not an Aristotelian, but a Platonist. His being and his ontology are Platonist. He is not interested in substance and the categories as subject and predicate. Instead, like Plato, language is not the fundamental mediator between beings and ideas. Instead, Badiou looks for the ontological in mathematics, in set theory. Dick is equally Platonist. He speaks correspondingly of the pure idea and understands knowledge in terms of Platonic anamnesis or un-forgetting. The medium of such un-forgetting, though, is primarily neither language nor the mathematical, but information.

Social theory

Let me add a coda to indicate that this book is a study in *social* theory. It may address intensive *culture*, but it is *social* theory. It is not empirical sociology, though empirical sociologists will be able to draw on it. Instead of an empirical comment on, say, post-secular movements, we carry out a social–theoretical exploration into the nature of the religious. It may address a number of questions addressed by philosophy, but it does so differently. And, for example, consider the notion of substance. Most all modern philosophers reject notions of substance and indeed metaphysics. As a social theorist, I am less interested in systematic arguments against Aristotelian substance, and more interested in how we can use the notion to understand social and cultural processes. Thus Marx, Weber, Durkheim and Simmel all had notions of substance. Marx spoke of value-substance, Weber of substantive rationality, Durkheim of the substance of religious life and Simmel of life-substance. In each case, substance is a question of intensive culture while form is a question of extensive culture. Thus, for Marx, value-form was exchange-value and the commodity; Weber spoke of bureaucracy in terms of formal rationalization; Durkheim of forms of religious life; and Simmel of social forms.

There is also an implicit theory of social change in this book. My view, with Marilyn Strathern (1992) and *pace* Durkheim, is that the earliest cultures were not intensive. This is because intensive cultures are fundamentally individualistic, while the earliest cultures are not individualistic but instead somehow relational. Even with modernization not all cultures have developed in the intensive/extensive frame. Chinese culture, for example, even though attaining very high levels of abstract thought and a rationalized bureaucratic state, never primarily entered into the Western dialectic – and this indeed *was* Hegel's dialectic – of extensity and intensity. Chinese culture remained primarily relational and never took on the agonism – of competitive scholars, dramatists and politicians – of the Greek tradition. Even though Chinese culture moved, as did Western cultures, from the clan to ever more universal political and cultural, it does not take on Western transcendental individualism. With Max Weber, I do think this comes from a very specific conjunction of Athens and Jerusalem that infused the West. It was the extensive rationalization of Weber's bureaucratic state and Marx's commodity that Habermas and critical theory understood as 'system' that stood in juxtaposition to the 'life-world', the intensive sphere of family, private life, sexuality and art.

In this context of the separation of intensity from extensity, I would like to signal two processes that will be increasingly pervasive in twenty-first-century culture. The first of these concerns the rise of China and India and other non-Western cultures. These are constituted largely exterior to the intensity/extensity dialectic. Their often relational cultures will increasingly challenge Western hegemony and increasingly pervade Western culture. The second is in recent decades an implosion, a coming together, a de-differentiation of intensity and extensity. 'System', previously extensive as it becomes self-organizing and processual, takes on intensive colours. The 'life-world' for its part is commoditized, branded and turned outward on to its external surface. Power, itself previously extensive through the commodity and the bureaucratic state, becomes intensive in new non-linear forms of domination. Whereas, previously, intensity was in some sense spiritual and extensity in, say, the commodity was material, now there is a new indifference in what might be called the *intensive material*. Capitalism itself becomes more or less metaphysical, while simultaneously remaining material. Information is on the one side mind, and on the other matter: it too is thus intensive-material. A lot of this was more or less foreseen some 38 years ago in Deleuze and Guattari's *Anti-Oedipus*

(1972). This critique of Freudo-Marxism famously inaugurated the notions of 'desiring machines' and the 'body without organs'. Here desire, previously intensive and born in the unconscious mind (*esprit*, *Geist*), now merges with the materiality of the machine. Likewise, the machine and Marx's material commodity take on an intensive flux. The body, previously the home of Cartesian materialist extensity, loses its physical organs and takes on the intensive topology of the virtual.

2

Intensive Sociology: Georg Simmel's Vitalism

Introduction

Lebensphilosophie, or vitalism, would seem, for social scientists and intellectuals more generally, to be back on the agenda. One of the most successful books in the social and cultural sciences in the past decade is Michael Hardt and Antonio Negri's *Empire* (2000). Negri is a Lebensphilosoph. He is a vitalist. Negri argues for a restructured, anti-Hegelian Marxism, replacing labour with life as a central category. More accurately, he understands labour *as* life. For Negri, both labour and life are conceived as movement or 'flux'. For him, class struggle is not for labour to oppose capital in the factory, but for labour to escape from the factory. The factory is prison. And class struggle becomes escape attempts. This movement of escape from the factory is conceived as flux, as becoming, as movement: in short, as life. This is the theory of Italy's *operaista* left. It has been appropriated by the movement of the unemployed in Argentina. It is the ideology of new media artists – such as Austria's Knowbotic Research (Reck 2003: 369) – making site-specific interventions throughout Europe. Negri, and contemporary vitalism more generally, is influenced by Deleuze and Guattari. The category of life, for Deleuze and Guattari (1972), is understood as 'desire': it is an incessant deterritorialization. Desire on this account is pitted against dominant social structures, conceived as 'the symbolic'. The symbolic, taken from the work of Jacques Lacan, is to a certain extent Durkheim's *conscience collective*, as it were, grafted on to the Freudian Oedipal complex. Thus against both the family and capitalism, the *Anti-Oedipus* pitted a metaphysics of flux and flows. Vitalist politics (see Chapter 6) are the politics of movement, of escape, of lines of flight.

Today's information or media society presuppose a more or less vitalist non-linearity. They suppose non-linear, open systems. Vitalism is best understood in contradistinction to *mechanism* (Prigogine and

Stengers 1984). Newtonian mechanism understands causation to be external to beings, to systems. Cause, in this sense, is unidirectional: it is linear. The external causation of 'metanarratives' such as Christianity, Whig history or orthodox Marxism is inscribed in such a logic of linearity. Vitalism, in contrast, is non-linear, presupposing not external- but *self*-causality. These are self-producing or self-organizing systems. Such self-organization is the *ordre du jour* even in many natural sciences today. Thus the vast growth of complexity theory: indeed, the assumptions of complexity, of self-organizing systems pervading biology, chemistry and physics. Thus the renaissance of cybernetics – the renewed interest in the work of Gregory Bateson and Claude Shannon.[1]

Vitalism has, I think, three central dimensions. The first is movement, or flux: this entails a metaphysics of becoming, of deterritorialization, what the Situationists called *dérive* (Debord 1993). Its second thematic is non-linearity or self-organization, corresponding to our contemporary processes of informationalization. The third constitutive dimension is monism. This monism contrasts with the dualism of so much of contemporary theory. There is a fundamental dualism in, for example, Heidegger's and phenomenology's fundamental distinction between beings and Being. This is 'ontological difference'. Vitalism is based not on a notion of ontological difference. Instead, it is based in an ontology *of* difference. Here there is no fundamental dualism of being and beings. Rather, all being is difference.[2]

If vitalist flux opens up a window on to globalization and non-linearity a window on to informationalization, then this monism corresponds to our actuality of *networks*, of the network society (Castells 1996), which is both global and informational. In this flat world of networks, the dualism of institutions that legislate to us is replaced by the monism, the self-legislation of today's reflexive subject, of today's reflexive modernization. Here the old dualism of traditional institutions is displaced on to the flat, the monist actor-networks, whose connections and terminals stretch across the times and space of the globe. Contemporary sociology is increasingly vitalist. Three of the most influential sociological theorists of the past 25 years are Bruno Latour (1993) and his flat, global actor-networks, Ulrich Beck's (Beck et al. 1994) reflexive modernity with its built-in chronic uncertainty, and Niklas Luhmann's (1997) self-reproducing systems. In each case, there is monism, self-reproduction and becoming – the three principles of vitalism. Three of the most central vitalist (or proto-vitalist) philosophers are Spinoza, Nietzsche and Bergson. Spinoza was a monist, presuming a pantheism, an immanent religiosity, in which, as Simmel (1995: 200) noted, the human subject is assimilated to God. In Bergson's *Matter and Memory* (1991: 133ff.), things, including inorganic things, not only – at least implicitly – self-organize, but are also blessed with powers of perception. For Bergson, *all* matter has memory. Indeed for him, memory is co-extensive with life. In Friedrich Nietzsche (1966b: 447–8), there is a metaphysics in which all beings, all entities have a will to power, have powers to this extent of self-organization.

Where does this leave Georg Simmel? Simmel was clearly a vitalist in his later work such as *Lebensanschauung* (1999c). He was influenced by vitalism in his inordinately productive middle period of 1900–08 (e.g. in *Schopenhauer und Nietszche* (1995)). He even wrote a review article on Nietzsche in his early period, as early as 1895 (Simmel 2000a). In what follows I want to underscore the actuality, the relevance of a Simmelian vitalism. I want to reconstruct a Simmelian vitalism in dimensions first of nature and then of value. Categories of both nature and value are pivotal in Simmel's *Lebenssoziologie*. Then I want to move into the social dimension. I want to suggest the pertinence of a sociological reworking of Simmelian vitalism. In doing so, the task is to make vitalism *sociological*. Maurizio Lazzarato (2002) has already accomplished this on an impressive scale via the work of Gabriel Tarde. Our task in this piece is, with Lazzarato, to point to some threads of a largely forgotten vitalist heritage in classical sociological theory. It is to underscore the meta-theoretical and hence philosophical assumptions of these. It is also to give a few indications of the relevance of sociological vitalism to our age of media and communication.

Forms: from cognitive a priori to social a priori

In *Lebensphilosophie*, noted Simmel (2000b), what Nietzsche was to morals, Bergson was to *nature*. This is an unusally pregnant thought. The point here is that Nietzsche brings a very sharp notion of *interest* into morals. This is a break with the disinterested character of the moral imperative in Kant's *Critique of Practical Reason* (1956) for a notion of morals dependent on the will to power. If this, Kant's second critique, addresses morals, his first critique (*Critique of Pure Reason* (1929)) addresses nature.

The first critique presumes that knowledge in regard to nature is predicated on a disinterested observer. For Bergson, the relation of 'the observer' to nature is one based very much on interest. Kant's idea of a science of nature is based on objectivity, or what Francisco Varela calls 'third-person truths'; Bergson's, in contrast, is based on Varela's 'first-person truths' (see Rudrauf et al. 2003). Bergson brought vitalism to *Naturphilosophie*. Simmel's idea of form was heavily grounded in Kant's *Naturphilosophie*. Simmel (2000c) wrote an early paper on Kant's pre-critical monadology: on the notion of matter in Kant. Simmel understood Kant's shift from monadology to critique in terms of a move from Leibniz to Newton. Simmel wrote an essay on Bergson, in which nature as a concept assumed centre-stage only with the advent of modernity. Thus for Simmel (2000b: 53), God is to Christianity what nature is to the Renaissance and Enlightenment. From the late nineteenth century, Simmel himself sees neither God nor nature but instead 'society' (*Gesellschaft*) as playing such a role. This is challenged by his later focus on vitalism. In each case – in this transition from God to nature to society to life – Simmel sees the hegemonic category as a 'value'. In each case it is a 'form'.

Kant's notion of nature is for Simmal as a doctrine of the culmination of the Enlightenment. This is a final idealist twist of the Enlightenment. In this that nature is understood via the categories of cognition. Simmel understood 'society' on the model of Kantian nature. For Kant, the categories of cognition and perception are *forms*. They are a priori forms. Without them, knowledge of nature is impossible. Kant breaks with Leibnizian monadology and metaphysics for Newtonian atomism. In monadology, simple substance is difference (Lazzarato 2002). In atomism, it is identity. In Kantian atomism, simple substance as identity is knowable through the forms, the a priori forms of cognition/perception. In Simmel's early and Herbert Spencer influenced sociological positivism, the question shifts. It becomes no longer how nature is possible, but how society is possible (Simmel 1992a: 42–61). That is, what are the a priori social forms? What *forms* make society possible? Simmel's question is not, how is knowledge of society possible? But how is *society* possible? Kant's initial question is epistemological. Simmel's is not. Forms are what make society possible. These forms that prevent society from disintegrating are also *functions*. So the first forms for Simmel and classical sociological positivism are also functions. They are not categories of knowledge (or perception). They are institutions like the family, economic institutions, the state, cultural institutions like the church, education or art. These function-forms, though, like the cognitive categories, are abstract. Like the Kantian categories, they deal with the material. For Kant, this material is nature conceived atomistically. In the case of sociological positivism it is socialized human people, who are also treated as if they were abstract, interchangeable atoms. The Kantian scientific observer of nature understood atomistic matter through cognitive–perceptive forms. The positivist sociological observer understood society's atomistic matter through institutional forms.

Causation is in an important sense external to things in both Kant and the early sociological positivists. Yet there is a major shift in that Darwinian causation largely displaces Newtonian causation. The sociological positivists' reading of Darwin takes us not to vitalism but to a sort of 'neo-mechanism'. Newtonian causation has to do with external force applied to a body. In Darwinian causation, this is displaced by the external cause of system needs. This is clearly a different order of cause, of functional causality (see, e.g., Cohen 1978). Such functional causality is not vitalist self-causation. By 1905–06 Simmel starts to move towards such a sort of Bergsonian 'creative evolutionist' (self-causation) position. Yet Simmel, in his statements on 'society' and on 'form', throughout his career, worked from such a model of Darwinian functional causation.[3] Simmel never changed his idea of form and society. The change lies in that what he saw more or less as objective fact in his early work becomes in his later work increasingly pernicious value.

For Simmel as positivist, forms are the social a priori: for Kant, they are the cognitive a priori. The later Simmel, as he moves towards vitalism, speaks less of an a priori. Vitalism does not think in terms of a prioris. It does not speak the Kantian language of the condition of possibility. Vitalism is not interested in the condition of possibility of knowledge. It is interested in how human and non-human beings know as they do. This is always connected to interests and to power. Thus, the later Simmel speaks less in terms of an a priori but in terms of 'objectifying' (*Objektivierung*). For Simmel, forming (*Formung*) is always *Objektivierung*. Forms, whether natural or social, are objectivized. They are constituted through a process of objectification. The raw material from which they are constituted is life: respectively, natural life and social life – before they become the forms of nature and society. Objectivation (*Objektivierung*) constitutes the object, constitutes nature out of the flux of sense impressions or appearances. Here 'the heterogenous variety of sense impressions formed into units' (Simmel 1999a: 133). This is the 'flux of continuous and contiguous appearances' that the cognizing subject makes into discrete units. Before the object we have 'matter (*Weltstoff*)'. Matter is the 'vorliegen wirklichen gegebene Welt' (the actually given world before us). It is 'allein wirklich primäre Dasein' (basic effective primary being).[4] In this sense, the disinterestedly objectifying Kantian categories transform vital nature into mechanistic nature.

Simmel argues that for Henri Bergson life is as matter flux and continuous movement. Simmel understands Bergsonian life is also comprised of *images*. That is, matter in flux appears as images, as '*Erscheinungen*'. His critique of Kant runs parallel to Bergson's. For Bergson and Simmel, we, as cognizing subjects, convert continuous matter-appearances into discrete and interchangeable units. We call these 'objects', though it is the subject that constitutes them. The subject then recognizes himself as a very special object, one that is blessed with powers of reason. When acting instrumentally we are merely thinking-objects: we are caused, like mechanism, in the Kantian realm of necessity. This sort of subjectivity that is caused, instrumental and atomistic is at the basis of modern natural law. Here Hobbes extended Galileo's assumptions of isolated atoms in tension with one another to human beings involved in a struggle of all against all (Strauss 1953). This is what Simmel and Nietzsche saw as the levelling dimension of democracy and the idea of society. In his late work on 'Conflict of Culture' and 'Tragedy of Culture', Simmel (1997) speaks of form, in poetry for example, that is not objectifying. He argues that we need form to have meaning or value at all. Thus there is, for Simmel, objectifying and non-objectifying *Formung*.

Simmel's Bergson essay works through the systematic contrast of mechanism and vitalism. The implication is that society is mechanism. Simmel's focus is temporality. He observes that Kantian time, as distinct from lived temporality, is part of the same transcendental apparatus that constitutes nature as form.

He endorses Bergsonian temporality as flux. Newtonian mechanistic time is reversible and vitalist time irreversible. Time divided up into discrete and interchangeable units is reversible in that one can substitute for another. Vitalist time, unlike discontinuous Newtonian time, is *kontinuerlich*. Memory has no role in Newtonian time. Here time is comprised of atoms that are removable and can be exchanged one for the other as equivalents. There is no path dependency in Newtonian time, which is not internal to but outside life (Urry 2002). There is no future and no past. Lived time is always attuned to goals, indeed to internally generated value. It is dependent on past memory. The past and future orientations in the Bergson essay are very close to what Heidegger (1986: 130ff.) wrote in the chapter on *In-Sein* in *Being and Time*.

Like Heidegger, Simmel (1999b: 297ff.) returns to the temporal in the context of death: in the chapter on 'Tod und Unsterblichkeit' in *Lebensanchaungen*. Simmel's antagonists are Christianity and Schopenhauer. Both proffer doctrines of the will that are a rejection of mechanism and atomism Simmel argues that Christianity was to Greco-Roman fragmentation and abstract differentiation what Schopenhauer was to modern mechanism. Yet neither Christianity nor the work of Schopenhauer, he notes, was a doctrine of becoming. The assumption is instead of timelessness, of indeed not death but immortality. The difference is that Christianity has a goal and meaning, while Schopenhauer's will has neither. For Simmel, finitude means most of all that we are beings (and forms) with boundaries. These boundaries are spatial, but more importantly they are temporal. Death most fundamentally sets up the temporal boundary that defines us as forms. Without this finite form there would not be the flux, the self-overcoming, the restlessness of life. Time and death are constantly rising up internal to us. This is in contrast to the external temporality of Christianity. For both God and (Kantian) nature, there is external motivation of the individual; there is also timelessness. In God's case, there is external teleology, in Kant's nature, external causality. In Simmel, man avoids both causal and teleological metanarratives. In both positivist causality and teleological metanarratives, man is an atom and an instrument. He is an atom in what Simmel sees as the normativity of 'society', in which man is reduced to a function. In contrast, Simmel's vitalism gives us a self as a self-organizing form, i.e. a form that deals with its own flux.

Value: Nietzsche and Simmel

Simmel was, from the start, a moralist – a sociologist and philosopher of morals. His first major book was, more than *Über soziale Differenzierung* (1989c), *Einleitung in die Moralwissenschaft*. This is the positivism of the early Simmel, for whom norms differentiate out and then take on functionality.[5] For Simmel as for Nietzsche, morals presuppose values. And, Simmel is as much a theorist of value as he is of form.

If the early Simmel's positivism was evolutionary, so was the late Simmel's vitalism. He read and endorsed Nietzsche as an evolutionist (*Entwicklungslehre*). His (1995: 179) fundamental distinction of Schopenhauer from Nietzsche is that between Schopenhauer and Nietzsche came Darwin. Positivist – Darwinian and Spencerian – evolutionism thematizes differentiation. Vitalist, or creative, evolution is a question of what Simmel called '*Differenz*'. Simmel (1995: 184) discusses Nietzsche's individualism in terms of 'Wertdifferenz' or value-difference. In this, difference itself (in the above-mentioned sense not of ontological difference, but an ontology of difference) becomes a value. Classical evolutionism takes place through the accidental generation of elements – be they social or natural – that then become reproductively functional for adaptation to an emerging and changing environment. The environment is thus an external cause of changes in structures or forms or morals. There is something mechanistic – or at least 'heterotelic' – about classical evolutionism. Vitalist evolutionism is self-generated, through life's overcoming of existent forms and creation of new ones.

In mainstream evolutionism, when values differentiate, the criteria for evaluation are functionality for the whole.[6] In creative evolutionism, the criteria are which values bring man as species-being to higher levels of life. The ultimate value is the quantity of life in man as species-being (Simmel 1995: 402–3). Difference and evolution are the heightening of life as value. Because life is the most important value, evolution for Simmel becomes a move from life to 'more-life'. The value and goal of life is more-life. It is higher stages of the fullness of life and its energies. At issue here is the value of man as a form, and the evolution of forms moving from *Mensch* to the ever-unattainable *Übermensch*. Indeed, the *Übermensch* is not a form in the classical sense, but instead the unattainable value that human life gives itself. The *Übermensch* is 'Mehr-Leben'. It is a process of 'Hinauszugreifen über sich selbst'.[7]

It is self-difference (*Selbst-Differenz*) (Simmel 1995: 374–8; 1999b: 223). This autopoetic difference stands opposed to heteropoetic differentiation.

We cannot overestimate the influence of Darwinian evolutionism here. First, humanism needs to change after Darwin. Previously, humanism was a matter of human values and reason replacing Christian values. But now humanism becomes understood in terms of man as a species per se in comparison to other animal species. This is true in Marx as well as Nietzsche. Only after Darwin does man become species-being. Secondly, while before we may have had a notion of the *polity* on the basis of human atoms as in, say, Hobbes, only now, after Darwin, do we have such a notion of 'society'. The heuristic of course is the organism, with functional roles and a division of labour. Nietzsche and Simmel philosophized morals in terms of species-values (*Gattungswerte*) that were indeed human values (*Menschenwerte*). Values always presume, not just an 'is' but an 'ought': not just a *Sein*, but a *Sollen*. It is *Leben* itself that is the internalized *Sollen* here: and that *Sollen* is *Mehr-Leben*. Life carries its furthering in itself. Its immanent imperative is to be more life (*Mehr-Leben zu sein*). Morality here is the value of the individual. This morality is not, as in Kant, to be found external to the individual in his *Tun*, or his doing. It is to be found in his being, his *Sein* (Simmel 1995: 388–9).[8]

All animals, Simmel notes, work through the 'eternal triad' of desire, means and ends. Simmel spoke of man, however, as the 'indirect animal' in that the chains of means between desire and end become ever longer. These chains of means he understood as *die Technik*, as technology. For Simmel, all forms started their life as means.[9] His point was that what start as means – in knowledge, art, ethics, law, play or sport – evolve to become ends in themselves. As forms they take on a certain *Eigengesetzlichkeit* or self-legislation: a certain autonomy. But some means are somehow intrinsically means, no matter how autonomous they become, no matter how much they find their own logic. Such a means is money, the means of exchange of goods and services. A second is technology. A third is the media. A fourth might be language. Let us ask what kind of form is money. In doing so we might imagine that money stood in a relationship to life for Simmel that is similar to the juxtaposition of the media and life today. At stake are issues of value and form. The money-price of an object is its exchange-value. Marx also called exchange-value the *value-form*. If labour was the substance of value, then exchange was the form. For Marx, it is labour that is at centre-stage. For Simmel, it is life. For Marx, as we saw, labour was the substance of value. Simmel writes that life is the 'substance' of value. Such value-substance is the above-described 'von innen bestimmten Lebensprozess' (inwardly determined life-process). Simmel's masterpiece, *The Philosopy of Money*, was about the value-form. Simmel's *Soziologie* was about the *social* form. Both value-form and social form are on the model of Kant's natural forms. Both social and value-form (and natural form) presume instrumental reason.

Let us take some of these Simmelian thoughts forward into the twenty-first century. Let us ask what kind of forms are at stake where media displace money as the abstract means that define our times. Where even money takes on mediatic form. Where even more than the media becoming commodified, money and the commodity become mediatized. Where the social itself begins to be submitted to the laws of media. Society, as commodified, does become abstract and instrumental in the sense that we defined Kantian nature. When society and money are submitted to the laws of the media, then things take on a logic, no longer of exchange, but of *communication*. In the age of the commodity and the social, things become commodified, i.e. they become units of exchange. Now in the media age they become units of communication. The commodity is a unit that is exchangeable for other units. It has an abstract generality. It is instrumental. When things become commodified they take on these characteristics. When things become mediatized – and become communicators – they take on agency. In an age of media, things communicate with one another. Objects – which are no longer constituted by subjects, but which take on their own ontological status – take on powers of judgement. They take on powers of perception. Ford was commodified, Nike is mediatized. The Fordist, commodified product works differently to the Nike-ist, branded product. The commodity is a form based on a certain density of exchange. The brand is a form, one that necessitates a certain density of *communications*. When this density of communications falls below a certain level, the brand becomes entropic and the form dissolves. We are getting closer perhaps to the core of what Baudrillard called 'sign-value'. An object has exchange-value to the extent that it can attract money (in exchange for it). An object has sign-value to the extent that it can *generate* communications. Cisco-Systems, Microsoft, Vodafone and News Corporation also have sign-value as communication-generators, though a different kind of communication-generators from Nike. Surely sign-value is convertible into exchange-value.

But it is still analytically distinct. Exchange-value works through interchange-ability and indifference of units, while sign-value works through *Wertdifferenz*. Though, here, value-difference itself becomes a means of domination. Simmel, in taking the idea of form beyond and substance beyond Marxian labour and exchange to life and to culture, gives us conceptual ammunition to better grasp these contemporary phenomena.

Social substance: from Labour to life

Simmel addresses life in terms of *social* life. This is the originality of *his* vitalism. For other vitalists, relations between things or between subjects and things are primary. Relations of perception are primary. For Simmel, life is already social. For Simmel, social life is literally social *life*.[10] In Wittgenstein, the idea of 'forms of life' means mostly ways of life. With Simmel, we come to understand forms of life as forms of *life*. With Wittgenstein, there is no life without forms. For Simmel, it is life that gives rise to form. Simmel does have a notion of social *life* (*gesellschaftliches Leben*), especially in his late and vitalist *Grundfrage der Soziologie* (1999a), which he juxtaposes life to *form* of *Vergesellschaftung*. This is the social life, or social substance that is *vergesellschaftet*. Simmel speaks of individual life in terms of 'Pulsschlag' (pulsebeat), in terms of 'Energie', in terms of the 'wogenden Rythmus der Lebenswirklichkeit'.[11] Other terms are *Inhalt, Substanz, Stoff, Materie, Bewegung, Wirkung*, and *Strom* and *Fluß*. Here we might understand *Wirklichkeit*, not as reality, in the objective sense, but more in the sense that we would now call 'the real' – as distinct from the symbolic and imaginary – as intrinsically unrepresentable. In the chapter on *Geselligkeit* in *Grundfrage* (1999a), he speaks of social life (*gesellschaftliches Leben*) as a bearer of all forces (*Trager aller Kräfte*). He speaks of this pre-societal, 'not yet social' *Wechselwirkung* (exchange-effect) (1999a: 68). At stake is an intersubjective pulsion: a primary or even primordial intersubjectivity. At stake is 'the content and at the same time the matter of societalization: the stuff with which life fills itself, in order to drive its motivations'[12] (1999a: 103–4; 1999b: 216–17, 222).

This sociological vitalism is necessarily also a metaphysics: Simmel's *Lebensanschauung* is subtitled *Four Metaphysical Chapters*. Nietzsche and Bergson are confessed metaphysicians. The late Simmel as metaphysician is in search of the in-itself (*an sich*). He is not the only one. Dissatisfaction with the Kantian *für-sich* led to the *an-sich* of Schopenhauer's will. Husserl was also driven by this, his *an-sich* being phenomenology's intuition of essences. Newtonian mechanism is paradigmatic of the *für-sich*. Ethics can be *für-sich* or *an-sich*. So can values, in regard to which Simmel speaks of 'Werte-an-sich' and 'Werte-für-sich'. Clearly, money was the model of *für-sich Werte*, i.e. values with external ends. Similarly, Marx, in metaphysical mode in his *Grundrisse* (1973), distinguished between *Wertsubstanz* and *Wertform*. *Wertsubstanz* like use-value is an *an-sich*. The same was true of Kant's imperative, which defines itself as having no end outside itself. Simmel similarly addresses society. 'Die Gesellschaft-für-sich' would be society as in positivism. In contrast stands 'Die eigentlich "Gesellschaft"-an-ihr', that is 'jenes Miteinander, Füreinander, Gegeneinander, womit materielle oder individuelle Inhalt und Interesse durch Trieb oder Zweck eine Formung oder Förderung erfahren' (Simmel 1999a: 106). To translate, social substance here is 'every with-another, for-another, against-another, with which material or individual content or interest is – through purpose or drive – experienced in its form or its demands'. Simmel is saying that we experience social form. That such form is generated by social substance as conflictual, associative and ethical intersubjectivity. And that such intersubjective substance is translated into form through various contents or interests that can be individual or material. He is saying that when such substances are translated into form, they may be experienced as forms or as demands.

Indeed, what we have here is not the elementary forms of religious life, but, so to speak, the 'elementary *substance* of *social* life'. It is drives, it is *Wechselwirkung*, perhaps non-linear effects, it is flux, it is conflict and coalition: it is immediate. It is perhaps the social relation before the advent of the social bond. The dyad before any *Vergesellschaftung*. This social relation – that is, flux without form – is important. Not so much because it is primordial, but because it can also be post-symbolic. That is, because it suits the post-symbolic matrix of the global information culture. The social bond, in the classical sense of Durkheim and Mauss, was always mediated by the symbolic. The symbolic has been embedded in our classic institutions, which are just at the moment undergoing rapid meltdown. The symbolic presupposed the hegemony of the national society, which itself is being eroded by global communications. Outside and in excess of the symbolic is of course the real. But this excess is now banalized and routinized in the communication, whose real signal is also outside the national and institutional symbolic and inside the global flows. We have a post-social relation now, the communication. This is a relation after the decline of the social bond. This sort of intersubjectivity is at stake in Simmel's pre- and now post-social dyad. This is technologically mediated communication, which takes the old social bond, and stretches, shrinks, accelerates and intensifies it to the point of explosion. No one more than Simmel gives us tools to come to terms with this.

Monadology: Simmel, Bergson, metaphysics

A half-generation older than Simmel and Bergson were the first modern vitalists: Friedrich Nietzsche and Gabriel Tarde. Tarde was a sociologist and a major influence on Bergson (Lazzarato 2002). The *école durkheimienne* aimed its arrows equally at Tarde and Bergson. There has been a revivification of Tarde's work in Maurizio Lazzarato's *Puissances de l'invention, Gabriel Tarde: La psychologie économique contre l'économie politique* (2002). Lazzarato shows that Tarde, the ur-sociologist argues in effect for a 'psychological economy'. This is a psychological economy that pertains to any sort of being: it applies to human beings as entities, to societies, to organic or inorganic matter. In each case the entity at issue is understood as a *monad*. One of Tarde's seminal works is *Monadologie et Sociologie* (1999). Tarde's importance now is perhaps most of all in connection with this monadology.

Let us develop this notion further. We need to recall here that Simmel's PhD thesis was entitled *Das Wesen der Materie nach Kants physchicher Monadologie*. This seems to be the original published title. The title of the defended thesis at the Königlicher Friedrich-Wilhelms Universität, Berlin, was *Darstellungen und Beurteilungen von Kants verschiedenen Ansichten über das Wesen der Materie*. I do not want to argue that Simmel was a lifelong and ardent monadologist. We need to make a number of qualifications. First, it was the second submission for his doctorate. The first was on the 'psychological' and ethnographic origins of music. This was a more straightforwardly evolutionist argument drawing on ethnographic material in an attempt to contest Darwin's opinion that man's language use grew out of an earlier musicality. Simmel argued that language came first and music, perhaps in part as a higher, more differentiated culture, came after. The thesis was failed by the examiners because of its apparently poor documentation, and the fact that it was hastily put together and contained too many

'*Schreibfehler*' (typos). The examiners also disagreed with Simmel's method, consisting of combining Darwin's evolutionary theory and 'theorems from *Völkerpsychologie*'. The examiners, who were sympathetic to Simmel personally, suggested that the candidate submit for his doctorate another essay: the one on Kant's physical monadology that had already won him a prize in a competition for essays on Kant at the University the year before. Simmel wrote the core of this argument for his PhD at the age of 21 in 1879. The submitted thesis was only 34 pages in length. In the thesis, Simmel (2000c) contrasts the monadology of the early Kant and Leibniz with the Newtonian atomism. He largely rejected Kant's pre-critical monadology for a sort of positivist 'speculative atomism' (Köhnke, 1996; Landkammer 2001).

Simmel's theoretical evolution is more complex than often realized. The received chronology is that Simmel evolved from an early positivist to a mid-career neo-Kantian and a late-career vitalist. Yet there is evidence of elements of vitalism *and* positivism in all of Simmel's work. There was clearly a shift in emphasis after his late reception of Bergson. Yet right from the start Simmel engaged with Nietzsche and Schopenhauer. He read these thinkers as a student, before he was 20 years of age, in the Fakultät für Philosophie und Völkerpsychologie at the University of Berlin. Darwin and evolutionism were themes for both positivist and vitalist Simmel. The speculative atomism of his early positivist evolutionism indeed *becomes* the vitalism and creative evolutionism of his late period. Simmel always understood substance in terms of flux and monads. And from start to finish there was a positivist idea of form. Social forms were already functions in Simmel's failed PhD thesis on the origins of music and in the early work on *Soziale Differenzierung* (1989c). These function-forms convert substance (as monadological flux) into atoms. Sociological positivism, as argued above, is a different sort of atomism from objectivist physics. When 'substance dissolves into function' we have atomism in sociology (Landkammer 2001).

This is, of course, early Durkheim as well as Simmel. But the young Simmel – already an admirer of Goethe and Nietzsche – was less a positivist than Durkheim: he was never the consistent atomist. There was a fundamental relativism in Simmel from the start that was foreign to Durkheim. This relativism was difficult to accept for Simmel's examiners for doctorate and *Habilitation* (Helle 2001). A vitalist dimension in Simmel's early work is also suggested by its pronounced psychological thematic. This again compares with Tarde's just-mentioned 'psychological economy', in which all monads – whether an individual, a society or a bit of inorganic matter – comprise irreducible relations of affect and perception. Trained in a Faculty of Ethnopsychology, Simmel's failed PhD thesis consisted, as mentioned, of psychological and ethnological studies of music. Before *The Philosophy of Money* (1977), he published a paper on 'Zur Psychologie des Geldes' (1889). He published articles such as 'Zur Psychologie der Mode' (1992b), 'Zur Psychologie der Frauen' (1989a), 'Zur Psychologie der Scham' (1989b), and 'Zur Psychologie und Soziologie der Lüge' (1992c), i.e. on the psychology of music, money, women, shame, lies and fashion. For Simmel, there was not this horror of psychology common to the sociological atomism of Durkheim and critical Kant. Simmel's first published sociology monograph, *Über soziale Differenzierung*, was subtitled *Soziologische und psychologische Untersuchungen* (1989c). At about the same time Simmel published *Einleitung in die Moralwissenschaft* (1991). The psychology of an individual or a collective (or non-human) is by definition relativistic. It is by definition perspectival in contrast to either Kantian objectivism or Husserl's transcendentalism. Both Kant and Husserl defined their work as anti-psychologistic. As Jung (1990: 33) mentions, Simmel starts in his ethics, 'not from an a priori but from experience', from 'feeling'. This is psychological. Moreover, knowledge was not a question of a priori; not a question of experience's conditions of possibility. But knowledge began from experience – it was sociological and psychological.[13]

A few further considerations of monadology may throw more light on what sociological vitalism might be. Kant (2007) wrote on physical monadology in the 1750s, some 15 years before his critical and Newtonian period. Kantian critique was first and foremost a critique of metaphysics. It is a critique of Kant himself in his earlier metaphysical guise. Both the two predominant social-theoretical traditions – positivism and phenomenology – are anti-metaphysical. In a very important sense the progenitor of positivism was Kant's *Critique of Pure Reason* (1929), while the progenitors of phenomenology were the *Critique of Practical Reason* (1956) and the *Critique of Judgement* (1952). Vitalism, for its part, must, however, be pre-critical (or post-critical): it must be metaphysical. 'Difference' in phenomenology – Husserl, Heidegger, Gadamer – is ontological difference: it is the difference between beings and being. In contrast, difference for metaphysics is the monad. Simple substance is difference. Differences or singularities are the monadological building blocks of the world.

The word 'monad' comes from the Greek, meaning 'unit' or 'one'. In Pythagoras's doctrine of number, the monad was the One. The monad is an irreducible self-determining entity. Unlike the atom, where causes typically come from the outside, the monad is self-causing. Leibniz's monads were, first, irreducible and, second, self-determining. Third, for Leibniz, and perhaps most important, monads were less analogous of body or matter than they are of mind. They are based less on *res extensa* or material substance than on *res cogitans*, mental substance. In Descartes, the idea of the soul or *res cogitans* is thinking substance, possessing self-certainty in immediate unity (Deleuze 1993a). The mentalism of Leibniz's monad corresponds to the mentalism of Bergson's memory. It corresponds to Prigogine and Stengers' (1984) idea of inorganic physical entities, which are capable of communication and more or less reflexive. This 'mentalism' is present in Tarde's idea of monads possessing affect. The monad is defined as its perception, from its particular point of view. In vitalist metaphysics, all entities are capable to some extent of thought. A fourth characteristic of monads is their *active* nature. This is unlike the classical idea of matter, which is passive and inert, where cause must come from the outside. Monads contain powers of which they themselves are the source. Monads are thus: (1) irreducible; (2) self-determining; (3) partaking of mind; (4) active. Fifth, though monads are irreducible, they consist of relations. The relations are with other monads. For Leibniz, these relations are perceptions. Perceptions entail a psychology of the monad: they presume that monads are agents of experience. Perception is very much at centre-stage for Bergson (1991) and Deleuze (1983) in his work on cinema. For both of these writers, relation is, in the first instance, relation of perception. For Simmel, this relationality is the above-described originary intersubjectivity, i.e. his sociological life-substance. For Leibniz, too, the monad consisted of relation of perception – the sum of its perceptions of other monads. More precisely, each monad was 'an infinite series of perceptive acts defined by a unique point of view or a unique law of series' (Woolhouse 1993: 55). A sixth characteristic of the monad for Leibniz and vitalism is memory. Each monad contains its past, present and future. For Leibniz, 'Each substance contains in its nature the law of continuation of its own operations and all that has happened to it or will happen to it' (Maigné 1998: 18). Mind, for Leibniz, is importantly characterized by memory. Thus the cause, which is always self-cause for Leibniz, is also a trace. It is unique to that monad. For Leibniz, a substance always bears traces of its earlier state. These traces as causes can be discovered in the substance. This element of the thing is mind, since matter itself cannot contain such traces (Woolhouse 1993: 54–5).

Vitalism and the monad are defined against Cartesian dualism. The monad presumes neither a Cartesian dualism of substance nor a Spinozan monism. Vitalism and 'monadology' presume that every substance is different from every other substance. Leibniz has, of course, a notion of extension. We encounter entities through their extension. Yet their difference does not consist in their extension. For Leibniz, 'a body is a momentary mind, but without memory' (Loemker 1968: 362). In this sense, vitalism is a sort of 'transcendental empiricism' (Massumi 1996). In atomism, matter is extended and inactive. It is caused. In monadology, matter is not inert substance. It is 'an action that relates itself to an extension' (Maigné 1998: 51). Each monad is an entelechy, a primitive active force. Seventh, monads are not extensive. As action, as indeed reflexivity, they are instead intensive. They are intensive and reflexive also in the sense that individual substances are responsible for their own actions. Monads are unextended bodies – said Leibniz – like points or instants (events).[14] They do comprise a configuration of the monads that make up their world. The inner movement of these 'parts' constitute the resistance of such bodies to outside forces. Inert bodies have no such resistance. Finally, Leibniz's monads can carry their entire future and past in them because they are operationally closed. Leibniz's monads 'do not have windows' (Alliez 1999). A self-organizing system is in one sense open in that it is self-organizing. Leibniz's monads are in this sense like Luhmann's social systems: self-organizing yet operationally closed, not possessing 'windows' (Lazzarato 1999). The equivalents of monads in Tarde and Deleuze have windows and do not possess their entire histories and futures inside themselves. They form connections, syntheses, branches. They are, in this sense, 'rhizomatic' systems. They are 'singularities'.

Conclusions: towards a global politics of flux

Georg Simmel died in 1918 at the very height of industrial capitalism. He wrote in an age in which the emergence of the social, in the institutional sense of functioning society, gave birth to the discipline of sociology. I write as a sociologist in the information age, an age in which the ubiquity of media and communications threaten the social. Vitalism, of course, must be transformed in the information age. For example, Simmel's societalization (*Vergesellschaftung*) seems increasingly in the information age to be displaced by mediatization. Simmel described a situation in which the thing, the individual and especially originary intersubjectivity were societalized: these substances were given form through societalization. In the information age, the thing, the individual and intersubjectivity are instead mediatized. In the age of globalization and information, intersubjectivity is characteristically 'at-a-distance'. It is technology that makes possible intersubjectivity at a distance. The mediatization of forms is also their technologization.

Yet, even as media, these technologized forms do not lose their sense-making capacities. The paradigm for meaning in industrial modernity is in Kant's idea of cognition: here the subject imposed forms that made meaning possible. Simmel, as we saw above, transposed such meaning-determination on to the institutions of society. Today it is the media as technological forms that are given meaning-making powers: but these are largely outside the control of the subject and of the social institutions. In the realm of morality, Nietzsche and Simmel took the transcendental Kantian *Sollen* (the 'ought') and brought it immanent to the internal flux of the self-different subject. In the age of flows, in the information age there is no *Sollen*. There is instead a pure facticity. There may be an ethics. But there is no *Sollen*. There is a flattened and brute immanence of the 'is'. Simmel's core value in an age of societalization was, as we saw, life, or to be precise 'Mehr-Leben', that is life struggling ever to heighten life. *Mehr-Leben*, as we saw above, is difference itself. Difference takes a different form in the information age. If the media age is characterized by culture-at-a-distance, then difference itself becomes difference-at-a-distance. The core value of mediatization is thus captured less in any kind of struggle than in Situationist 'dérive' or Negri's politics of escape from the factory. These core values are the essence, the *an-sich* of mediatization. What about the *für-sich*, or instrumental rationality? For Simmel, when a product is manufactured in industry it is a form. If the *an-sich* is substance, the *für-sich* is form. In Simmel's age of industrial capitalism and societalization, this form is the commodity, or exchange-value. In the information age we have sign-value. Sign-value, in Baudrillard's sense, is not the *an-sich*, but the *für-sich* of mediatization. Sign-value thus has to do with the reproduction of the global mediascape. In the information age, difference as vitalist substance is here transformed into dead form. *Puissance* is transformed into *pouvoir*. But what sort of form is at stake in the new modes of media domination? Media domination yields a shift from the externally causing power of mechanistic form, to power that is wielded through self-causing, cybernetic forms. Self-cause entails not just outward cause, but an inward flexion. The result is that power as form becomes power as the formless, as Georges Battaile's *l'informe*, that is immaterial power.

Marx spoke of a labour process and a process of capital accumulation. The labour process is somehow frictional and concrete. The accumulation process is smooth and abstract. The labour process has to do with substance, with *flux*. The accumulation process has to do with *flow*. The externalized flows of the information society are already abstract – information, communication, finance flows; flows of technology, media, immigrants, even desire or libido. Is contemporary mediatized politics about transforming flow into flux? Are tomorrow's politics about transformation of the value-dissolution of flow into the *Wertdifferenz* of flux? Information is constitutively and already informe. But it is also already abstract, immaterial. The question is what kind of forms and what kinds of flux are at stake? What kind of forms and what kind of *life*? Labour is a process. Life is a process. '*Prozess*' is a word that Simmel used often in regard to life. So *Wertsubstanz* as labour or life is a question of process. But information is a flow, not a process. Money flows. Money is not a process.

Simmel speaks of flux and not flow. Flux is a tension; it is intrinsically struggling and conflictual. Simmel's originary intersubjectivity comprises such flux. In the information order there is a generalized *externalization* of process, of flux, of flow, and indeed the nervous system on to, as McLuhan had it, the global networks of information and communication. And it is the media that channel this flow. The media are, at the same time, socio-technical systems. Mediatization is this collapse of form into technology. Technology in Simmel's age had to do mainly with means of production. These are means that are not forms. Unlike the value-form or money or the commodity, they do not function in sense making. They function in production. Technology in our age is a matter of means of communication. Our machines are communication-machines. Flow is *Strom, Fluß*; to flow is also *rinnen*. But flux has to do with electricity, with 'ständiger Wechsel, dauernde Veränderung'. Flux is not smooth. For example, in the *Lebensanschauung* Simmel speaks of 'die ewig fortströmended Reihen der Inhalte oder Prozesse' (1999b: 225).[15] Flows are a lot smoother. The idea of life as flow seems more like the smooth idea of will in Schopenhauer (Simmel 1995: 308ff.). Flow is a-telic. It is not packed with tension, with *élan vital*. Flux is autotelic, while Flow is a-telic or heterotelic. So many of today's global mobilities are heterotelic, determined by the likes of Microsoft and News Corporation. Today's neo-vitalism must convert this into an auto-telic register. Today's neo-vitalism is an attempt to put flux back into the flow. To put flux into flow is to put reflexivity (flux is always reflexive) into globalization. Today's political imperative may be in this sense to develop a global politics of flux versus flow. Georg Simmel, in giving us a *Lebenssoziologie* of intersubjective flux, might be one source for such a politics.

Notes

1 Wiener, and what Hayles (1999: 103) calls first-generation cybernetics, uses the self-causation, which can be understood as steering in the form of feed-back loops, which constantly bring the system back to equilibrium. Vitalism presumes disequilibriate systems. Vitalism presumes an ontology of becoming. Wiener's self-causation seems to assume a normativity of stasis and hence being.

2 I do not want strongly or necessarily to assert here that Heidegger is a dualist. The distinction between being and beings does not, of course, reproduce the Cartesian distinction between *res extensa* and *res cogitans*. Indeed, for Heidegger, being is not substance. My point is only that there is a major cleavage between theories that presume ontological difference and those that presume an ontology of difference.

3 In functional causality the system's environment that selects system attributes. Yet the system must somehow generate these attributes. Hence functional (evolutionary) causation has an element of self-generation that mechanistic causality lacks. Yet functional causality is basically extensive. In functional causality, what is being caused is something like a species, whereas in vitalist causality it is an individual.

4 This idea of life seems perhaps as much a question of disorder as of self-organizing systems. In the question how is society possible, the fear is of anarchy. Simmel's vitalism was never as all-encompassing as Tarde's or even Nietzsche's. It was always a bit more humanist. In affirming life with Simmel, we are looking at flux as much as self-organizing monads. Contemporary vitalism seems to have these two poles. In Deleuze and Guattari's *Anti-Oedipus* (1984), for example, life is conceived primarily as flux or desire. In say, Prigogine and Stengers' *Order Out of Chaos* (1984), life is primarily self-organizing monads. Simmel, of course, as we see below, also has a strong notion of life as form and not just life as substance. Indeed, there are two types of forms in Simmel monadological and atomistic.

5 Josef Bleicher, in a personal communication, insightfully notes that Simmel's *Moralwissenschaft* is a science of morals more than it is a moral or ethical doctrine. Simmel, Bleicher observes, took the idea of *Moralwissenschaft*

from Dilthey, who himself took it from J.S. Mill's moral science. For the neo-Kantians this *Moralwissenschaft* had also become the *Geistes-* or *Kulturwissenschaften*. Dilthey and Simmel both, Bleicher argues, move from such a neo-Kantianism to a focus on life. There was, as Bleicher maintains, a vitalist strain in Simmel even in his middle period. Simmel's lifelong preoccupation with Goethe was very much vitalist. In Goethe's notion of colour, the object (in opposition to the object in Renaissance perspective) seems to possess its own light. Vitalism in cultural and social theory, it seems to me, does have a concern with value. Though it breaks, I think, with notions of judgement. It is also not at all primarily a morality or an ethics. It is profoundly anti-Kantian. Values and norms in vitalism are important for their 'facticity' rather than as part of ethical or moral discourse. Because of the path dependency of vitalist social systems, facticity is of the utmost importance in making practical interventions in social life. Vitalist facts are already alive: they contain their own light. See Chapter 7.

6 At stake here is reproductive functionality, because evolutionism – perhaps creative evolutionism too – always has not somatic cells at centre-stage, but instead germ cells.

7 This is very hard to translate. It suggests a self that is process. And this process is of a sort of chronic revolution of this self as process, through a reaching out and above that is, at the same time, a reflexive inward movement.

8 The point I am trying to make here is that vitalist morality/ethics/value is at the same time more ontological *and* psychological than Kantian ethics. In Kant's second critique, the moral imperative is understood in terms of autonomous and not heteronomous legislation. Yet it is still legislation and in this sense 'external' to the individual. In its a priorism it is the condition of possibility of moral action and in this sense also external. Vitalism, for me, has no sense unless it is defined against Kant.

9 Husserl, in the *Origins of Geometry* (1982), traced the Euclidian doctrine as starting out in a logic of means. Heidegger's 'Die Frage nach der Technik' (1954) spoke about abstract means in his idea of *Gestell*, while in Being and Time of concrete means in the idea of the tool and *Zuhandenheit*. Also Marx's means of production are, on the one side, abstract as exchange-value and, on the other, concrete as use-value. Simmel of course spoke at length of concrete objects too in his *Philosophie des Geldes* (1977).

10 What I mean here is life as social substance. The point is that there are two notions of the social in Simmel: one as form, which is constraining and life-destroying, the other as substance.

11 'Wave-like rhythm of effective life-process'.

12 'Inhalt, und gleichsam die Materie der Vergesellschaftung; diese Stoffe mit denen das Leben sich füllt, Motivierungen die treiben'.

13 Here again at stake are Varela's first-person truths (see also Obrist 2003). Durkheim and Kant give us third-person truths. Varela, however, like Niklas Luhmann, would deny that these entail relativism or the privileging of subjectivity per se.

14 Deleuze and Guattari's 'body without organs' is perhaps such an unextended body. It is the body as *intensive*.

15 'The eternally forward-coursing succession of contents or processes'. This can, of course, also be read as a smoother flowing of a stream. Yet Simmel does

follow Nietzsche in understanding 'Mehr-Leben' in terms of tension and discomfort and abrasive processes. Indeed, for Leibniz, the subject is substance. And the subject contains in itself its predicates. These predicates can be understood as a series of events. If these events are understood in the above-described Nietzschean/Simmelian sense of *Mehr-Leben*, then indeed substances are in flux. The same would hold for social substances like societies, if they are to be doubly open systems. The same might hold for the 'world-system'.

3

Intensive Philosophy: Leibniz and the Ontology of Difference

Leibniz, Aristotle, ontology

Georg Simmel, we just saw, gives us a basis for an intensive sociology. Unlike 'epistemological' positivism, Simmel's vitalist sociology is very much ontological. Simmel, who understood his own work as 'metaphysical', was influenced by Leibniz. We introduced Leibniz's monad in the context of Simmel's *Lebenssoziologie*. Leibniz's monad is at the foundations of ontological knowledge (though cf. Badiou 2005). When Heidegger says, writing in the heyday of neo-Kantian positivist epistemology, that we have forgotten the question of ontology or being, he directs us back to Aristotle. Aristotle says at the outset of his *Metaphysics* (1998) that the purpose of philosophy, of 'first philosophy', which is metaphysics ('second philosophy' is natural philosophy), is to understand being. Thus first philosophy is ontology. Aristotle then states, with much of the Greek tradition, that primary being is substance or primary substance. Substances are what do not change in a being or thing. If we say that 'Socrates is musical', being musical is a property or quality or predicate of Socrates that can be changed without the underlying substance – Socrates – changing. Substance literally 'stands under' a being or thing.

Aristotle asks the question, then, what is substance? He gives four possibilities as to what can be substance. These are matter, Platonic idea, genuses and essences. He rejects matter because ultimate matter is formless, because substance must be differentiated and have a 'this-ness', and because these characteristics are absent in undifferentiated matter. He rejects both the Platonic ideas and genus because neither entails that substance must be instantiated in a particular in order to exist. He considers the possibility of matter and concludes that matter is not substance. Matter is an undifferentiated substrate out of which substance is formed. Matter, connecting to the Latin *mater*, for mother, is that from which something or someone is born.

Every substance also consists of matter. But matter cannot tell us how one substance differs from another. Aristotle (1998: 26–7) settles on essence as the key to substance. Essence here is the formal cause of substance: that which makes anything what it is and persists under conditions of change. This essence Aristotle calls form (*morphe*). But these essences or forms are not sufficient to understand substances. And this is because they cannot exist as pure forms, like Plato's idea. Forms must be instantiated in matter. Substance is, *pace* Plato, irreducibly hylomorphic, a composite of matter (*hyle*) and form (*morphe*). Thus, in Heidegger's ontology, being must be instantiated in beings. Now Leibniz's *monad* is Aristotle's *substantial form*. The monad, which Leibniz calls 'simple substance', is not the same as Aristotelian substance because the monad has no material side. The monad is form; it is what makes substances different. Even though the monad is immaterial, there is no monad without matter (Deleuze 1988: 8). That is why the monad is not just a form, but a substantial form. An Aristotelian substance is a form and a material body at the same time. While a substantial form is not a material body, it *has* a material body.

The matter and form in each substance are that substance's material and formal causes. We may be aware of the four Aristotelian causes from, for example, Heidegger's essay on 'The Question Concerning Technology' (1954: 13–14). They are material cause, formal cause, efficient cause and final cause. Two of the causes – the material and the formal – are not so much prior to a substance (or thing) but comprise it. The final cause is the purpose that the thing serves and the efficient source is the force or impulse that precedes it and brings it about. So Aristotle's substantial *form* that is Leibniz's monad comprises also the formal cause of a substance. This formal cause acts continually to differentiate the substance, to constitute a given substance's 'this-ness'. This formal cause is not exterior to the thing or being. It is not an external and extensive cause, but intensive cause; it is intrinsic to the thing. It is the thing-itself as self-causing. Leibniz's simple substance, i.e. the monad, is not identical to its formal cause. Yes, it is a substantial form. But substantial form in Aristotle and Leibniz is different from this substantial form's formal cause. Leibniz does not insist that the substance's self-causing activity is just due to formal cause. Substantial forms have powers of perception and they are endowed with sufficient reason. But their causal activity is due, says Leibniz, to 'appetition' (Copleston 2003: 297).

Equally anti-Platonist and Aristotelian is Leibniz's thinking about language. Plato's dualist dismissal of the material world must also be a dismissal of language. Plato, like Aristotle, was familiar with language and grammar through the rhetoric of the Sophists. For Plato, the material world was a poor imitation of the real world of ideas. Rhetoric and drama, and hence language, were only an imitation of this imitation. For Aristotle, they were not an imitation but instead a *mediation* between ideas or forms on the one hand, and matter on the other. Thus Aristotle appropriates the grammar of the rhetoricians' grammar to the understanding of being. The grammatical predicates are appropriated in Aristotle's *Metaphysics* (1998) and his *Categoriae and de Interpretatione* (1963) as the ten categories. The Scholastics later called these categories *antepraedicamenta*, and Aristotle (1963: 4–5) spoke of them as being predicated of a subject. Nine of the categories – quantity, quality, relation, place, time, position, state, action and affection – were such predications. The tenth category is substance. Substance in language and categorical thought is the *subject* of which the other categories are predicates. Aristotle called this primary substance. For him, each primary substance is different from every other. It is the substance's formal cause that makes it different. Yet the substance consists of intensive form and extensive matter. Every being, every Aristotelian substance is an intensity and an extensity. Aristotle's predicates are extensities. In an important sense the material side of a given substance is the substance's predicates. To know a being through its predicates is to know it epistemologically. To know a thing as an intensity is to know it ontologically.

In our strict post-Aristotelian sense, ontology is both intensive and extensive. Thus Heidegger's ontological difference embraces Being *and* beings. If you take away Being for a pure materialism, you lose ontology. If you take away the empirical (or beings), you lose ontology. Ontology is about the transcendental–empirical couple. It is about the relation of being and beings. This said, formal cause more than material cause is at the heart of ontology. For ontology, unlike epistemology, every being is different (Witt 1989: 175ff.). In material causation it is the parts, the constituents, that cause the whole. In formal cause it is the whole that causes the parts. In sociology, and the human sciences more generally, this makes sense. Here positivism works from part–whole causation while phenomenology – and here I include the systems–phenomenology of, for example, Niklas Luhmann – work through whole–part causation. We see this whole–part, hence intensive or ontological causation, in sociological ethnomethodology (Garfinkel 1984). Ethnomethodology understands societies or social groups in a way similar to what Ludwig Wittgenstein called forms of life. Each is different from every other. Here the whole is the form of life itself, and the set of background assumptions that 'members' have. Such members make sense of given events or communications inside that form of life through this background knowledge of the whole: and in this knowledgeable sense-making action contribute to either continuity or change in any part of that whole (Garfinkel 1984: 76–7).

Epistemology and knowing things as they are for us with an objective observer survives and thrives in mainstream positivism. Edmund Husserl, against the positivists initially, prescribed a phenomenological return to things themselves. Moreover, Husserl (1993: 64) held that we are not objective *vis-à-vis* those things but have an 'attitude' towards them. Positivism's objective observer was in a different (dualist) world from the things that he/she observed: in this sense, the positivist's observer was without an 'attitude' towards those things. In phenomenological study you are in the same world with the objects of knowledge and thus necessarily have an attitude towards them. Phenomenology and ethnomethodology as well as much of anthropological ethnography proposes not nomothetic positivism but a more ideographic approach, presuming the singularity of forms of life. Positivism abstracts a set of general qualities or characteristics or predicates from a society, such as ethnic composition, education and income. Phenomenology instead looks at societies not as things for us but things in themselves. Thus phenomenology looks not so much at social predicates but at members' predications. As phenomenologist you do not remain objective in regard to and outside the form of social life you are studying. Instead, you immerse yourself as much as possible in the interior of the form of social life. From the outside and positivism, you look at societal functions. From the inside, you look at communications: you study members' knowledge, which helps to put meanings to these communications. You do not treat the society you are studying as a causal mechanism, but develop instead a thick description of a particular and singular life-world.

Another line of descent from ontology in cultural theory is in the work of Gilles Deleuze. Here Heidegger's Being and beings is displaced by Deleuze's distinction of the virtual and the actual. We encounter Deleuze's actuals, which are more or less generated by the virtuals. At stake in Deleuze (1968: 82–4) is not so much Heideggerian ontological difference, but instead, like we will see in Leibniz, an *ontology of difference*. This ontology of difference only applies in the realm of the virtual. It holds that all virtuals are different from one another. Like Leibniz's monad, Deleuze only accords the status of existents to virtuals. Actuals are derivative and composites, and are ruled by a logic of equivalence and extension. It is these homogeneous actuals that we encounter. Deleuze's virtuals are constantly in process; they are – in contrast to more or less static actuals – not beings but becomings. Deleuze's virtuals work as much like self-organizing and 'machinic' systems as like formal cause. They are as much *l'informe* as *forme*, and they work in the register of the material and, in Deleuze's *Logic of Sense* (1993b), for example, of structure. Unlike Heideggerian *Dasein*, which is the ontological dimension of human being, Deleuze's virtuals are in a sense 'post-human' and to be found anywhere. Alongside this post-humanist ontology are the media and technological ontologies of thinkers such as Friedrich Kittler and Bernard Stiegler. In Kittler (1997), the algorithm of generative media occupies this sort of ontological depth. It is not visible, but it generates the actual: it generates what we encounter across our various interfaces. Stiegler, for his part, takes Heidegger's *Dasein* and recasts it as *techne*. All beings in Stiegler's (1998) media philosophy, including human beings, are technical beings. Drawing on Gilbert Simondon's (1958: 61–4) work on literally the 'mode of existence of les objets techniques', Stiegler gives us a sort of technical *Dasein*: a mode of existence of technical beings. This technological ontology – also seen in the work of Pierre Levy and, as we will see in Chapter 8, Philip K. Dick, often comprises ideas of Platonic anamnesis. Here, with Plato, thought becomes such anamnestic unforgetting. Thus, thought is memory and our memory extends to before we took human form – it is infinite. Such anamnestic knowledge and its pre-human and post-human bases seem to be pervasive in the information age, with its centrality of memory-banks and archives of all kinds. For Plato, this anamnesis is a question of us getting rid of the matter to attain a pure remembrance of the forms. But media ontologists like Stiegler are aware of the irreducible materiality of information, in which every anamnesic act must be instantiated in a material substrate. Again we are back not to Platonic forms, but to Aristotelian substance.

Sensation, perception, knowledge

A good place for us to begin to grasp Leibniz's ontological knowledge is through his critique of John Locke in Leibniz's *New Essays on Human Understanding* (1996). This book, a point-for-point rebuttal of Locke's *An Essay Concerning Human Understanding* (2008), was the book on which Kant focused the most concentratedly in his reading of Leibniz. The book places us, like it did Kant, at the crossroads of where empiricism meets rationalism: where epistemological knowledge meets ontological knowledge. Let us use this comparison to signpost the key themes in Leibniz's intensive philosophy. As a rule of thumb, we might say that Locke starts from extensive sensation and works towards the association of ideas in his epistemological doctrine of knowledge, while Leibniz starts from intensive perception and also works towards ideas in his doctrine of ontological knowledge.

Book I of Locke's *Essay* is *Of Innate Notions*. Here Locke contests the Cartesian and Scholastic assumptions that the human mind has innate ideas. Descartes' assumption is that man innately knows basic logical propositions. These innate ideas include, for various philosophers, mathematical truisms such as that three is greater than two, the certainty that the self exists, and, for some, the innate ideas of God, of identity and of impossibility. God imprints such ideas on man from birth. Locke disagreed with notions of imprinting. Locke (Hewett 2006) was a liberal and close associate of the Earl of Shaftesbury, the founder of the Whig movement, and a strong believer in individual freedom. He thus disliked the traditionalist and hierarchical morality implicit in innate-idea philosophies. The doctrine of innate ideas made it possible for one person to teach another unquestionable truths, a 'dictatorship of principle' from one man over another. Locke argues against such innate ideas as that it is not possible for something both to exist and not exist. He says if we are not aware of these ideas, then how can we know that they are really innate? For Locke, instead the mind is a 'white paper', a *tabula rasa*. The mind from birth is without content. There were precursors of such *tabula rasa* notions in Aristotle and Aquinas. Locke, for his part, believed this *tabula rasa* was imbued with faculties and that these faculties, especially our faculty of reason, were at the same time powers. For Locke, there is no God-given content in our minds, only God-given faculties. These faculties are the senses, memory, the ability to use language, and most importantly the ability to use reason. To be born with innate content would be to be born with rules that could already process information. Locke's faculties (which later are Kant's faculties and Marx's labouring capacity or labour-power) allow us to take in information through the senses and, step by step, to develop rules for processing. All knowledge in this faculty-laden 'white paper' comes from experience and originally from sense perception. Ideas and knowledge are built up from empirical familiarities with objects in the world. The *tabula rasa* is also pure potentiality. Yet 'experience', 'sensations' and 'reflections' are the basis of all ideas and all knowledge.

For Leibniz, we are born with concepts, but they are surely not clear and distinct. We are born with vague concepts that become, through progressive change, more clear and distinct. But for Leibniz this clarity and distinction, which are properties of *perception*, are of not just of a few basic ideas, but of all the other simple substances in our world. Thus perception, which is not so much sense perception as incipient reason, is at the heart of Leibniz's ontological notion of knowledge. Whereas Locke has the faculty of sensation and then other faculties, which do work on the sensations, Leibnizian perception, as it becomes clearer and more distinct, effectively takes on the powers of the reasoning faculty itself.[1] Such a notion of clear and distinct perception is more central in Leibniz even than in Descartes. What Descartes understands in terms of mechanical cause of one body on to another, Leibniz understands in terms of perceptions. Descartes' mechanical and material bodies are the outer-cladding of Leibniz's monads. These monads, whatever bodies they may have – whether inorganic, organic or human – are 'simple substances' or 'souls'. Monads famously have 'no windows, no doors' and are not thus caused from the outside. Lockean sensation, though it is an effect of bodies on the mind, is in contrast material and mechanical. What we should understand as 'perception', Leibniz writes in section 17 of *The Monadology* (1991), is not explicable by mechanics (Maigné 1998: 23). Indeed, mechanical causation does not have the status of ontological existence. Instead, simple substances 'express' 'in their own manner what occurs outside itself'. This does not happen through the influence of these outside beings but instead by 'expression from the depths of (a substance's) own nature'. Substances receive this 'nature', 'this inner source of the expression of what lies is without' from a 'universal cause' (Leibniz, cited in Bobro 2009: 2). These 'expressions', Leibniz states, 'from the depths of our own nature are called perceptions'. Two points are important here. The first is that Leibniz's substance, unlike Aristotelian substance, does not consist of form and matter; it is not hylomorphic. In Aristotle, substance is a unity of substantial matter and substantial form. In Leibniz, simple substance is only substantial form. These substantial forms or monads have material cladding, have material bodies, but *they are* not hylomorphic. The second point is that whereas Lockean sensation is caused from the outside by bodies, and hence is extensive, Leibniz's perception comes from the inner depths of an individual's own intrinsic being, and is intensive.

Leibniz stands in contrast to Locke in terms of what we experience. Experience is not at all as central a concept for Leibniz as it is for Locke. In German, for example, empiricism is *Erfahrungswissenschaft*, taken directly by Kant and others from Locke as literally 'the science of experience'. For Locke, we experience objects or events or bodies; for Leibniz, we experience things that are already imbued with reason. Leibniz (1996: 134ff.) normally calls this not experience, but perception. In such perception, for Leibniz, we are monads perceiving other monads. We perceive these monads more or less clearly depending on the development of our reason. Yet these things we experience already have *their* reason. Knowledge has to do with the clarity of our reason perceiving their reason. This is part of Leibniz's doctrine of 'sufficient reason'. Locke speaks of the 'self' as a 'conscious thinking thing' that 'is sensible'. He speaks of material and immaterial substance. God, for him, is an immaterial substance. What receives sense impressions from matter in the outside world, for Locke, is not material itself. It is mind and not brain. Thus it is the *mind* that is a 'white paper' or *tabula rasa*. Yet a doctrine of substance is not central to Locke's theory of the human understanding as it is to Leibniz's. Locke is not overly concerned with thinking substance. He talks instead about 'bare faculties' that have the power of thought. For Locke, experience, that is sensations and reflections, is the source of all of our ideas. For Locke, the knowledge of our own existence is 'intuitive knowledge', the most certain kind of knowledge that we can have. Yet this is not based on innate ideas but instead on the mind perceiving an agreement between two ideas without the intervention of any other idea (Leibniz 1996: 109–11). For example, the Cartesian cogito would be an agreement between the idea of my self and the idea of to exist. For Locke, though this simple kind of intuitive knowledge is quite certain: it is not logically certain, but we judge it to be certain. Its certainty is thus not logical but a question of *judgement*. This is a question of judgement of an association of two (or more) ideas. When what Locke calls intuitive knowledge is certain, it is certain, contingently, because we judge this association to be certain. So Lockean truths, even when certain, are *contingent*. Leibniz's truths are necessary. They are as necessary as the inferences in a syllogism. In Locke, reasoning works through empirical judging of more and less certainty of idea association. In Leibniz, reason works like a syllogism. Lockean certainty comes neither through innate ideas nor from syllogistic reasoning, but from contingent judgement. Indeed, judgement should be seen first and foremost in contradistinction to syllogism. Both are modes of reasoning: the one (syllogism) necessary, the other contingent.

If knowledge of simple ideas is 'intuitive' for Locke, knowledge of more 'complex ideas' is 'demonstrated'. Again this is not through syllogistic reasoning but through reasoning 'in steps'. In this we associate, say, two ideas, each of which must have intuitive certainty by the intervention of other ideas that are 'proofs'. This 'demonstration is shown to the understanding'. For example, Locke argues that 'no government allows absolute liberty'. This is quite certain knowledge but is not 'intuitive' and needs to be demonstrated. Government is the establishment of society on certain laws or rules, hence there cannot be absolute liberty. Here the two ideas are government and liberty, and they stand in a negative association. Lockean knowledge starts from sensation. A sense faculty takes in sensations from the material world. Faculties of memory and reasoning reflect on these sensations and produce ideas. It is the association of these ideas – that is always a question of judgement – that comprises knowledge. Leibniz's (1996: 331) understanding works not through judgement but through syllogism. Syllogisms comprise propositions. Knowledge and truth are necessary and propositional.

Leibniz says we can learn the innate: that we have an innate idea of number, which we can learn (1996: 85). Locke understands the mind as impressed with images, with sensory images. Leibniz says, in response, that the senses are not adequate to show the necessity of necessary truths. Leibniz, contra Locke, insists further that ideas are not originally derived from sensations. He notes that we can be confused in regard to what we are feeling and images may be hard to tell apart, whereas ideas are clear, distinct and certain. Lockean sensation is extensive. Leibnizian perception is, as we saw, intensive. Lockean sensation is imprinted from the outside by what Michel Serres (1968: 24–9) calls an 'extensive multiplicity'. Leibniz's perception has its source in the inside, in an 'intensive multiplicity'. Perception, and for Leibniz not just humans but also non-humans can perceive, will give a confused version of this intrinsic multiplicity, while reason gives a much clearer version.

Leibniz's God is a 'Universal mind whose understanding is the domain of eternal truths' (Remnant and Bennett 1996: xviii). Leibniz's God 'understands'. And truth always has to do with something like the understanding. Understanding (in Leibniz's French 'entendement', later Kant's Verstand) is intellection, but it is psychological. Locke gives us knowledge through a psychology that is assimilated to the senses, to sensation. Leibniz gives us knowledge through a psychology that is assimilated in the other direction, to logic. The eternal truths of Leibniz's God are similar to the abstract objects of logic. This is the basis of Leibniz's thematization of the logical properties of language, of subject–predicate logic, and Locke's disinterest in knowledge as grammatical thinking.

Locke does address 'Ideas' in Book II of the *Essay Concerning Human Understanding* (2008). He speaks of simple ideas and complex ideas. He speaks about substances: of 'the way we group substances into species'. He speaks of three types of actively built complex ideas – 'substances', 'relations' and 'modes'. Here substances are things in the material world that exist independently, 'such as lead and water, but also including beings such as God, humans, animals and plants, and collective ideas of several substances such as an army of men' (Hewett 2006: 2). For Locke, universal knowledge is about abstract ideas. He often calls these abstract ideas 'essences'. But for him such 'essences' operate through 'extrinsic denomination'. He says we can know the nominal essence of something but not the real essence. Knowing the real essence would be 'intrinsic denomination'. Here the nominal essence is the complex idea a word stands for and the real essence is 'the true properties and constitution of the thing' (Hewett 2006: 3) we describe by the word. The abstractions and words we use to distinguish substances into sorts or species is based on 'their nominal and not their real essences'. For Leibniz, of course, denomination is intrinsic, and we can know the real essence of things. In Locke's extrinsic denomination, we know substances through their predicates, this relation being one of judgement. In Leibniz's intrinsic denomination, it is substances that include their own predicates.

Intensive causation

Unlike David Hume, who forcefully argued that there is only one type of cause, Locke does not have a rigorous notion of cause. Locke held, with Aristotle, that causes are substantial powers. '*Power* being the source from whence all Action proceeds, the Substances wherein these Powers are, when they exert this Power into Act, are called *Causes*; and the Substances which thereupon are produced [...] are called *Effects*' (Locke 2008: II, xxii, 11). Locke saw causes and effects in terms of not universals but particulars. He did not insist on necessary connection or uniformity and lawfulness. Such a modern idea of cause would have to wait for Isaac Newton, and was such an important basis for Kant's first critique. Locke recognized fewer elements of Newtonian cause than Descartes, who – along with Galileo and Francis Bacon – rejected substantial form and Aristotle's and the Scholastics' fourfold notion of causation. Descartes retains only Aristotelian efficient cause in his mechanical notion of the causes of motion of bodies. Leibniz rejects both Lockean notions and Cartesian mechanical causation. But he focuses his own arguments against the causal theory of 'physical influx'. Proponents of this theory include some of the Scholastics, but also moderns such as Hobbes, Gassendi and Robert Boyle, the latter of whom had a great influence of Locke. 'Physical influx' presumes the passing of something from one substance on to another substance: a passing of 'material particles' or of 'species (immaterial) qualities' from one substance to another. For Leibniz, as for Aristotle, such an influx of material particles is an influx of 'accidents'. And cause is far too serious a question to be a simple matter of 'accident passing'. Cause instead must not just be brought about by particulars, but be reasoned and partake of an incipient universal. For Leibniz and Aristotle, there are two sorts of entities that can be predicated of a substance: there are 'attributes' or properties, which are permanent common characteristics that pertain to all individuals of a given species, and there are 'accidents, which are transient and individual characteristics'. For Aristotle, accidents, such as colours, weights, motion, exist only when they are accidents of some substance. Aristotle maintains that cause cannot be by accident but by 'nature'. Accidents are predicates and do not figure among the four Aristotelian causes. Predicates, whether as properties or accidents, are not causes. They might be possible effects but not causes.[2] 'Accidents cannot stroll outside of substances' (Leibniz, quoted in Bobro 2009: 5). The monad is at the centre of Leibnizian causation, and monads do not have doors and windows for accidents to 'stroll' in. Leibniz described physical influx theory as 'barbaric': our soul does not receive 'certain species as messengers as if it had doors and windows'.

Indeed, accidents 'emanate' from substances. As substances express the things in the world, they do so as accidents (or properties). A substance 'emanates' accidents and properties, as the subject generates its predicates. Thus God emanates His reason in constituting the world of simple substances. Leibniz is, like Locke, far too committed to the reasoning individual to accept divine determination. For Spinoza, individuals are modes of divine substance. God is the only real substance, while all else are just modes of God. For Leibniz and Locke, in contrast, the individual has considerable powers; God gives no content to our minds but just powers, causal powers. For Locke, these powers are the faculties of the mind; in Leibniz, the potential for clear and distinct perception. The difference again is that, for Locke, the substances in the world are material and contingent. For Leibniz, they too possess reason: first there is a reason for how they are as they are. And, second, these substances are all involved in active self-causing via their perception. To self-organize like this is to possess perhaps very limited powers of reason. The bottom line for Leibniz – more than the actions of God – is always multiplicitous substance (Serres 1968: 103ff.), possessed with significant casual powers. 'Activity is the essence of substance in general.' Leibniz speaks often about the 'nature' of a substance. This nature is a substance's substantial form. These substantial forms work through perceptions, while driven by appetites. The causal power of the substantial form (the monad) works through appetite.

Accidental form can change without loss of identity. Substantial forms cannot change without loss of identity. For example, in 'the horse, Bucephalus is old', 'old' is Bucephalus' accidental form, and its substantial form – horse as much as Bucephalus – cannot change without loss of identity. A substantial being, then, has form and also causal powers. Its form includes: (1) the structure in which it is arranged; (2) its properties or functions; (3) its characteristic activities; and (4) its 'operations' (Aquinas). All these comprise the unity that is its nature (Woolhouse 1993: 68). For Leibniz to say that there is no existence without a reason is to say 'no effect without a cause'. Here (sufficient) reason is a logical ground. Reason-imbued perception is the same as a logical ground. Thus the relation between cause and effect is not an accident but a necessity: a necessity as strong as logical necessity. In this a complete knowledge of the causes would yield the premises from which, by reason alone, the effects could be concluded (Hulswit 2005). So Leibniz's monads are self-causing with reason. For a substance to self-cause is for it to contain its own predicates. Predicates, not just as material properties but also as temporal events, are contained inside the subject. Think, for example, of Alexander the Great. A Lockean Alexander has a past and future as qualities, as extrinsic characteristics. A Leibnizian Alexander *is* his events: *is* his past and future.

Matter, for Descartes, is extended substance. It is primary and unanalysable. Leibniz rejects Cartesian extended substance. For Leibniz, only intensive substance exists: matter is not substance at all. 'Extension is instead a "relative and analysable concept".'

Extension is a relation. Matter is constituted by relations between primary existents. These primary existents are simple substances or monads. A given monad expresses its relation to the other monads in its world as properties and material extension. Matter or extension is thus not an existent, it is derivative. In this sense, a monad causes its own body. The monad is not a body but has this body that it has caused. Leibniz's notion of substance entails a relation of form and matter. Here, first, every material body must have at its core some sort of intelligible substance. Leibniz writes in 1665, at the age of 19, that 'the substance of a body is in union with a sustaining mind', and again some 50 years later that 'the body is just a well founded phenomenon': that we must look at the 'entire nature of a body not just extension – but its substantial form' (Woolhouse 1993: 94–5). He wrote that in physics and 'corpuscular philosophy', the principles of mechanics are not fully explicable through extension and presume an intensive core. This means not only that at the core (or the fold) of every body is a substantial form, an intensity. It also means that there is 'no soul without an animate body'. At the heart of matter thus is 'the organizing nature of substances as they develop and change'. The substance causes its matter. There are no windows from the outside to the inside, but there is some dynamic blasting of the outside from the inside. Thus the bodily material is 'animated' or ensouled … it is 'organised by an entelechy or form'. Hence material aspects or attributes ('accidents'), that is predicates, are organized by, distributed and determined by the entelechy and its energy.[3] The material attributes and functions of the organic body do not come together to make composites, as they do in mechanical materialism. The organic body instead follows from the intensive logic of the soul. No action or change can be deduced from an extensity; that is, 'if man contains only a figured mass of infinite hardness, he cannot in himself embrace all past and future states' (Woolhouse 1993: 67–8). If a man is only a composite of qualities, he will be moved from A to B by external forces. But the individual is much more than a composite of qualities and his internal force moves him from A to B. This intensive causal force will work not in Newtonian reversible time, but in an irreversible temporality. Thus the monad Alexander bears in his 'soul', traces of the past and marks of all that will happen to him.

Leibniz's God is wise: He is an intellectual God. God has reasons for things: for beings, for human and non-human things. This God also is substance, is real, is substantial: He is universal mind. He is not a 'scribe who writes truths onto our souls', but substantial as universal mind. Leibniz's God is the supreme monad: His reason is approached only by mathematics and logic. Leibniz's God is to be not feared but loved (1996: 144). Thus the name of the protagonist – Theophilus of the *New Essays* – is literally 'God-lover'. Man is to fear a God of power but love a God of intellect. We are to love God for his infinite reason. God's predicates are not power and arbitrariness but perfection and reason. Classical sociological theory, particularly that of Max Weber, has made much of the notion of 'theodicy'. Leibniz of course is the great thinker of theodicy. For a Hobbesian or Lockean, for whom God will have created a world of contingency, there can be no problem of theodicy. There is a problem of theodicy only if God's premier predicate is not power but instead infinite reason; there can only be theodicy if God's word is the word of reason and the highest perception. The Kabbalism – in both Leibniz and, we will see, Walter Benjamin – must presume a God of reason rather than one of arbitrary will. If reason is a primary predicate of God, then theodicy is necessary to account for the presence of wickedness and suffering. It is helpful to think of this in terms of the 'virtual' and the 'actual'. Leibniz's God creates men as virtuals. Humans, for Leibniz's God, are not Hobbesian atoms; instead they are substantial forms. These substantial forms then self-actualize, they self-organize: some will self-organize as wicked, others as good. Each human, and not God, is responsible for his/her own self-organization.

God is a monad – His perception and his appetite comprise a perfect monad that cannot be improved. Monads are not common but proper nouns. For Leibniz and in Benjamin, God created an intensive world for man, which in the Fall descended into extensity. God in His intellect, in His highest reason, His infinite reason, has full understanding of the world of intensities. To reason, as we have noted, is to predicate. Intensive reason folds back the predicates into the subject. This in – folding of predicates – is the principle of Leibnizian individuation. The full concept, the idea and the highest achievement of reason is this principle of individuation of the thing. Only God has the full concept, i.e. the principle of individuation of a thing. This is not the thing's emergence because the thing emerged in Creation. It is its mode of self-organization: and its predicates appear as 'moments' in this self-organization. Leibniz is fond of using Alexander and Caesar as examples of such individuals. Only God sees in the individual – the 'haeccity' – of Alexander the 'basis and reason for all the predicates [qualities, activities] that can be affirmed of him'. Only God will see in Alexander's substance that he will conquer X and Y. Thus for Caesar, 'the action is contained in the concept'. Here the proper name is the 'infinite series of its predicates' (Fenves 2001). God has full knowledge of the extrinsics – the con- quering of X and Y – and the intrinsics – the intrinsic activity is the self-modification of the monads Alexander and Caesar. It is their reflexivity, their self-cause.

The monad is born in Creation. Just before the Monadology's section 7 on the windows, Leibniz (Maigné 1998: 18) says 'Monads ne sauraient commencer que par la creation et finir par annihilation'. This gives us a final step in the sequence of creation, revelation, fall and redemption that we will visit in the next chapter on Walter Benjamin. Now step five is annihilation. Whereas Benjamin lives the language of the Fall, Georges Bataille and also Nietzsche speak from the other side of annihilation. In annihilation is there not just a Fall into extensity, but the destruction of the monad. God lives in Leibniz's world and He still lives on in the wasteland of Benjamin's baroque. But what sort of excess might be at stake when the monad and God, and indeed metaphysics itself are annihilated?

Language: intrinsic predication

In Book III of Locke's *Essay*, entitled *On Words*, we can see the comparative absence of linguistic thinking in Locke. Here we see that words are not so much propositions, but 'names for ideas in the mind'. Locke is not keen, for example, on the linguistic propo- sitions entailed in Aristotle's syllogistic thinking. His focus is on association and judgement. The ideas are made up from reflections on sensations. There are, for example, simple ideas that are 'pas- sively acquired' like 'sweet' and 'round', and complex ideas that are actively built, like cause, effect, number, substance, identity, diversity. Leibniz's language thinking works from the predications of substances and is, unlike Lockean extrinsic domination, a question of intrinsic denomination (Leibniz 1996: 291–3). The world, for Leibniz, can be described in a set of subject–predicate propositions. Each 'names a monad and attributes to it a state or a perception'. The monad as 'primary entelechy' is the substantial form of a body. For Locke, these linguistic descriptions are nominal; for Leibniz, they are real. Leibniz also speaks of algebraic descriptions and number as a fea- ture of an intrinsic being.

Thus there is a contraposition of Locke's nominalism and Leibniz's realism. Lockean nominalism speaks of substances and modes; sub- stances are subjects, modes predicates. Leibniz's predicates are often *verbs*: they are activities. Locke's predicates, i.e. the qualities of things, are entities that *we* attribute to nouns. The Lockean qualities of things thus have no reality outside our minds. Leibniz's predicates do have reality outside our minds; indeed we can combine qualities to define substantial entities in advance of experience (Remnant and Bennett 1993: xxiii–xxiv). The qualities are not extrinsic to but in the objects. We have just touched on adjectival qualities – hot, hard, green, etc. – and activities such as conquering a foreign land. But what about general terms: kinds, species, essences, virtues (1993: xxvi)? For Locke, these are mental particularities: the general and universal do not belong to the existence of things but are the workmanship of the understanding (Leibniz, 1996: 292). For Locke, abstract ideas, and the names associated with them, come from the sorting of individuals according to similitudes. These abstract ideas are of the sort of kind, genus and species. Locke spoke of 'nominal essences': 'the features we take to be necessary and sufficient (Remnant and Bennett 1996: xxvii) for a thing to be properly describable as gold are this nominal essence'. Yet if we 'take away the abstract idea by which we sort individuals and rank them under common names, then the thought of anything essential to them vanishes'. For Leibniz, these 'abstractions', or their equivalent, are real essences in the sense of 'a certain number of forms or moulds wherein all natural things that exist are cast', and we can reasonably conjecture about these inner constituents of things. Leibniz thinks symbols are important. A good symbolism is a great aid to the understanding – from iconic systems of writing that enrich the imagination to algebraic systems of writing that 'unburden the imagination'. Here iconic language and mathematical symbols pertain to the nature of things.

For Leibniz, there is no difference between the individual substance and the general in mathematical objects. Mathematics is like an infinite language. At stake is not the extensive but the intensive dimension of the infinite. For Leibniz, the pure word is a 'new calculus for the determination of the incalculable' Mathematics is a higher symbolic mode of description than is predicate logic; thus demonstration through predicates is not as absolute as that of numbers or geometry. Geometry, for its part, is in an important sense extensive. The material (hence extensity) for Descartes comprises three basic qualities: extension (size), movement and figure. Geometry works in the logic of figure and not singularity. For example, triangles can be identical. In contrast to geometry, numbers give a window on to discontinuity. Thus Peter Fenves (2001: 273) notes a parallel between numbers and Walter Benjamin's proper name (see

Chapter 4). The discontinuity of whole numbers is the basis for Leibniz's monad. This symbolism of mathematics is closer to the divine than any but paradisal language. This is because historical languages emerge from the resemblances between the characters of languages and things. There is no such resemblance with mathematical symbols. Second, words begin with some points of agreement between speakers, with convention, again in contradistinction to mathematical symbols. Moreover, mathematical symbols are indeed symbols and not signs, in comparison with the semiotic dimension of historical language, in which the sign is divided between signifier and signified, neither of which is symbol. Language has thus a more encompassing domain of extensity than mathematics. The signified is to do with conventional meanings, itself whose condition is the differential relations between signifiers. But whole numbers, or at least prime numbers, open a window on to the infinite. Even more so does Leibniz's infinitesimal calculus, whose 'range is "the infinite and continuously determined relation"'. This is the relation dx/dy. Over the whole range of $y = f(x)$. What is the relation at any point? This is a continuous relation over a curve. The derivative gives us instantaneous acceleration. If the discontinuity of number is an ultimately dissatisfying starting point, then the differential calculus goes much further. The relation at stake would be between y, the monad and all the xs – the infinity of xs – in that monad's multiplicity. This is the infinity of monads. We know that each of these is from a perspective because each of the infinity of xs stands in a dx/dy relation with the monad y. Each of the curves $y = f(x)$ is infinite in that it is not emergent but begins at the beginning. And it is infinite in its stretch into the future. But at any given moment, at any given again infinitesimal moment, the state of the relation of y and each of the xs can be given in the derivative dx/dy (Serres 1968: 255–62). Here the y is the equivalent of the singular subject and the xs stand for each of the predicates. We can only indeed talk of y's past as relational too, now in terms of earlier states of dx/dy. The same is true of the future. This is an infinite number of derivatives in regard to the whole, the unity y, which gives its multiplicity. dx/dy is a fairly general expression for its concept. The y is the substance, the subject, and all the xs are its predicates. They are the series, the infinite series of its predicates. Also predicated of y are an infinite series of material predicates. The Newtonian calculus gets close to answering this. Its ys are perhaps also singularities but are understood on their extensive side, in which an external force x is applied to y. Hence the motion of Newton's material substance is altered and the relation of the original motion to the force is acceleration – instantaneous acceleration. Unlike in Newton, in Leibniz's case the main force comes from the inside.

Peter Fenves, in *Arresting Language* (2001), opens up Leibnizian predication into a whole theory of representation in his discussion of Leibniz and rhetoric. In his logic, Leibniz reduces Aristotle's eight categories to three; he similarly reduces the figures of rhetoric to three: metonymy, synecdoche and metaphor. Here, in metaphor there is a relation of similitude, in metonymy a relation of causality, of it would seem extrinsic causality; in synecdoche a relation of part and whole. Leibniz's focus is on a type of synecdoche called 'antonomasia'. Antonomasia is a temporal sort of synecdoche, in which in place of the proper name (the individual, the monad) is the trope of an epithet. This epithet is a species, an appellation, a quality. In antonomasia, a fated sort of temporality is driven by this trope. Of Leibniz's three types of tropes only synecdoche – and thus antonomasia – works from the (from whole to part) logic of an inclusive predicate. Here the subject, the individual, includes the predicate, the epithet or even species. Metaphor and metonymy are, in contrast, extensive: the former working through similitude, the latter through causation. In synecdoche, the whole is the name; the unity and the parts are the multiplicity of its appellations.

At stake in metaphor, metonymy and synecdoche is a relation of representation or *standing-for*. This is a rhetorical relation, different from the logical relations of mathematics and philosophy. So even if metonymy is causal in the sense that A causes B, A causes B only in terms of B *standing for* A. These are *sensible* relations, taking place in the domain of sensation rather than intellect. We are then contrasting the intensive standing-for of synecdoche with the extensive standing-for of metaphor and metonymy. In Leibniz, all three categories of trope comprise an abstract noun, an appellation that is transformed into a proper name. Antonomasia is a trope particularly concerned with naming (Fenves 2001: 172ff.). Here even God can be named through appellations, because God's proper name is of course hidden. Classification and extensive causality take place in the intellect, while standing-for is situated in the domain of the senses. Standing-for (in German, *vorstellen, darstellen*) is literally a relation of *representation*, which explicatory causality and classification are not. Representation is aesthetic or rhetorical: it is of the senses. Explication is of the order of the intelligible. Explication and representation entail two different types of predication. In explication in the sciences, predication is propositional. In representation in rhetoric and poetry, predication is expressive. Expressive predication is not so much about intelligibility as sensibility.

An historical language is in this sense a 'canal of tropes'. An historical language is like an individual: it begins as heavily weighted with material extensity; it is imbued with chatter and common sense. But it becomes more perfect in its self-causing infinity. Here the active and causative substantial form is this canal of tropes. The first trope that affects this sort of change in an historical language is metaphor, through which language's characters work onomatopoetically. At this point, language's characters are pictographic and work through relations of similitude with things. Here it is the common noun that emerges. Then the canal of tropes will undergo more evolution in metonymy, working now no longer through similitude but in now a not mimetic but semiotic representation in which the part stands for the whole. We are still in the register of the common noun or name, and haven't yet attained the language of singularity or difference of the proper name. But finally in synecdoche, in which now the whole stands for the part, the best of the common, the most heavily weighted of the common will become the proper. For example, Aristotle becomes 'the philosopher' and Homer 'the poet'.[4]

We recall that predication is at the same time intrinsic and extrinsic. This is first in that symbols must be sensible and thus are partly material/extrinsic. Second, in denomination, predication refers at the same time to both intrinsic and extrinsic multiplicities. Now antonomasia is predication via the proper name of an intensive multiplicity. In antonomasia, a substance (the proper) not just articulates but also *causes* its tropes. Here synecdoche works like Aristotelian formal cause, metonymy like efficient cause and metaphor perhaps like material cause. Metaphor works like material cause in the sense that the things are the material from which the originary, onomatopeotic common names are made. Antonomasia follows a logic for Leibniz of *fatum*, whose root is to say and which connotes fate (Fenves 2001: 178). Thus what happens, the fate of the individual – of the proper – will unfold in terms of the necessity and the reason of who it is that is doing the saying. Teleologically it is God who is doing the saying. Thus in synecdoche (antonomasia, we remember is a type of synecdoche) the saying of God is determining the capabilities of created beings. The word of God is a unity in determining the diversity and difference of substances: that is, determining the intensive multiplicity of the series (the series of predications). This is final cause, God's power and the reason of the Word. Created substances, for their part, participate in a self-causing antonomasia. The individual must fulfil the fate of his name: a name that is at the heart of substance.

In Latin, antonomasia is *pronominatio*. This is not yet the proper name; it is not yet a rhetoric of ontological difference. Yet it is this *pronoun* that is at the heart of Leibnz's monad. Here we start from the Cartesian pronomial 'I'. This is not just Aristotelian substance as subject of all its predicates; it is the thinking substance of modernity's individual. This Cartesian pronoun is at the origins of the monad. Descartes' *cogito* is a very special kind of substance: a very special staring point for metaphysics. Thus the 'I' as a pronoun is a replacement for the noun. It is not a quality of a substance, as are adjectives (Locke's nominalism) and verbs (Leibniz's realism) but it stands *in place* of substance and subject. A common noun stands for itself, i.e. it stands for a generic noun. A pronoun stands for a *singular*. The 'he' stands for Gottfried and John and René, as do the 'I' and the 'you'. The 'I' is a replacement for the common noun 'in the absence of a general term' (Fenves 2001: 46). So unlike the verb and the adjective, which are general predicates of the singular subject, the pronoun is not a predicate at all, nor is it a general term. It is a placeholder for the singular subject. This 'I' becomes the subject matter of modern metaphysics. The substantial form is the subject matter for Aristotle's metaphysics. For Descartes, primary being is instead the 'I'. It is through the 'I' that Descartes' mediations take place: his metaphysical meditations. Descartes' 'physics' is comprised of perhaps not atoms, but instead surely species, or composites, or common nouns: his metaphysics of the 'I' is incipiently a question of singularities. The 'I' is not a common noun: it stands in for any singular 'I'. Leibniz's antonomasia describes a movement from this stand-in, this pronoun, to the proper noun. Through its series of intensive predications, there is a movement from the stand-in to the singular. Or the stand-in attains singularity as self-causing through its series of (rhetorical) predications. The 'I' thus is that contradiction: a generalized singularity.

Who is the 'I'? It is 'every singularity but no one in particular'. It is a 'formal indicator' of, as Fenves (2001: 117) writes, 'the reality of *res*; the substantiality of substance'. The 'I' is the 'index through which the idea of substance as such can be deciphered'. In each case of antonomasia, there is a movement from the appellative to the proper. Descartes only needs the innate ideas, the certainty that I think. Descartes begins, by discarding all assumptions, with systematic doubt, especially with doubt of sense perceptions. All he knows for certain is that he doubts. If sense perceptions are unreliable, then what we are left with is this doubting intellection. The doubter must also think, and in order for there to be thought, there must be a thing, a *res*, that thinks. Finally this doubting, thinking thing must exist. The innate idea that I think entails not just the verb of thinking, but a substance that thinks. Further, to know that I think means to apperceive myself thinking. It is to stand in a position of second-order observer in regard to myself. This *apperceptio* is relational. It is the 'I = I'. The 'I' can know it thinks but it cannot know the basis on which it is an 'I'. Only God can know this. It can, on the other hand, know all the other 'I's, thinks Leibniz – all the other monads – 'to which it stands in relation' (Fenves 2001: 48). This relation is the 'I' = dx/dy of Leibniz's differential calculus. Perhaps more accurately the 'I' = 'I' is the dx/dy. The 'I' = 'I' is the relation of apperception. The 'I' describes this philosophically and mathematically. This 'I', this monad, this intensity is defined itself via two qualities by Leibniz: perception and *appetito*. This appetite that drives perception – the perception of the series of rhetorical images – is desire: it is will-to-power. This is at the same time energy as vital force. It is not the extensive energy of physics, but metaphysical, intensive energy. It is not the external energy of cause, but the internal force of self-cause.

Substance and system: from exchange of equivalents to exchange of difference

Leibniz's return to Aristotle was subsequent to the whole Cartesian revolution which Leibniz fully took on board. This is science based and mainly reflects Galileo's physics – his two chief systems of the world; Kepler's celestial physics; Harvey's corpuscular motions of heat and blood; and indeed later Newton's mathematical principles of nature. Leibniz's own foundations in the scientific revolution were reinforced by his extensive contact with Robert Boyle and the foundation of the Royal Society for the Advancement of Experimental Knowledge in 1660, and his friendship with Christiaan Huygens. Leibniz was not just an Aristotelian but fully immersed in modern notions of extensity. As a schoolboy he was steeped in study of the materialist atomism of Francis Bacon and Pierre Gassendi. Even at that point he was conceiving the individual (monad) privatively, in contradistinction to the mechanistic assumptions of such to materialist atomism. Later, in Paris, Leibniz was close to Huygens. The Dutch mathematician, philosopher and physicist had been himself a friend of René Descartes. Leibniz at this point was a Cartesian in his valorization of the extensive world of mechanism, and in basing his own positive doctrine of the monad and individual on Descartes' *cogito*. For Gassendi, born in 1592, atoms possessed different natures: they were like species, not qualitatively equal. His emphasis was on how atoms, of different kinds, formed molecules. If Galileo's focus was on the collision and clash of atoms, Gassendi's was on their role as the building blocks in nature of composites. Descartes, for his part, understood extensive unity less qualitatively than quantitatively. For him, quantities of matter moving together form a unit. This led to a corpuscular theory. In atomism, matter is not infinitely divisible. At a certain point – the minimal unit of the atom – it can no longer be divided. For Descartes and Leibniz, matter is infinitely divisible: as they infinitely divide corpuscles which then change their mechanical properties. Boyle, born 20 years before Leibniz, was interested not so much in mechanical but in chemical properties. He spoke of chemical elements that form compounds. In each of the above cases, the assumption was that some sort of similar material units are to be exchanged: such exchanges often taking place through the rearrangement of parts – of elements, corpuscles or atoms.

For Leibniz, *mechanics* address the *physical* stages of a *system*, which are lawful consequences of earlier stages. Metaphysics, in contrast, addresses the *perceptual* states of a *substance* that are lawful consequences of earlier states. Here in mechanics physical change is a question of 'transposition' or rearrangement: the rearrangement of parts. In contrast, metaphysical or substantial change comprises alteration of properties (Rescher 1991). In section 15 of *The Monadology* (1991), under appetition, Leibniz contrasts appetition with motion. Here physical change – which is a rearrangement of parts – may take place through motion or it may be a rearrangement comprising figure and extension. This rearrangement of parts is, in effect, an *exchange* and in each case this exchange (rearrangement) restores the equilibrium of the system. In each case there is an external cause that either sets into motion or accelerates or rearranges the parts (i.e. figure or extensity) of the system. Metaphysical change is a question of '*appetition*'. Thus, 'if motion carries matter from one configuration to another', 'appetition carries the soul from one image to another' (Leibniz, *Phil Schriften* v III, p. 347, cited in Rescher 1991: 81). Here the body and motion are connected with the figure in the sense of configuration. The mind works through perceptual states: the energy of appetition drives the series of perceptual states. It does so in the same sense that motion drives the series of 'physical stages'. Appetition is the force of substantial form. In motion, force comes from the outside. The physical stages – the series of physical stages – it drives are those of displacement from A to B, changes in figure and configuration, and changes in extension. All of these 'three prime qualities' of the material are physical stages. Yet even along all the physical stages, the system is not altered. In each case, there is an exchange and a return to equilibrium. In contrast, in appetition in each step of the series of perceptions, substance itself is altered. These perceptions may be understood as 'abbreviations', in the sense of the abbreviations of the infinity of perceptions in each state of the series. The monad's present world is thus abridged: it can be abridged or abbreviated mathematically as dx/dy: it may be abbreviated in language as a poem. Thus appetition is the drive that moves substance from one family of perceptions to another. Rescher (1991: 79) writes in his commentary on Leibniz's *Monadology* that there is an internal principle of change in appetition that functions as the 'law of series of monadic states'. Appetition is the force of novelty through a self-development of the soul towards a fuller view of the universe.

Motion presupposes empty space (as does extensity more generally). Newtonian space is such an empty space. The space of the monad, in contradistinction, is a plenum. For Leibniz, empty space has no real existence; it is analysable and is itself a 'derivative from the organization of "punctiform monads in their qualitative interrelation". The "world" thus is a plenum, an integrally connected system of coordinated monads'. This plenum is seen in its details. Thus epigram 12 of *The Monadology* addresses change and states: 'il y ait un détail de cequi change, qui fasse pour ainsi la specification et la variété des substances simples'. This is on the inside of the monad, which 'enfolds a multiplicity of affections and rapports' (section 13). So a monad does not experience time as movement in space. Instead, time is the change of the plenum; it is the change in the monad's perceptions of the plenum (Leibniz 1991: 72–3).

Even Classical mechanism – for example, Democritus' atomism – understood natural phenomena as 'a result of the *collision* of small material bodies, corpuscles or atoms' (Woolhouse 1993: 58). Thus the idea of 'mechanism', of extensity, as understood by Hobbes, and many of the corpuscular theorists entailed not just organized Newtonian cause and effect, but generalized *collisions* of atoms. Michel Serres, in his *Le système de Leibniz et ses modèles mathématiques* (1968: 304ff.), speaks of 'extensive multiplicity' in terms of a 'combinatoire of exchange'. That exchange entails substitution. If one thing is subtracted, then another must be put in its place. This is in order to preserve stability or equilibrium. That is 'la conservation d'un schéma général des êtres' is only 'des échanges de parties définies' (Serres 1968: 305). What this yields is not time but 'movement', Serres notes (1968: 306), 'au sens de la géométrie ou de la cinématriqiée' – this in Henri Bergson's sense of cinema as mechanism. Here extensity or extensive multiplicity is an infinite series of exchanges of equivalents. In such an extensive multiplicity equivalents are causes and caused. The way in which they cause and are caused is very much like collisions. The collisions of equivalents cause and are caused. The effects of such cause are a rearrangement of parts; a rearrangement of such equivalent parts. This entails assumptions of system equilibrium. For one part to go to one place and another to another involves something very much like exchange. In the repetition of exchange, i.e. the collisions of causation, as exchange of equivalents (A takes the place of B and B takes the place of A) there is stability. Hobbes' war of all against all was based on the collisions of Galilean atomism. The Hobbesian position also incipiently describes the free market. All exchange must be the exchange of some sort of equivalents. Otherwise it is not exchange at all. Market exchange is the exchange of abstract equivalents. This is a set of substitutions that yields no real change at all. So in Leibniz either there is exchange of equivalents and reproduction, that is no change, or there is self-generated change in the intensive multiplicity. At stake too is Newtonian reversible time. Wind the clock forward in this extensive order of exchanges or wind it backwards and you get back to the same place. Nothing could stand in greater contrast to the irreversible time of the monad. In Chapter 5, we will draw on this idea to look at today's capitalism. We will understand this in terms of a shift from an extensive capitalism of the exchange of equivalents to a capitalism based on the exchange of difference.

Atoms or corpuscles or extensities collide and exchange. They thus *cause* one another. These collisions are causes. They come together as composites to make compounds, which are then dividable into units of equivalence. Yet extensive entities only ever express a present state. They only move through space. Take away the attributes – extension, figure, movement – and the extensity will disappear. Intensive multiplicity is comprised of differences and extensive multiplicity is a multiplicity of equivalents, that makes up a system, an equilibriated system. If Descartes gives us extensive multiplicity in his material world, and Spinoza gives us intensive unity, then Leibniz gives us intensive multiplicity. This is an ontology: a question of what truly exists. And what truly exists is a multiplicity not of equivalents, but of differences. And what I can know as an individual is not this extensity of equivalents but my own intensive world of monads, of singularities.

Leibniz's monad is – and this seems to be one of Serres' theses – a bridge between its inner substantial and outer material space. It is a bridge – though it has neither doors nor windows – between its inner intensive and outer mechanical space. It is a bridge between its metaphysical world and its physical world. In each case, this works through the regulation of correspondences. Thus in the *Theodicy*, Leibniz (1985: 197–8) writes that substance is the 'immediate cause of all its [outward] actions and its inward passions'. In section 7 of *The Monadology*, he says that monads cannot be affected from the outside by either substances or 'accidents', i.e. matter. He disagrees with the Scholastics, for whom accidents are a sort of wandering about 'qui se promener dehors des substances'. These accidents comprise the material body of monads. This body too is excluded by the window-less and door-less interior space. They cannot get in, cannot affect the monad because the monad has no internal motion ('mouvement interne'). The material compound and atom are composites with moving parts. The monad changes not through the series of movements of internal motion, but instead through moving from one perception to the next.

The monad and its body is like a material house whose outer shape, façade and indeed even particular structure, is driven from the inside. The monad's house is of course the house of being. It is an ontological house, each one different from every other driven by ontological difference. Into the house, purely as material artefact, come images. But images cannot penetrate into the interior of the monad's windowless house. In *New Essays on the Human Understanding* (1996: 110ff.), Leibniz writes that if a soul had windows it would be like a writing tablet; it would be corporeal like Locke's empty writing tablet.[5] Then the images would produce Lockean sensations, not the Leibnizian perceptions of the soul. The Lockean house, in contrast, would seem to be more consistent with Renaissance perspective, which in painting and architecture is operative through windows and images. In 'physics', the outside of the house is a cause that has effects on the house. In art, the image of the real outside is projected on to the window of the Renaissance house, the hylomorphic Renaissance house that is a unity of substantial form and material composite. And it is then registered on the *tabula rasa* of the faculty of sensation. Corbusier's modern house is no longer hylomorphic: it is pure matter, pure extension. This is the extensive house; the composite house is effectively a machine, with internal parts. It is a *machine à habiter*. We enlarge this house of sensation, we go inside, we examine the parts. In the Lockean faculty of material sensation, these images come in through the windows and, as it were, act as a force to rearrange the parts of the *machine à habiter* that is this composite microcosm. Sensation comes in mechanically through the windows. Whereas the window works through external cause, Leibniz's house works through internal causation. This is the topological house of Deleuze's (1993a) 'fold'. Deleuze's *Fold* is subtitled *Leibniz and the Baroque*. Leibniz's house as simple substance with material cladding is such a baroque house. Here the cladding, the material and extensive body of the house in-tends inwardly as a topological infolded surface. If Renaissance Art works through the mechanical image from the outside (the 'light-on') formed on the windows of the house, in the baroque and topological house the energy comes from inside the house. So does the light. Deleuze thus speaks of the light of a baroque El Greco painting shining through from the interior of the painting.

Renaissance art and Corbusier's house work in the register of the extensive multiplicity of the mechanical *system*. The ontological house and the El Greco generate their cladding, like the predicate generation of Leibniz's *substance*. We will see in subsequent chapters what the erosion of this substance–system distinction will bring. In Leibniz we have substance as active self-formation and change and system working from exchange, collisions, composites and equilibrium. Here system modification – whether in extension, figure or movement – comes from the rearrangement of parts. Exchange itself, as Serres notes, is such a rearrangement of parts. This is true of capitalist exchange. Marx focused on this in Volume Two of *Capital*, in which exchange leads to general equilibrium in the simple reproduction of the total social capital. Yet still we have the separation of material base and ideational superstructure. In Leibniz there is of course this separation. Classically, Descartes gave us this juxtaposition of *res cogitans* and *res extensa*, thinking and extensive substance. What Leibniz does is to explode the unity of thinking substance into a potentially infinite intensive multiplicity of fragmented monads, each of which then takes on its own powers. In Leibniz, extensive multiplicity loses its independent existence and becomes a cladding generated from intensity. Yet the origin of such intensive multiplicity is mind. There is the intensive ideal, on the one hand, and the extensive material, on the other.

In today's global informational culture, intensity and extensity are increasingly fused together. The result is that *substance increasingly becomes system*. Substance, and for that matter ontology, become system. What were separate worlds of the substantial or intensive on the one hand, and the extensive and material on the other, become fused as the *intensive material*. The entirety of the work of Gilles Deleuze is driven by such a notion of the intensive material. This is why Michel Foucault could say that Deleuze was the philosopher of the twenty-first century.

This is an effective de-differentiation of mind and matter, of substance and system. We see this in Deleuze and Guattari's desire and desiring machines that rework Leibniz's intensive 'idealism', in the sense of reasoning appetition, in the register of the material. We see this in the body without organs, again in the new register of the intensive material. We see it in Deleuze's (1983) time-image in his analyses of cinema, which fuses the mechanical and material image with intensive time. This is a materialism, not of mechanism, nor even a dialectical materialism but an intensive materialism of difference. True *neo*-marxism is such an intensive materialism. In Simmel, in Chapter 2, we also understood intensity in terms of the materiality of social life. The fusion of substance and system, of the intensive and the material, is seen above all in information and communications. Information in its difference – and there must be difference, as Bateson says, for it to be information – is necessarily intensive. Yet as economic base and instantiated in silicon chips and server farms, it is quintessentially material. System itself, as we see in the work from Luhmann (1997) through Bateson (Hayles 1999) to Varela, becomes substance. For Leibniz, predication and meaning were integral to substance and foreign to system. Now we have meaning in Luhmann and Francisco Varela[6] in semantic machines: in machines of predication. Substance leaves its place in the human subject and itself becomes system – becomes non-linear, self-organizing, now far from equilibrium system. System itself now becomes intensive. Such intensive system works not through exchange of equivalents but through the exchange of *difference*. Sociologists will have learnt an extensive, externally caused and normative idea of systems in the work of Talcott Parsons. But Parsons was a sociologist of the industrial age. Luhmann, in contrast, gives us a sociology of the information society. System itself has now become intensive. Machines (media machines of information and communication) have taken on powers of predication.

Notes

1 Although Leibniz does speak of 'apperception', effectively the perception of perceptions, in such a context.
2 Thus some of the Scholastics had 'sensible species', i.e. accidents, Leibniz observes, going about outside substances as causes.
3 We are reminded here of the 'ego instincts' and 'id instincts' of Freud's early work; Leibniz's 'drives of the intelligible' are the equivalent ego instincts.
4 All of this argument heavily draws on Fenves.
5 Locke, as discussed above, very much understands his writing tablet, his 'white paper' as mind, and hence essentially immaterial. We saw above too that Locke has a notion of immaterial substance. Leibniz chooses to read the Lockean *tabula rasa* as corporeal. He seems to think that, despite Locke's disclaimers, it *acts* like matter.
6 See Varela et al. (1993: 200–4).

4

Intensive Language: Benjamin, God and the Name

Leibniz and Benjamin: from the monad to the word

There is a lineage from Gottfried Wilhelm Leibniz to Walter Benjamin. Benjamin addressed the monad in the preface to his *Origin of German Tragic Drama* (*Trauerspiel*) (1977b) in one of his most fundamental statements on method. In his work on Baudelaire's Paris, Benjamin treated the nineteenth-century arcades as monads to the extent that they were closed, and to which there were no windows or doors for anything to get in (Gunning 2003). But whereas intensity as philosophical thought is pivotal for Leibniz, for Benjamin at centre-stage is *language*. In this movement from philosophy to language, from the idea to the word, there is at the same time a move from ontology to the messianic and religious. To make this move from ontology to the messianic is, with Benjamin, to open up the possibility of *critique*. If ontology with Heidegger operates in the dimension of the already-there, the religious-messianic operates in the register of the to-come. This is not ethics, or the 'what-should-I-do', but the 'what-can-I-hope' in what, for Immanuel Kant, was enlightenment. The point of the messianic was for Benjamin, not a matter of theology, but instead critique: critique of modernity and above all critique of capitalism. So this chapter traces the movement from intensive philosophy and the ontological idea to intensive language and the religio-critical word. It does so via two key Benjamin texts. One is the 'Epistemo-Critical Prologue' to Benjamin's *Origin of German Tragic Drama* (1997b). The second is his essay 'On Language in General and the Languages of Man' (1977c). The first text sets up the movement from the idea to the word: from intensive philosophy to intensive language. And the second explores the nature of this intensive language.

The German title of the book for our first text is *Ursprung des deutschen Trauerspiels*. In German, *Trauerspiel* does not mean 'tragic drama'. *Trauer* means to mourn and *Spiel* is a play so a *Trauerspiel* is a mourning play. This is conceptually important. The main conceptual counterposition of this book is that between classical and ancient Greek tragedy, on the one hand, and modern (seventeenth-century) mourning play, on the other. The mourning play is an allegory for modernity and modern capitalism itself. If it is called 'tragic drama', this pivotal counterposition – between ancient and modern – loses its definition. The pivotal contrast between ancient and modern lies in the fact that Classical tragedy is 'full', and a plenitude, while modern mourning play is empty, entailing lack or loss. It is this loss that is the object of the mourning. This theme plays out elsewhere in Benjamin, especially in his work in nineteenth-century Paris. He comments that in Paris, the ancient is present in and underneath the modern, while in Berlin there is only the modern. Berlin, in contrast to Paris, he comments, is 'cleaned up' and 'cleaned out' (Frisby 1985). It is cleaned out and empty. Modernity and the commodity are similarly empty. In the fulfilledness of ancient Greece in the era of tragedy, there is the integration of Dionysian and Nietzsche's Appolonian. In the mourning play, there is instead the baroque wasteland of modernity. The melancholy of *Trauerspiel*, and modernity more generally, is the mourning of this plenitude. The contrast is between the ontological fullness of Classical Greek antiquity, the plenitude of Athens. And modernity's mourning is also the mourning for the Second Temple of Jerusalem. It is a mourning whose other side is the messianic hope of the to-come. For Benjamin, thus we have the centreposition of, on the one hand, ontology, whose paradigm is the plenitude of Greek antiquity and, on the other, the messianic-religious, whose void is at the heart of European modernity. The nearly one-half of *Trauerspiel* that is devoted to the tragedy versus mourning play contrast engages at many points with Nietzsche's *Birth of Tragedy* (1966a). Benjamin's theme is that Nietzsche approached classical tragedy from the standpoint of the aesthetic while he sees mourning play from the standpoint of the religious. Now Benjamin defines his own work in the Prologue to the *Trauerspiel* book as arts-philosophy (*Kunstphilosophie*), and most of his *oeuvre* addresses not religion, but the high and popular arts. Benjamin's point is that his – and not Nietzsche's arts-philosophy, which is in our terms ontological – works through the allegory of the messianic-religious. Nietzsche's paradigmatic figure will be the fulfilled, indeed over-fulfilled *Übermensch*, while Benjamin's flâneur operates in a melancholic void.

This juxtaposition of Niezschean ontology and Benjamin's critical and messianic arts-philosophy is a question of method. This – which extends to cultural criticism and cultural theory more generally – is the explicit topic of Benjamin's Epistemo-Critical Prologue. The first part of the Prologue is a critique iterally of lepistemology. In Benjamin's German, the term for epistemology is *Erkenntnistheorie*. In this sense, the first half of the Prologue counterposes such *Erkenntnis* (or cognition) to truth. Here cognition and epistemology means knowledge through nominalist classifications, while truth – either in poetry or *Kunstphilosophie* – deals with the intensive, the inner reality of things. The second half of the Prologue, for its part, moves effectively from ontological to religio-messianic truths. In this Benjamin addresses the monad, the idea and the word. Benjamin understands the monad as a pure intensity. He wants to displace Leibniz, like Nietzsche, into the messianic. He does this through recasting the 'idea', the pure intensity of Leibniz's monad, into the *word*. In doing so, he recasts intensive philosophy as intensive language. Benjamin writes that 'the word as idea is the violence of the name'. By name, Benjamin means, not the common noun but the proper name. The common noun partakes of the language of classification and nominalist epistemology. The (proper) name is not generic but singular, not nominal but real. Yet Benjamin's name is not ontological. Ontological language deals with the intensive singularity of things in their dimenion of the 'is', of the already there. The name deals with this singularity in its dimension of hope, its dimension of the to-come. Benjamin insists on the 'violence' of the name. In this sense, the Prologue is of a piece with his 'Critique of Violence' (1977d), written four years earlier. 'Critique of Violence' is about the justice inherent in the violence of the messianic and revolutionary politics. This violence of the messianic political is also, we see, the violence of the word: of the name. It is the violence of intensive language.

If *Trauerspiel* gave us the 'fall' from Greek plenitude into the modern void, the 'On Language' essay treats not tragedy but the Old Testament's *Genesis* and the Fall from Paradise. Here Paradisal language is fulfilled, naming language. Only with the Fall do we need messianic pronouncements of the Prophets. In 'On Language' we see how Benjamin's name, unlike the pure intensity and immateriality of Leibniz's monad and philosophy's idea, is both immaterial and material: both extensive and intensive. In the absence of materiality we cannot encounter language. Here Benjamin understands extensive language as means, as instrument, while intensive language is not a means but a *medium*. With the Fall from Paradise, naming-language becomes such instrumental language. It is eating of the Tree of

Knowledge that brings about the Fall. The Tree of Knowledge was put in the Garden of Eden in order that God could judge man. In eating of the Tree and thus trying to take on God-like powers of judgement, man fell from Paradise. For Benjamin, the instrumental language of the Fall is also the language of judgement. Judgement works like classification, only in place of classification's common noun stands judgement's universal norm. In judgement, particular cases are brought under universal norms to be judged. Nothing could be further from the singularity of the name. The title of Benjamin's essay is 'On Language in General (*überhaupt*) and the Language of Man'. Language 'in general' here refers to the language of all beings: the language of God, the language of things and the language of man. In this context, God's language is purely immaterial and works through creating. Things' language is mainly material and works through the images that the things give off. For its part, man's language is both immaterial and material. Man communicates immaterially to God by naming material things. In a further separation from ontology, Benjamin rejects the activist assumptions of intentionality of (phenomenological) ontology. Man as naming animal stands in a relation, not activist intentionality but more passive 'contemplation' to things. The things speak to man in their own language of material images. Man, as what Foucault (1966: 314ff.) called the transcendental–empirical double, then registers these images and translates them through the name.

Intensive method: from epistemology to truth

Benjamin begins the 'Epistemo-Critical Prologue' with a quote from Johann Wolfgang von Goethe's (1970) *Materials on the History of the Doctrine of Colour*. Here Goethe explores the counter-position of art, on the one hand and science (*Wissenschaft*) on the other hand. In this *Wissenschaft* embraces both philosophy and the *Geisteswissenschaften*. Goethe states that knowledge (*Wissen*), on the one hand, and reflection (*Reflexion*), on the other, are insufficient on their own in order to constitute a whole (*Ganz*). In knowledge, on the model of science, the internal (*Das Innere*) is missing; in art the external is missing (*das Aüßere*). Goethe says we need to think of science as art to derive such a wholeness. In as much as art is *wholly* represented (*darstellt*) in every work of art, so should science reveal itself (*sich erweisen*) completely in every individual object (*Behandelten*) it deals with. Thus for Goethe neither extensive science nor intensive art is adequate. Art is 'monadological' because all of art is present in every work of art. He is advocating that science be so too. In the 'Prologue' (*Vorrede*) Benjamin himself wants to give a method to what for him is *Kunstphilosophie* (arts-philosophy). He (1974a) thinks that the Romantic *Kunstphilosophie* of Friedrich von Schlegel and (Georg Friedrich Phillipp von Hardenburg) Novalis is too much a question of systematization and hence too science-like, too extensive. Benjamin extols the virtues of a number of medieval forms, such as the doctrine (*Lehre*), the esoteric essay, the propadeutic and the treatise, which he holds up in contrast to the nineteenth-century fondness for the philosophic system. Such systems-thinking, Benjamin maintains, reaches for universalism, which has more to do with knowledge than truth. Medieval science writing, such as the treatise, does not feature intention and the accumulation of knowledge, whereas systems philosophy does. Instead of activist intention, such medieval science texts entailed contemplation (*Kontemplation*). Here contemplation works not through the 'uninterrupted' 'coercive proof'. It works instead through representation, which is not purposive and lacks intention. Such *Wissenschaft* is more like art and is effective through 'digression'. It 'makes new beginnings, returning in a roundabout way to its original object'. The treatise, for example, is like a medieval mosaic: a 'fragmentation into capricious particles', which are 'distinct (*Einzelnem*) and disparate'. The treatise thus bears 'testimony to the transcendent force of the sacred image (*Heiligenbildes*) and the truth itself'. Systematic philosophy, says Benjamin, lacks the didactic authority of 'doctrine'. Goethe's writings on colour were such a doctrine (*Lehre*). Though Benjamin prefers doctrine to systems philosophy, he prefers the treatise. The treatise has less didactic authority; further, it 'refers implicitly to those objects (*Gegenstände*) of theology without which the truth is inconceivable'. *The Origins of the German Mourning Play* is a sort of *Trakat*, or treatise in the philosophy of the arts. Centre-stage among the arts, here is literature: poetry and theatre. This early work of Benjamin is as much arts-philosophy as empirical arts-history. It deals as much in philosophical method as with literature itself. Thus Benjamin's idea of the treatise deals with representation rather than eliminates it; is concerned with truth rather than cognition; works like a mosaic through fragments; comes through historically calcified language; and is effective through contemplation rather than intention.

Monad and method

For Benjamin, 'truth', in contradistinction to knowledge, is 'actualized' (*vergegenwartigt*) in the 'round-dance of represented ideas' (1974b: 209). 'Knowledge', for its part, entails possession (*ein Haben*,

Besitz). Thus in science, which takes place in the register of knowledge, consciousness takes *possession* of the object. In Benjamin's proposed representation-philosophy, the reader does not take possession of the object, but instead the object forces him/her into reflection. For Goethe, art, unlike science, works via reflection. Benjamin contrasts two methods: a 'knowledge-method' and 'truth-method'. Knowledge-method is possessive of its objects, even when it addresses the metaphysical. Truth-method, less intentionally and more passively, contemplatively, lets the object represent itself. Knowledge gives us method as a way of acquiring objects. Truth presumes a prior existence of something that is representing itself. Knowledge establishes unities only as a coherence between the intellect (*Verstand*), which develops concepts (*Begriffe*) that give coherence (*Zusammenhange*) and the extensive world of empirical objects. That is, knowledge intentionally acquires objects through the intellect's concepts, bringing those objects into coherence under the grasp of the intellect. Truth-method lets an object represent itself. When an object does this, it does so through its spiritual (*geistlich*) being: it does so through its form, which gives a unity to truth. The activist concepts of the intellect are set in contrast to the contemplative ideas presupposed by truth. These ideas are not formed by the intellect, but are pre-existent and given to be reflected upon.

Benjamin's most explicit discussion of the monad is close to the end of the Prologue. Some one-half of the 16 sections of this *Vorrede* are dense with theory. The others either are criticisms of classificatory knowledge or address the Baroque and *Trauerspiel* more directly. *The Monadology* section is the last of the meta-theoretical sections. Benjamin introduces the Leibnizian monad to develop a notion of the 'idea'. Indeed, the major figures of the Prologue are 'truth', 'the idea', 'representation' and the 'phenomenon'. What are perhaps its two core sections are entitled 'The Idea as Configuration' and 'The Word as Idea'. Benjamin introduces the monad to try to think about the idea in general and tragic drama in particular. For Benjamin, the idea is a monad: it is a pure intensity. He also draws on the monad to develop his thinking on 'origin'; about the origins of a phenomenon. Throughout the Prologue, Benjamin insists that every idea is a totality. With Leibniz, he thinks that every single monad (idea) contains, in an indistinct way, all the other monads. Benjamin says the structure (*Bau*), thus of the idea, is monadological (1974b: 228). The structure of the monad is a world, a not empirical but ideal world. The structure of the idea is the idea-world. Benjamin talks about these two different worlds: of facts or phenomena, on the one hand, and ideas, on the other. The monad is a more or less distinct idea. For Leibniz, there are, as we saw, various levels of distinctness in a sort of continuum. God as singularity is the monad that contains in a perfectly distinct way all the other monads. Man contains these less distinctly. Man when asleep or unconscious still less distinctly. Animals even less distinctly. Inorganic substance – in Leibniz's sense of substance (i.e. ideal) – we would add, least distinctly. Benjamin's Mourning Play is a quite low-level idea or monad: its world is vague and indistinct.

Benjamin will take Leibniz a step further. For Leibniz, the monad is its world from the point of view of its perception or apperception. Benjamin extends this to *representation*.[1] Benjamin says that the perception of the monad is at the same time a representation 'in ihr (the Monade) ruht prästabilisiert die Repräsentation der Phänomene als in deren objektiver Interpretation' (1974b: 228). That is, interior to the monad, the phenomenon's representation is, as it were, reposing, in its pre-stabilized form, as in the monad's objective interpretation. In this it seems we have two monads in relation: one that is interpreting and the other that is interpreted. The implication is that the interpreting monad is historical philosophy, or more accurately philosophical history (*philosophische Geschichte*). This is what Benjamin is pursuing in the *Trauerspiel* book. What he is doing is kunst *philosophische Geschichte*. Thus Benjamin's monad is representing the intensive being of the phenomenon as perceived from the idea. His point is that the idea must 'penetrate into' historical phenomena. Ideas must penetrate into the real world. This 'real world' is a 'task' which one must 'penetrate' (*dringen*) in order to 'open up' (*erschlosse*) an objective interpretation. This task is also the task of the translator, which Benjamin cites in this section. Benjamin's Leibniz was such a translator, who 'immersed' (*Versenkung*) himself in this real world and founded 'infinitesmal calculus' (1974b: 228). The calculus is a translation, the capturing of the metaphysical kernel of nature. This task (*Aufgabe*) is also, says Benjamin, to show this image of the world in its 'abbreviation' (*Verkürzung*). The infinitesimal calculus is thus an ideal *Verkürzung* of the phenomenal world. What are the words Benjamin uses for the material world? 'Facts', 'real world', 'nature', 'world of phenomena', 'things', 'objects'. Benjamin is most interested in that part of nature that is history. For Benjamin, 'natural history' is 'inauthentic' (*uneigentlich*) history. Benjamin's studies are mostly historical: the work on Baudelaire and Paris, Goethe's affinities, Romantic *Kunstkritik*, *Trauerspiel*. Or they are 'contemporary historical'. In contrast to such 'natural history' stands, of course, 'messianic time'. Spatially in the idea-world, the monad perceives, represents, abbreviates and indeed redeems. Yet of course the monad also has a temporality. Thus Leibniz discusses Caesar or Alexander as monads: as subjects (substance) that have internal, temporal predicates. These internal predicates, we saw in Chapter 3, stand in contrast to the external predicates of nominalism. Thus for Leibniz your predicates do not modify you: instead you *are* your predicates. A monad can comprise these predicates, which are at the same time the monad's world of other monads in what, for Benjamin, is a 'configuration' or a 'constellation'.

It is not just language but history that is at the heart of Benjaminian intensity. The idea is a monad: 'the being that enters into it (the monad) has a past and subsequent history'. 'Das Sein, das mit Vor- und Nachgeschichte in sie geht'. The monad and the idea then contain not only a spatial world, but a temporality, a past and future. This is not natural, but instead pure history ('reine Geschichte'). Such pure history is at the centre of the notion of Benjamin's notion of 'origin' (*Ursprung*), which is historical. This is central to the *Trauerspiel* book, whose full title of course is *Origin of the German Mourning Play* (*Urpsrung des deutschen Trauerspiels*). It harks back to an older philosophy, it would seem a treatise, whose task is 'to grasp the becoming of the phenomenon in its being'.[2] It is a monad – like idea that must penetrate its object and immerse itself in it. It must further, via philosophy's concept of being, 'absorb' (*Aufzehrung*), literally to 'swallow up' the history of the phenomenon. This swallowing-up becomes a 'tearing-into'. Here, in contrast to Benedetto Croce's idea of *Entstehung* (emergence) stands Benjamin's idea of 'origin'. *Entstehung* (beginning, development, upshot, growth out of) is an historiographical method that, like Benjamin, breaks with the logic of nominalist and nomothetic classifications, for the singularity of the historical event. Croce contrasted such abstract classification with his historical and 'genetic' classification. Yet in contrast to 'origins', the historicity of 'emergence' and genetic classification is inscribed, not in its being, but in a 'naked' facticity. When phenomena are original (*ursprunglich*), what is determined is 'the form in which the idea will confront' the historical world'. *Entstehung* is in contrast purely a question of, not form, but the material. The *Urpsrung* is in this sense 'an eddy in the stream of becoming: its current (*Rythmik*) tears into (*hineinreßen*) history's genetic material' (*Entstehungsmaterial*) (1974b: 226). The 'original is never revealed in Croce's naked exist- ence of the factual'. Genetic historiography *á la* Croce does not see 'facts with an innermost structure of origin and idea'. Thus in history the same individual can stand under the sign of *Entstehung* or *Ursprung*. In the first, the 'individual (*Einzelnen*) comes under a concept, and comes under it unchanged'. In the latter, the individual 'stands under an *idea*, it becomes something other than itself, a totality. This is Platonic salvation/redemption (*Rettung*)'. Thus in genetic history, like in abstract classification, the individual comes under the concept, it stands as if particular to universal. When it comes under the idea, it comes to comprise a totality, a world of ideas (1974b: 227). The philosophical history, the arts-philosophical history that Benjamin is carrying out in *The Origin of German Tragic Drama*, is – in this sense of origin – *intensive* history.

Against classification: naming and cultural critique

The concept and knowledge presume a method of classification. The idea (and truth), notes Benjamin is 'nicht klassifizierend': it 'defines no class'. *Trauerspiel* and, for example, tragedy are not classes. They are not empty classes. As ideas they instead comprise 'metaphysical substance': they are something like substantial forms. *Trauerspiel* and tragedy are not concepts to be defined across a range inductively. This is how systems of classification work. Benjamin opposes this sort of 'continuous' and 'systemic' mode of thinking. It is only when systems in, for example, Hegel and Plato cross over into the intensive and the singular that they start to address truth. Benjamin attacks classificatory modes of cultural criticism, which look inductively across a 'range' for commonalities and differences, and whose result is often 'an average'. The concept, working though inductive classification, yields what Heidegger ridiculed as *Das man*, with the average, with Kierkegaardian 'chatter' (*Geschwätz*) (Duttmann 2000). Classificatory systems grasp 'the word' only as concepts, embracing a span of 'particulars'. They remove the word from the sphere of the idea. *Ursprung* and the idea are to be looked for, not in the mean, mode and median of classification, but in 'the extreme and in excess'. We look not into the average, in which particular stands under universal, as in Weber's ideal type. Instead Benjamin's particular is so extreme that it evades the grasp of the universal and transforms itself from 'unchanged' particular into changeable singular, itself monadologically comprising the totality of a world. It is this extreme particular that will make its appearance later as Benjamin's *Shockerlebnis*. It is this 'extreme and excess' that will be understood as 'the event'.

'The Word as Idea' (*Das Wort als Idee*) is at the heart of the Prologue. For Benjamin, the being of ideas is given in the word (and indeed naming). He starts by disagreeing with thinkers for whom the being of ideas is given instead directly in phenomena. These thinkers – mainly the Romantic *Kunstkritiker*, such as Schlegel and Novalis – espouse a method of 'intellectual intuition'. For Benjamin, this word, in which the idea (and not the concept) is given, is comprised of representations (*Darstellungen, Räpresentationen*). Representations are not intellectual intuitions: they are media that stand between intuition and phenomenon. Intellectual intuition foregrounds intention, while monadological perception (and representation) is intentionless. In such intentionality, the *Kunstkritiker* are working via the concept and not the idea. For them, the types of phenomenon that incorporate the being of such ideas are intellectual 'archetypes' or 'prototypes'. For Benjamin, these too entail intention, while 'truth' is 'intentionless'. These notions of intuition betray the 'neo-Platonist paganism' (*Heidentum*) of such 'esoteric philosophy'. This is also an implicit parting of ways of Benjamin with phenomenology. The in-itself is displaced for Benjamin from the thing to language.

The being of the phenomena is, for Benjamin, irreducibly representational (or 'linguistic', naming). The being of the idea is given through the process or event of naming. It is given in representation and language. That it is '*given*' (*gegeben*) means that it is not 'taken' through activist intentionality. This is Benjamin's departure, not just from phenomenology but also from vitalism: from Bergsonian intuition and Nietzschean paganism. What Nietzsche found in Dionysian polytheism, Benjamin finds in the word of the One. If for Nietzsche tragedy is born from Dionysian dithyrambs, for Benjamin it has a prophetic past. Nietzsche's 'ontological' *Übermensch* will resemble the tragic hero. For Benjamin, the tragic hero of fulfilled language must die, must be sacrificed because of the impossibility of fulfilled language after the Fall (*Sündenfall*). For Nietzsche, the spirit of tragedy and art of revalued values is possible in, for example, Wagner. For Benjamin, historical, and Kabbalist, a rebirth of intensive language in Germany is not possible. The best that is possible is *Trauer* (mourning) and flashes of the idea in 'the extreme', in the event. If in phenomenology and the Romantic Critics it is the thing that incorporates the idea, for vitalists Nietzsche and Bergson it is the process or the becoming of life. For Benjamin, it is not the thing nor life, but language and the medium that is home for the transcendental, both as process (naming) and as form (representation).

'Truth', Benjamin writes, is not a relation (*Relation*) and especially not a relation of intentionality. In both positivism and phenomenology, things have windows and doors: they undergo Newtonian causation and phenomenological reduction. Benjamin's *Kunstphilosophische* method dispenses with intention (*Meinen*) and *Erkennen*, and instead advocates an 'Eingehen und Verschwinden', that is, an 'entering in' and 'disappearance'. The rays of intentionality impossibly aim at truth from the outside, while 'die Wahrheit ist die Tod der Intention' ('truth is the death of intention'). Instead we enter in, and we disappear in the fabric of things. 'The structure of truth "demands a mode of being", which – apart from its greater permanence (*Bestandhaftigkeit*) – in its "intentionlessness", resembles the simple existence of things'. We humans have the passivity of things. We do not take truth from the phenomenon, but are given truth in the name: in the passive process of naming. This passive process is at the same time violent. The name stamps truth on the phenomenon with violence. Thus Benjamin writes, 'truth does not consist of an intention through which the empirical finds a determination'. Instead truth consists of 'the emboss-ing violence of the being of this empirical'.[3] The idea not only pene-trates the phenomenon of the empirical: it stamps or embosses violently its character, its emblem on it.

What is this violent being of truth? What is this being 'from which all phenomenality is withdrawn'? It is *the name*. 'Das aller Phänomenalität entrückte Sein, in dem allein diese Gewalt eignet, is das des Namens' (Benjamin 1974b: 216). The violence of the name is the word as idea. The word is normally phenomenal when it is also a question of the empirical language of man or the language of things. But the word without phenomenon can only be – and this is the basis of *Genesis* – the creative word of God. This also means that the idea is a creative function of God and a truth-function of man. Yet there is neither creation nor truth without the word. God's word as idea is creation, while man's word as idea is truth. What comes primordially, before any First Philosophy of the idea – before ontology – is religion. 'Adam, the Father of man is the Father of Philosophy.' We humans are meant to be not creators, but truth tell-ers: and our truths, as less science- or system-philosophers than arts-philosophers, are not primarily as ontologists but as thing-namers. Ours is less the task of the philosopher than the task of the translator. It is, Benjamin says, the name that determines the givenness of ideas. These ideas are given not so much in primordial language (*Ursprache*) as in primordial perception (*Urvernehmens*): primordial perception of the images of things. In such primordial perception, words possess their naming (*benennende*) nobility, undiluted by cognitive meaning (*erkennende Bedeutung*). Primordial perception, is through the naming through the word as idea, undisturbed by the extensive and cognitive word. Plato's idea cannot be given without the word. Plato's doctrine of ideas is possible because the 'literal sense ('Wortsinn') of the solely mother-tongue speaking philosopher, did not have links with the word's apotheosis ('Vergöttlichung des Wortes')'. Indeed, 'Plato's ideas are basically – from this standpoint – nothing other than word-concepts'. Thus if words have both material and symbolic moments, the 'idea is the symbolic moment of the word'. The task of the philosopher – and Benjamin obsesses endlessly with tasks (*Aufgabe*) – is to restore this state of affairs, in which 'the idea comes to self-understanding'. This reflexive idea is the name. 'Philosophy', however, does 'not speak in the tones of revelation' (*offenbarend*), so philosophy must 'think in the register of memory' (*Erinnern*). Thus Platonic anamnesis is a matter of philosophical contemplation. 'Then the idea is released from its innermost reality (*Innersten der Wirklichkeit*) as the word ... claiming its name-giving rights'.

Philosophy, Benjamin observes, has always been a struggle for the representation of ideas: whether they be represented in the concept or the word. In the concept, philosophy thinks with intention, in the word with contemplation. At stake is 'a few, ever again the same, words'. Logic, aesthetics and ethics attain their significance not through the continuous concept of systems-philosophy, but as 'monuments in the discontinuous structure of the world of ideas' (1974b: 213). Philosophy is thus a question of not intention, but 'reflection': of reflection on phenomena to remember their being. Intentionality is impossible towards essences that have no doors or windows. Ideas do not touch each other. Benjamin writes 'every idea is a sun, and ideas are related to one another as suns' (i.e. untouching). The harmonious relationship of such constellations of essences is truth.[4] The configuration is of an idea surrounded by concepts. The concept that here mediates (*Vermittlerrolle*) between ideas and things resolves the thing or phenomenon into elements. In the absence of phenomena, ideas are obscure. But in the presence of the gathering of phenomena, the ideas come to life, like 'the mother who is only in her "fullness" in the "circle of her children". As for the things, the phenomena, for their part they are 'redeemed' (*gerettet*). When the concept claims its own supremacy as universal, it enters the pitfalls of classification. But the concept can also come under the spell of the idea and the name. Then the idea relates to the phenomenon in terms of its objective interpretation. The idea thus seizes (*erfassen*) phenomena and via the concept transports them to a different world: the world of the idea as constellation. Thus the concept, when it is released from the egotism of cognition, is the salvation of phenomena and the representation of ideas. Ideas actualize (*vergegenwärtigt*) themselves in concepts. Concepts, at the same time as they represent ideas, actualize them.[5] For phenomena, ideas are 'their virtual ordering (*virtual Anordnung*) and their objective interpretation'.

Concepts, we just saw, gather elements from phenomena and represent ideas. Philosophers as well as critics have no choice but to deal in concepts. Poets do not deal in concepts, but in other sorts of representations. Truth, in Plato's *Symposium*, is the essential content (*Gehalt*) of beauty. Beauty, for its part, is indispensable to the definition of truth because there is no truth without representation. The *Symposium* dresses beauty as Eros, which has longings for truth. Here truth is not beauty in itself but for Eros, who is the seeker of truth. This, in the same sense as the beloved, is not beauty in-itself, but is beauty for the lover. In this 'every representational moment of truth is the refuge of beauty' (Benjamin 1974b: 211, my trans.).[6] It is this palpability that 'provokes the pursuit of the understanding', 'from which beauty flees'. Thus the Romantic Critics, who Benjamin finally rejects in his doctoral thesis, worked through the concept, in pursuit of the poet. Yet the intellect – when working through the name – 'bears witness that truth is not the exposure (*Enthüllung*) of beauty's secret', but is the 'revelation (*Offenbarung*) that does justice to this secret' (1974b: 211). This is also, says Benjamin, what great philosophy does. The great philosophers see the world in terms of the order of ideas: Plato's ideas, Leibniz's monad and Hegel's dialectic, in each case describing the 'unfolding of idea into the empirical world'. Here the artist and scientist (*Forscher*) stand in contrast to one another. The artist 'sketches a miniature picture of the idea-world', whereas the scientist 'arranges the empirical world in order to disperse (*zerstreuen*) it'. Yet it is in the *Ideenwelt* in which the *Forscher* divides the empirical world into concepts. The philosopher and artist are thus both engaged in representation, whereas the scientist is involved in analytic subdivision. The scientist's 'shallow universalism' stands in contrast to philosophy's and art's representations and thematic repetition. The scientist's chain of deduction stands opposite to the philosopher's and artist's art of interruption (*Absetzens*) (1977b: 32).

What I am describing is a sort of Benjaminian method for the cultural and perhaps also social sciences. This method is monadological, where the main thrust of monadology is to treat culture in its difference. To take memory and ideas seriously. And to treat all cultural beings, human and nonhuman, people, animals, objects and bits of information, in terms of their relation to the world they open onto. Benjamin, like Georg Simmel, rejects Kantian and positivist classification for a return to Leibniz's monad. If Kant's understanding is positivist and nominalist, his realm of ideas is Leibnizian and based on difference. But whereas in Simmel it is social relations that take on the colours of Leibniz's ontology of difference, in Benjamin it is the word. So in Simmel the Leibnizian idea is instantiated in social relations, in Benjamin it is instantiated in the word. This means that cultural objects for Benjamin are to be treated in terms of their world, but this world is mediated by the image-language that these objects 'speak'. This image-language is also rooted in the memory incorporated into these cultural objects. It is our task – as theorists, artists, architects, to listen to and translate this language into symbols, whether linguistic or mathematical, and indeed to translate them into other images and sounds and practices and built spaces. In this sense too, this chapter on Benjamin looks forward to Chapter 6 which outlines a possible future for cultural studies. It is this sort of really ontological method, a method of an ontology of difference that is at stake.

Language: things, man and God

Benjamin develops a more explicit notion of intensive language in 'On Language in General and the Languages of Man' ('Über die Sprache überhaupt und die Sprache des Menschen'). What the 'Epistemo-Critical Prologue' does for knowledge, 'Über die Sprache' does for language. In some ways this essay is foundational for the Prologue: that is Benjamin's theory of knowledge is rooted in his idea of language. The Prologue was written in 1928, and 'On Language as Such' was written in 1916. The three main divisions of 'Uber die Sprache' address first language, things and man; second, God, creation and man; and third, man's Fall from Paradise. In between, Benjamin presents his theory of the proper name, the idea of translation and gives us some directions for the arts. This essay, written more than a decade before the *Tragic Drama* book, does not address truth per se, or the notion of the idea. It is knowing and naming – knowing through the proper name – that form a bridge between them and are at the centre of Benjamin's understanding of (intensive) culture.

Kaballah: instrumental versus intensive language

Benjamin begins the essay by contrasting semiotic or extensive language with kabbalistic (intensive) language.[7] At the very outset, he addresses the language of law, and of technology. He insists that such language is not a question of how judges or engineers speak. The discourse of lawyers and engineers, indeed discursive language, more generally, is instead *extensive* language. In intensive language there must be the 'imparting of a spiritual content' ('Mitteilung' of a 'geistige Inhalt') (Benjamin 1977c: 141). This spiritual content needs to come from the *being* of law, from the being of technology: in our sense from the not epistemological but ontological being of law and technology. Benjamin insists from the start – as he does in the *Trauerspiel* Prologue – that language is different from the idea. This is because 'even God's idea cannot bear fruit' (*fruchtbar*). God creates not through the idea but through the *word*. For Benjamin, unlike the trees in the Garden of Eden, the idea does not bear fruit. The essay hangs on the contraposition of, on the one hand, communication through language (*durch die Sprache*) and communication in language (*in der Sprache*). His initial example is that the German language itself is what is communicated, not through it but in it. While communication through language has to do with interests, strategy, instrumentalism, what is communicated in language is language itself. What can the communication of language itself mean? Communication *in der Sprache* is communication of a 'geistige Wesen', i.e. a spiritual being. Language communicates not just itself *in der Sprache*, but also the metaphysical being of things. What is communicated though language is rather a physical or corporeal being. For the part of language, in communication *durch die Sprache*, language is a mere means (*Mittel*). In communication *in der Sprache*, language is a medium (*das Medium*). To say language communicates itself means that it communicates itself as a medium. This is not, say, German grammar or German as a linguistic system or the rules of discourse in German. What is communicated is not the extensive totality, but the intensive being of the German language. Yet the being of the thing communicated and the medium are not as different from each other as might appear. The content of an expression German *in der Sprache* consists of the spiritual being of the things and persons that are named through it. In contrast, German as extensive language (*durch die Sprache*) consists of the physical beings that are classified through it. Here Benjamin speaks of the 'signs' of extensive language and the 'symbols' of intensive language. Whereas, then, extensive or semiotic language is found in the instrumental discourse of law and technology, the symbols of intensive language for their part span the range from poetry to everyday life. Demetz (1986) is right to characterize Benjamin's work as a 'metaphysics of language'.

Benjamin's contrast of language, of, on the one hand, *durch die Sprache* and, on the other, *in der Sprache* is similar to Kant's classical distinction of means versus or finality (*Zweckmäßigkeit*). In *The Critique of Pure Reason*, nature is a means. In *The Critique of Judgement* (which addresses art), nature and art are finalities (Lyotard 1994: 63–4). Benjamin's language as not means but medium is such a finality. Like Kant's work of art, it has neither to do with interest nor with its content (Derrida 1987: 73); Benjamin's intensive language has no verbal content (*Inhalt*). Verbal, like pictorial, content would, for Benjamin, be extensive. Benjamin takes this a step further. Communication through a means is mediated, whereas communication through a medium is unmediated. As unmediated it is immediate. In what sense is it immediate? This type of immediate or intensive language is, for Benjamin, how Adam named things in the Garden of Eden. This Adamic language is immediate, as we will see below, in that God here is the spiritual, the metaphysical, that is unmediated, while the physical is mediated. The thing has an appearance for us; as we see it in physics or mathematics or commodities in markets it is mediated. But the experience of the spiritual (*geistlich*) being of the thing is immediate. For Benjamin, this immediacy is akin to 'magic', as Winfried Menninghaus noted in his *Walter Benjamin's Theorie der Sprachmagie* (1995). How is it 'magic'? Benjamin suggests it is first magic in its 'infinity'.[8] In this idea of infinity, Benjaminian magic goes beyond the metaphysics of substantial forms. He moves towards Kabbalism and Franz Kafka's mystical Judaism (Benjamin 1977a: 430). It refers to the magic of all *Sprache*, not just the word-language of humans, but the non-word language of images and signs of things. It also seems to connote a magical materiality as well as an immateriality. Yet it is not the infinity of man or things or even God that is at stake here. It is only language that is magical.

Language is magical in so far as it contains the 'infinity' of beings. This is not the extensive infinity of beings as particulars, but the 'unique' infinity of each being. In so far as it contains God's, man's or things' unique infinity, language is magical. But what is this unique infinity? Let us think of this through the categories of the 'Epistemo-Critical Prologue' discussed above. The uniqueness must come from something like each being's point of view. This point of view, which is the being's (monad's) identity as well as its perception, is also its representation. Benjamin's beings are magical in so far as their perception is representation. Such representational perception is only possible in beings that are linguistically endowed.

In this context, how can we understand, on the one hand, things and, on the other, man? To begin with, the linguistic being of things is not equal to their entire ontological being. This is different from man, whose linguistic essence is his spiritual being. Things have language: they communicate to man their linguistic being, but not their entire spiritual being. Things also communicate with each other. Things speak in the language of images, while man speaks in the language of words. It is through images that things can convey their ontological and singular nature to man. Thus things communicate to man in images, which man then translates into words. Benjamin (1996b) later wrote a famous essay called 'The Task of the Translator'. It is man who is this translator, and it is when man carries out this translation in intensive and not extensive language, that he fulfils his ontological nature as the naming animal. Benjamin thinks through this logic of naming through *Genesis* of the Old Testament. In *Genesis* God creates both man and nature (things) from material. God created Adam from earth – Adam means 'red earth', just as Christ means 'messiah'. In contrast, God does not create light from material, but only from the word: 'Let there be light'.

Things, God and man (man's soul) are all, in 'On Language', for Benjamin 'infinite'. By this he means that they are all somehow *linguistic* infinities. Each of God, man and things is, however, a linguistic infinity in a particular mode. The infinity of God's word is 'unlimited and creative' (*schöpferisch*), while the infinity of human language is 'limited' and 'analytic' (1977b: 143). In this, God's linguistic infinity is to do with creating while man's is to do with knowing. This is an intensive knowing and truth of both poets and *Kunstkritiker*, like Benjamin himself.[9] If man, thus, is the truth-representing being, then what about things? Their infinity must be even more limited than man's. It must be neither creative nor knowing, but something else. The linguistic infinity of things thus lies neither in creating (God) nor in representing (man), but in their *giving*. They give themselves to be named. In the sort of phenomenological sense encountered in Paul Ricœur, things open up in their giving, as man closes off (operationally) in his naming. Things are thus giving and open infinities. Here, things, man and God are monads. Monads, as we saw in Chapter 3, are distinguished by their point of view: by the different worlds that each monad's unique point of view comprises. Things and man are *limited* infinities in so far as each has its point of view. Only God's point of view is unlimited. Human and thing-infinities are not limited temporally. As infinities they are – like Leibniz's monads – eternal. As such infinities, man, things and God are substantial forms that are negated in processes of self-actualizing. God actualizes his ideas – through the word – in the creation of men and things as infinities. Thus God is a very special infinity indeed: the One whose actualization creates an infinity of infinities.

From images to symbols: man's fate

002:007   And the LORD God formed man of the dust of the ground, and breathed into his nostrils the breath of life; and man became a living soul.

002:019   And out of the ground the LORD God formed every beast of the field, and every fowl of the air; and brought them unto Adam to see what he would call them: and whatsoever Adam called every living creature, that was the name thereof.

002:020   And Adam gave names to all cattle, and to the fowl of the air, and to every beast of the field.

These passages from *Genesis* are of special importance to Benjamin's 'On Language'. In the language of the name, man is communicating himself to God. It is men, and not things, that communicate themselves to God in the name. Through the name, man communicates to God (1) the spiritual essence of the thing, (2) man's own self, and (3) the spiritual essence of language. For their part, the things of nature communicate their spiritual being only through man's name. This stands in contrast to what Benjamin seems to understand as a *'community of things'*, which communicates differently. Through man's naming, the thing's spiritual essence is communicated to God. Man, as the representing being, represents the truth through the name. The name is thus the linguistic essence of language; it is the language of language. This would be different from the language of technology or law, with which Benjamin introduces the essay. The name, as the language of language, is of a higher density (*Dichte*) than the language of law or technology. The point for us is that Benjamin approaches the name not through art or through philosophy, but through *religion*. If, for Nietzsche, truth and intensive language are found in the representations of art (in, say, *The Birth of Tragedy*), for Benjamin they are in religion.

It is in the context of the name that Benjamin directly addresses intensive and extensive language. 'Thus the intensive totality of language as the absolutely communicable spiritual essence and the extensive totality of language as the universally communicating (designating) essence culminate in the name.'[10] Let us unpack. Benjamin is saying that the language of the name (i.e. Adamic language) is not only intensive, but also extensive. It is intensive in its absolutely communicable *spiritual* being. It is extensive in its universally communicating (in the nominalistic sense of denominating or designating) essence. Second, its intensive essence is communicable and its extensive essence is communicating. It is in its extensity that language is universal. In its intensity it may be singular. Third, neither God's language nor the language of things, but only man's language has both such consummate intensity and extensive universality. '*Der Mensch allein hat die nach Universalität und Intensität vollkommene Sprache*' (italics in original).

At stake in Benjamin's implicit *Religionsphilosophie* is Creation (*Schöpfung*), Revelation (*Offenbarung*) and Redemption (*Erlösung, Rettung*). We have addressed creation. What about revelation?[11] Benjamin writes that the consideration of man as naming being leads us to *Religionsphilosphie*. He says that the 'inner concept of the spirit of language' (*Inbegriff der Sprachgeistes*) leads us to *Religionsphilosophie* and to revelation.

Here he brings in the eighteenth-century pre-Critical language-philosopher (*Sprachphilosoph*) Johann Georg Hamann. Hamann, a Christian Kabbalist, tells Benjamin that 'language is the mother of reason and revelation'.[12] It is God who creates: this much is clear. It is God who creates the beasts and man from earth, and the fish from water. But who or what *reveals*? In perhaps the first instance, the Bible reveals. The representations of the Bible yield revelatory knowledge. God creates through the Word: God creates man through matter. Man perceives creation. Man, at his most fully human (his most inner self) works through the name. It is man who reveals. But how about matter in this context? Things are more material than man: as man is more material than God. Man has a voice and communicates through sounds (*Laute*), while matter – and the beasts – are '*stumm*' (dumb). In his sounds and words man is created in God's image. We have already spoken of the contrast between Nietzschean art and Benjaminian religion. Just before the 24-year-old Benjamin wrote 'On Language', he wrote a short never-published essay on 'Tragedy and the German mourning play'. Here he contrasted the fulfilled time of Classical tragedy with the unfulfilled time of the mourning play. This latter is a forerunner of messianic time. When he later contrasts his mourning play and Nietzsche's tragedy, Benjamin (1977b: 102) focuses on the aesthetic nature of Nietzsche's reading of tragedy, which he criticizes for its Wagnerian ethos. Benjamin is making a distinction between the aesthetic and the religious. The aesthetic is fulfilled and, in Heidegger's sense, ontological whereas the religious is unfulfilled and points to a messianic to-come. The point in 'On Language', is that the language of man is found in a religious register whereas the language of things is more aesthetic. Art is more material in its composition than religion. Art has more in common with the linguistic being of things ('dinglichem Sprachgeist') (Benjamin 1977b: 147). Like art, the community of things is material, a 'stoffliche Gemeinschaft'. Man's community with things is immaterial[13] and, like in religion, is a community of spiritual beings. Yet both communities are magical. There is also a 'Magie der Materie'. What art does in its representations is to enable this magical and material community of things to speak.[14]

Thus God creates through the word, through a very particular medium and man knows things also through the word as a medium of knowledge and truth. Also God makes things knowable in names while man actualizes this knowability through naming-knowledge.

The Godly and the human approach one another even more closely through the *proper* name (*Eigenname*). The proper is where man most closely approaches *göttliche* creative infinity.[15] There is something thus more finite about the normal naming of things than proper naming. God may have created things as namable. But the proper naming of another man directly partakes of the word of God. To name in the *Eigenname* 'is the word of God in human sounds'. The *Eigenname* is man's community (communion) with God's creative word. Note that things commune with each other and with man's naming word, but not with God's creative word. For Adam to name his son Cain is an *Eigenname*. 'A man's name is his fate.' And this is singular. We recall that Leibniz's monads such as Alexander and Caesar were also names. They were thus substances or subjects that contained their own predicates and hence their fates. Their predicates were not as in nominalism external to their subjects. In the proper name man is pairing knowledge with creation. This is especially true in naming his sons and daughters. They are born material, but through the name take on their own being. In doing so he is also assigning fate to substance: that is fate to the subject.

Benjamin addresses the properties of things and how things communicate. If things are dumb and silent in their communication, then how do they communicate? How do these entities, which are much more 'spontaneous' than man, communicate? In *Genesis 1* God makes only man, and not things, from earth. For things, whether animal or vegetable, God says 'let the earth bring forth' (Gen. 1:12, 1:24) beasts and grass. To be brought forth from the earth is to be more material than man, who is made directly by God from earth: he is 'breathed life' into by the Lord and thus becomes a 'living soul'. Man as extensive being is made of earth: God's breath of life is what makes man an intensive being. If not God but earth brings forth animals and vegetable nature, then both their material and their maker are material and extensive. These things, whose creator and own matter are material, communicate to man – says Benjamin – through 'images and signs'. But they must communicate to one another exclusively through their (magic) materiality. Although without man's intervention there will be neither poetry nor art, God puts into things the kernel of the naming name ('Keim ernennende Namens'). This kernel, once present, speaks silently to man in signs and images (not in symbols). Man translates these images/signs into sounds and words. To do so he translates the restful (*selig*) aspect of the things. This is a double process once man is summoned to name. First, man gazes, i.e. *Anschauuen*. He works through intuition in regard to the images and signs. Man intuits the images/signs of things. Man thus receives (*empfangen*). Then man conceives, he knows (*erkennen*) through the name. Man receives/perceives and then man conceives. He translates signs/images into words. In Paradise, as Hamann notes, this is easy. Because 'all that man heard, saw, felt, i.e. all sense perception was living word. And for man to name was as "easy as a Kinderspiel"' (Benjamin 1977c: 151). In doing so, man takes language to a higher level of intensity.

The Fall: from naming to judgement

001:031   And God saw every thing that he had made, and, behold, it was very good.

002:008   And the LORD God planted a garden eastward in Eden; and there he put the man whom he had formed.

002:009   And out of the ground made the LORD God to grow every tree that is pleasant to the sight, and good for food; the tree of life also in the midst of the garden, and the Tree of Knowledge of good and evil.

002:016   And the LORD God commanded the man, saying, Of every tree of the garden thou mayest freely eat.

002:017   But of the Tree of Knowledge of good and evil, thou shalt not eat of it: for in the day that thou eatest thereof thou shalt surely die.

If *Genesis 2* addressed the Garden of Eden, Adam, naming and unashamed nakedness, then *Genesis 3* concerns the serpent and the Fall. The fall of man, for Benjamin, is due to a shift in language from the truth language of the name to the language of judgement. Judgement itself and experience is purely extensive and physical. It is the Tree of Knowledge that brings this about. After God creates Adam from earth and breathes life into him, He places him in the Garden of Eden. Previously in *Genesis 1*, there were men and women and nature, but not Paradise. There was no naming language or even discussion of language. God made Adam for the Garden of Eden to name and to eat from all the trees, including the tree of life. But He warned not to eat of the Tree of Knowledge because it 'is the tree of *knowledge of good and evil*'. It is indeed the serpent that 'seduces into the *nameless* knowledge of good and evil' (1977c: 152, italics added). The Tree of Knowledge was placed in the Garden in order for God to judge man, Benjamin notes. Yet man thinks the apples will impart *to him* the *faculty of judgement* of good and evil. Benjamin thus contrasts the 'naming (*nennende*) word' and the 'judging (*richtenede*) word'. Man eating from the Tree of Knowledge and moving into the register of extensive and judging language is, for Benjamin, at the origins of Law itself. 'This monstrous irony (i.e. man transforming himself into judge) is the mark of the mythical origin of law.'[16] In Paradise, in the Garden of Eden there was no law: no need for law or judgement. God saw what he created at the end of the sixth day and said 'it was very good'. The Tree of Knowledge was the presence of evil in the Garden. At stake is knowledge from the outside: 'the uncreated imitation of the created word'. In contrast to the 'created word' – i.e. man's naming-word – this judging word is uncreated. The judging word is the 'birth of the human word in which the name no longer lives intact'. There is an identity between the serpent's promise (*Verheißung*) and the superficiality (*äußerlich*) of the extensive 'word'. The superficiality of this communicating word of judgement leads to what Kierkegaard called *Geschwätz*. Now at the same time the *Schwätzer*, the sinner, is submitted to judgement. *Geschwätz* is also Heidegger's *das Man* and the rumour-mongering judgements of the tabloid press. The judging word means the *Verknechtung* (enserfment) of language in *Geschwätz* and the enserfment of things in 'folly' (*Narretei*) and the Tower of Babel. God, of course, is angry and expels man from the Garden. In post-paradisal language, language became a mere means, a mere sign.

What happens to nature in the Fall? The Garden of Eden is a state of bliss. Experience and nature is blissful (*selig*). In the Fall from Paradise's unity to post-Adamic multiplicity (*Vielheit*), God curses nature too: He curses the soil. Now nature too must be redeemed (*Erlösung*). Redemption is a doing. In any event, after the Fall, nature 'laments (*klagen*)'. There is a 'sadness (*Traurigkeit*) in nature'. Nature laments language itself. Nature mourns (*trauert*) because it is now known by the 'unknowable', i.e. it is known not by knowable naming language but the unknowable 'hundred' judging languages of man.

Benjamin speculates that while poetry is perhaps founded in the naming-language of men, painting and sculpture are possibly closer to the language of things. Of a material *Gemeinsamkeit*: a nameless, non-acoustic language in the plastic arts. In Paradise this material community of thing grasped (*befaßt*) the world as a unity, as an undivided whole. The language of things is likened to songs, to bird-songs (*Sprache der Vögel*). But art – in contrast to everyday things – will stand only in the deepest relation to the doctrine of signs ('tiefster Beziehung zur Lehre von den Zeichen').

Critical theory and the intensive religious

Immanuel Kant spoke in terms of, on the one hand, a sphere of necessity, in which we have epistemological knowledge and instrumental reason and, on the other, a sphere of freedom. The sphere of freedom is a metaphysical realm: its ideas of reason, which are distinct from the epistemological categories or concepts of the understanding, include the idea of the thing-itself, but also ethics, the ideas of infinity, God and freedom. The thing-itself, Kant says, is not knowable: that is, metaphysical or ontological knowledge is not possible. But also in this sphere of freedom are ethics and God. In his essay 'What is Enlightenment?', Kant sees Enlightenment not just in terms of 'What can I know?', but also in terms of 'What should I do?' And 'What can I hope?' The 'what-can-I-know' he limits to the epistemological knowledge of the thing. The 'what-should-I-do' is of course of Kantian ethics and its categorical imperative. The 'what-can-I-hope' pertains both to Enlightenment utopian thought and implicitly the transcendental God of Judaeo-Christianity. Ontological knowledge too is in Kant's sphere of freedom. But the what-should-I-do and the what-can-I-hope take us not just outside the realm of epistemology but also outside *ontology*.[17] The dimension of intensive culture that Benjamin addresses in his considerations of language and the name equally bring us out of ontology into the realm of the what-can-I-hope. This is not the what-should I-do of ethics, but the what-can-I-hope of the messianic and the religious. Ontology, with Heidegger, is about knowledge, about also an art and language not of loss and messianic promise, but of plenitude and fulfilment, of the already there. This what-can-I-hope is at the basis of critical theory – from Marx via Adorno to, today, Giorgio Agamben.

In this sense, Jacques Derrida is a critical theorist. His critical theory of deconstruction and difference is formulated explicitly as a critique of ontology: of Husserl and Heidegger. Heidegger's famous notion of 'ontological difference' addresses the difference between beings, on the one hand, and being, on the other. This is the difference between the epistemological (beings) and the onto-logical (being). Derrida redefines difference no longer in terms of that between epistemology and ontology, but between ontology and that which is beyond ontology. Like Benjamin, he understands this in terms of mourning – in this case mourning the ghost, the spectre of Marx. Even more like Benjamin, he defines this first in terms of language and then in terms of the religious, the messianic-religious. Benjamin's name is Derrida's writing. Here writing and difference is partly defined in terms of the difference of the 'epis-temological' subsumption of signified by signifier, of particular by universal. But mostly it is defined in contradistinction to Edmund Husserl's phenomenology, and its fully ontological knowledge of the thing-in-itself through the transcendental reduction. Derridean writing is in excess of the ontological knowledge of the thing itself. Partly through a deferral into what we can now understand as the to-come (Derrida 1989). This is very much like Benjamin's word or name, which is an essence, i.e. not at all an ontological essence but instead promise, hope. In this sense, the ontological realm for Heidegger and for Hegel was, though very much opposed to positiv-ist epistemology, determinate, was comprised of determinations (*Bestimmungen*). This deferral, this coming out from under the idea, made Derridean writing largely indeterminate. Thus in Derrida, from the start, there was deconstruction, not of epistemology but of ontology.

This is more explicitly a critique of ontology in Derrida's (1967) endorsement of Emmanuel Levinas' critique of Heidegger. Again, like Benjamin, the word becomes the messianic-religious here. In 'Violence and Metaphysics' (1967), Derrida addresses Levinas' rejection of ontology or First Philosophy through an eth-ics of unconditional responsibility to the Other: to an unknowable and unnameable Other. Derrida/Levinas understood ontology as metaphysics and insisted on its violence – this was a violence of underpinning a possessive individualism of property, a potentially brutal state and of the exclusion of this Other. If ontology for Derrida and, by implication, Levinas was 'Greek', then this Other was 'Jew'. The 'Jew' here is the position without position from which to deconstruct ontology. Here Kant's what-can-I-hope again becomes the messianic. Here we see 'the Greek' as obsessed with the will to knowledge and 'the Jew' obsessed with, well, *justice*. Now this extra-ontological nature of the religious comes back much later in Derrida's (1992) essay, 'Force of Law'. He draws on Walter Benjamin's 'Critique of Violence', and its counterposition of law and justice. Here law is effectively the normativity of a social ontology, while justice is the excluded Other: inscribed in messianic time that also is – for Benjamin – the temporality of revolutionary violence. Thus we have religion and justice against law. In our sense, such religion-inscribed justice and *Kunstkritik* stand alongside ontology – sometimes in opposition, other times in creative tension – as dimensions of intensive culture.

Notes

1 With Peter Fenves, we discussed Leibniz on representation in Chapter 3. We spoke of representation as effectively a modification of predication. For Leibniz, representation follows predication. For Benjamin, representation is primary.
2 'Das Werden des Phänomens festzustellen in ihrem Sein Benjamin' (1974b: 229).
3 'Nicht als Meinen, welche durch die Empirie seine Bestimmung fände, sondern als das Wesen dieser Empirie erst prägende Gewalt bestehet die Wahrheit' (1974b: 216).
4 'Tönende Verhältnis (der) Wesenheiten ist Wahrheit.'
5 'The set of concepts that represent an idea actualize these ideas as a configurations of them (the ideas).'
6 All translations in this chapter are my translations.
7 There is a very different notion of the transcendental in Judaeo-Christian and Greek thought. In Judaism and Christianity God is a personal God: the transcendental is personal. He is also singular. Thus 'there can be no other God before me'. The Greek transcendental is not personal but abstract and general. Christianity was in many senses a much more personal transcendental than even Judaism. Yet Judaism's and Christianity's transcendental was increasingly rationalized, increasingly Hellenized, through various iterations of Philo, Augustine, Maimonides, Aquinas. The origins of Judaism's transcendental are in ancestors' myths. For Emile Durkheim, only in more advanced, post-totemic religions did the soul, gods, appear. These were incorporated in ancestor myths. Only then did something like the individual soul appear. Gerschom Scholem appeared to capture this mythic aspect of Judaism in his arguments against the more rationalized Judaism of his contemporaries.

Kabbalism harks back to the first century AD, when Philo of Alexandria brought the Greek *logos* into Judaism as God's creative principle. Philo subsequently had more influence on the evolution of Christian than on Jewish thought. Kabbalism also drew from the again Hellenized and pre-eminent medieval Jewish philosopher, Maimonides. For Maimonides, every idea grows from its foundation in God and 'all the beings of the heavens and earth came into existence only from the truth of God's being'. On this view, God was neither matter nor spirit but created both matter and spirit. But Maimonides, for Benjamin's influential friend Gerschom Scholem, adopted the Greek principle too. The Jewish God Yahweh, may be fully transcendental but He is not abstract, He is a personal God. Though this name cannot be said, Yahweh has a name and this is singular: 'thou can have no other gods before me'. Maimonides brought in abstract reason from the Greeks and in important respects recast God as abstract reason, as an impersonal god. He did this, observed Scholem, through eliminating Judaism's remaining myths. Judaism of course, as we move from clans to tribes to nation (the Twelve Tribes), will become a world religion with a transcendental and yet still personal God. Thus perhaps we can understand the mythical dimension in Scholem's and Kafka's Judaism. Although the word 'Kabbalah' originated in medieval Spain, the core ideas of Kabbalism go back to the second century AD. Kabbalism is always looking for intensive, inner meaning of texts, from the study of the Torah, looking for the mystical aspect, through the rabbinic literature. Kabbalah features the oral transmission of such mystical and esoteric knowledge from the patriarchs, prophets and sages. Scholem, five years younger than Benjamin but also a student with him at the University of Berlin, was the founder of the modern academic study of Kabbalah. His doctoral thesis was on the oldest known Kabbalistic text – the Safir ha-Bakir. Scholem held that nineteenth-century Kabbalism had its roots in a Jewish Gnosticism. But Scholem wanted to retain the irrational force, the mystical component of Judaism in his Kabbalism. This is why he features historiographic study of Kabbalism rather than reasoning from first principles. For both Scholem and, effectively, Benjamin, the Kabbalists were interpreters of pre-existent linguistic revelation of the divine. The major difference is that, for Scholem, only Hebrew could yield the truth in such revelation, while for Benjamin all the languages of man could reveal such truth.

8 And indeed there is something of infinity in Benjamin in comparison with the radical finitude of Heidegger or, say, Jean Luc Nancy (1990: 12–13). This is perhaps because Platonic memory as anamnesia and memory/history are far more important to Benjamin, as is the messianic future.

9 Benjamin (1974a: 45), in his PhD thesis, rejects the systems thinking of the Romantic *Kunstkritiker*. Benjamin himself is a very different kind of *Kunstkritiker*.

10 'So gipfeln in Namen die intensive Totalität der Sprache als des absolut mitteilbaren geistigen Wesens und die extensive Totalität der Sprache als des universell mitteilended (bennenden) Wesens' (1977b: 145).

11 Let us note here that often in the English translation we have the word 'revelation' when Benjamin is saying merely to show. And that he uses *Rettung* (salvation) as often as *Erlösung*, the former with its more Christian connotations.

12 'Sprache ist die Mutter der Vernunft und Offenbarun.'

13 'Das Unvergleichliche der menschlichen Sprache ist, daß ihre magische Gemeinschaft mit den Dingen immateriell und rein geistig ist, und dafür ist der Laut der Symbol.'

14 This looks very much forward to the materialism of Benjamin's late essay on mimesis.
15 'Die tiefste Abbild diese göttlichen Wortes und der Punkt, an wem die Menschensprache den innigsten Anteil an der göttlichen Unendlichkeit des blo-ßen Wortes erlangt, der Punkt, an dem sich nicht endliches Wort und Erkenntnis nicht werden kann; das ist der menschliche Namen' (1977b: 147).
16 'Diese ungeheure Ironie ist das Kennzeichen des mythischen Ursprungs des Rechtes' (1977c: 154).
17 It is telling that Benjamin formulates the question of justice not in terms of the what-should-I-do of ethics but the what-can-I-hope of the (messianic) religious. Hence also Derrida's (1990) 'Force of Law' and much of the literature around St Paul, especially Milbank (2008).

5

Intensive Capitalism: Marxist Ontology

Introduction: from commodity to difference

Capitalism would, on the face of it, be seen as integrally extensive. At the heart of Marx's analyses of capitalism is the commodity, and these commodities are extensive. The capitalist commodity is abstract and homogeneous: it is interchangeable with a number of different concrete goods, again very much on the model of the atom, the smallest unit of extensity. This is a machine in which the extensity of the means of production engages with the extensity of labour to produce an extensive product. Capital itself is indeed a 'social relation', a social relation that works through the abstraction of the commodity and of labour power. Marx's labour theory of value understands capital to be comprised of congealed, homogeneous abstract labour time. The commodity and exchange are constituted in the field of the extensity.

What this chapter argues is that Marx's capitalism is now becoming *intensive*. If extensive capitalism is the production of extensity by extensity, then intensive capitalism is the production of intensity by intensity. If the watchword for extensive capitalism is the atom in which all atoms are like all other atoms, the principle for intensive capitalism is the monad, in which all monads are different from all other monads. Extensive capitalism entails the abstract homogeneity of capital: of (1) the goods produced, of (2) the means of production and of (3) labour or labour power. It is characterized by (4) a regulative, rule-regulated, work process of homogeneous, repetitive tasks. In intensive capitalism, what is produced is less the Fordist homogeneity of commodities, in which each is the same as every other, but instead the production of singularities. This is the production of *different* kinds of goods and services. What this means is that what Marx called the labour process is largely succeeded by the 'design process'. The value of a good or service is here comprised of the work that goes into it. In the labour process, goods produced comprise abstract homogeneous labour time. In the design process, labour time is heterogeneous. It is not characterized by the same repetitive tasks. Whereas labour process time is like Newtonian time, that is a succession of repetitive identical presents, design-process time incorporates different moments, in which each present comprises simultaneously pasts and futures, in which the past (of memory) and the future of anticipation is comprised in each present. This intensive design process will produce goods and services that are not homogeneities, not commodities, but singularities. Thus extensive capitalism works from a logic of identity, of sameness, while intensive capitalism works from a logic of difference. What is the same in extensive capitalism is not just the things that are produced, but also the units that comprise those things. Thus extensive goods and services comprise units or parts that are identical to one another. And intensive goods and services comprise units that are different from one another.

The Marxian economy of use-values (and indeed Marcel Mauss's gift economy) consisted of products and a work process which were concrete and singular. In Classical, extensive Marxian capitalism featuring exchange-value, work and products are abstract and homogeneous. Exchange-values abstract from the particularities of use-value and consist of homogeneous units of exchange. What is produced in intensive capitalism is not commodities but invention (Lazzarato 2002). At stake now is still abstract, but now *heterogeneous* information. Capital now begins to accumulate as difference. It makes sense to speak of 'use-value', 'exchange-value' and *'difference-value'* of things. Here a product has value in its difference from another product. A brand, for example, takes on value in its difference: its economically significant difference from another brand, or of a given branded product from competitor products in its sector. Difference and value is constituted through the difference of the products of one producer from one another, the difference of the congealed units of labour (design) going into the product, and the difference in the desire of the user or consumer.

This chapter will investigate intensive capitalism. The philosophy of the economy has importantly been a philosophy of value. We see this both in Marx's *Capital* (1967) and Simmel's *Philosophy of Money* (1977: 5–6). But Marx's *Capital* gives us largely a theory of extensive value. As Bernard Stiegler (2004b: 169ff.) suggests, today's capitalism needs a new critique of political economy. This chapter is part of such a new critique. In the first section, we rethink Marxian value in an intensive vein. We do this by reading Marx through the spectacles of the four Aristotelian causes. Working through this fourfold causation,

Heidegger in 'Die Frage nach der Technik' (1954) develops notions of extensive and intensive technology. We will attempt more briefly to apply this to capitalism. In capitalism, what we are looking for is not so much what, the essence or being of technology, but instead an economic ontology of *value*. Whereas Chapter 3 on Leibniz focused on the philosophical intensity of truth and Chapter 4 on the religious intensity of hope, this chapter addresses the economic intensity of value.

This chapter's second section investigates intensive capitalism in the context of the rise and the crisis of neo-liberalism. We will address neo-liberalism analytically in terms of the institutional economics of Ronald Harry Coase. Neo-liberalism, which arose in the 1980s, has been, unlike classical liberalism or the Keynesian welfare state, about competition *between* monopolies and the attack on public goods. Coase's economics justifies monopolies on the basis of transaction costs and provides arguments against public goods – welfare and environmental goods – on the basis of well-defined property rights. What neo-liberalism does is to try to internalize into commoditized transactions the negative *externalities* that it generates. We want to understand intensive capitalism, with Paul Krugman and Yann Moulier Boutang, in terms of the chronic spillover of externalities. These externalities are side-effects and more or less contingent entities that are themselves intensities. At stake here are not only the negative spillovers of 'bads' or environmental risks, but, both at the level of the Internet and urban space, positive externalities of information. In this sense intensive capitalism is not just a risk society but an 'externality society'. At the centre of this is a challenge to Coasean property rights in the context of a reconceived commons.

Neo-liberalism has undergone systemic breakdown due to the negative externalities of finance in 2008. The Coasean firm tends to multiply its product divisions, leading to the firm central management taking on effectively financial functions. This is part of a more general 'financialization', as determined by not the rise of finance in general, but of investment banks and an anonymized trading function. The upshot is resource allocation based not on the value of assets but on equity prices. The single-minded pursuit of market capitalization (i.e. maximizing share prices) drove the leveraging and hyper-expansion of the corporate and mortgage-backed bond market. We will examine the politics of this financialization.

The chapter concludes with a discussion of what seems to be the implosion of intensity into extensity in contemporary capitalism, so that we are no longer dealing with the extensive material on the one hand, and the intensive immaterial on the other. Instead we are dealing with the *intensive-material*. At one time, communication was intensive and machines and mechanism were extensive, but now information and communication machines – i.e. the intensive-material – are at the heart of our economy and society.

Causation and value: Aristotle and Marx

Aristotle, as we discussed in Chapter 3, spoke of efficient, material, formal and final causes. These are the causes of substances. And we are dealing with something along the lines of substances in the economy. Aristotle's examples of *efficient* cause are the sculptor making the statue and the father causing the son. Creation is at the centre of efficient cause. Hence Shakespeare would be efficient cause of *Hamlet*. This is creation in the German sense of *schöpfen*: whether creation by God (gods) or creation in the arts. Efficient cause might create substance for Aristotle, but it is in *formal* cause where the energy, the self-causing agency lies. If we think of cause in the modern or contemporary sense, then efficient cause is closest to mechanical cause from the outside and formal cause is closest to self-organization from the inside. Material cause for Aristotle (1998: 12–13) enters into the composition of the substance, which is of course hylomorphic, but it is not a motive force like efficient and formal cause. Efficient cause – for Marx labour-power – plays a greater role in the economic *value* of the object than it does in its ontological nature. This is partly because efficient cause, as in Marxian production of value, is not about nature: it is instead a *social* relation. What concerned Aristotle was *substance*; the thing at the centre of Marx's attention is capitalism's *commodity*. Its efficient cause is labour. The commodity is primarily an abstract thing, comprising abstract labour. It comprises abstract and homogeneous units of labour *time*. This is labour as efficient cause in classical Marxism's extensive capitalism (Marx 1967: 77). In contrast, Aristotle's sculptor works in concrete labour time. This labour time is comprised neither of homogeneous (extensive-capitalist) nor heterogeneous (intensive-capitalist) units. The concrete labour process, and the temporality of Aristotle's sculptor, is indivisible and not comprised of units at all. In intensive capitalism, financialization brings a major component of labour outside the succession of presents of Newtonian clock time and into a perpetual future: a future of warrants, of payments on bonds, of market capitalization as the value of those commodities that are joint stock companies.

In Aristotle, *material* cause is the stuff (the *hyle*) from which substances are made. It is amorphous stuff that only becomes hylomorphic when subjected to form and formal cause. Aristotelian formal cause forms and, in this sense, causes matter (Aristotle 1998: 374–5). Once matter becomes hylomorphic and thus becomes substance, formal cause continues to act, self-causing such substances. What is *material* cause in extensive capitalism? If efficient cause is the above-mentioned labour time, then matter is '*congealed* abstract homogeneous labour time'. It is only now that the commodity has *value*. This is the 'labour-value' that goes into it. It is different from use-value and exchange-value, both of which have to do with purpose and final cause. Substance – or matter – here *cause* form. The value-form or commodity is quantified through exchange-value. Exchange-value is a question of function rather than structure. Exchange-value is determined through teleological or functional causation. But the commodity form is at the same time structurally caused through the congealed labour time of value substance. Material cause is structural cause. In intensive capitalism, matter will consist not of congealed homogeneous labour but processual heterogeneous *life*. Matter does not congeal in metaphysical capitalism: it is processual. The unit of matter becomes not the commodity but the bit of information. If matter in use-value is concrete and indivisible, matter in the value-form of extensive capitalism is, from the point of view of the labour comprising it, abstract matter comprising congealed homogeneous abstract units. Matter in intensive capitalism remains abstract, but mutates into units of information and communication, each of which is different from every other. Matter itself becomes intensive and inseparable from thought and language.

We speak today of the mutability of genetic material. Yet there is a surprising 'stickiness' of phenotype, or form even. In biology, the failures of the human genome project attest to this stickiness. Despite the seeming infinity of genetic mutations, phenotype persists, and phenotypic space is vastly empty. This paucity of phenotypes in the context of seemingly unlimited genetic information-generating possibilities attests to the continued power of *formal cause*, and to the limitations of cause from material structures. So how do we explain this stickiness of phenotype, of form? This is not explicable by teleological cause of natural selection. Niches can change, environments can change radically, but forms persist; species can persist for millions of years (Dover 2001). In global geopolitics, strong nations persist relatively independently of the environmental niches they inhabit. The point is that causality is now as much about the preservation of form, including social forms, as about their destruction and mutation. And the problem is perhaps even more than explaining change – how can we explain continuity or this stickiness? For Aristotle, formal cause gives rise not to species but to individuals. It is formal cause that makes things, that makes substances what they are. It is their formal cause that makes them different from other substances. Formal cause self-causes from the inside: it is intensive cause. Formal cause, in part because all of the causes are also reasons, is always the *differentia specifica*: it is and it generates the specific difference.

What can it mean to say that form causes itself? In Aristotle, you have more or less timeless forms, genera and species. These are essences that explain the shape of individuals. In modernity, form is not timeless, yet a form's temporality is in an important sense reversible. The same is assumed in modernist architecture and planning – think of Corbusier. The assumptions are equilibriate. There are parallels here in the notion of reproduction that we have in the structuralist sociology of Bourdieu. In Bourdieu, we have equilibriate reproduction of the society and social class. Now, however, we are no longer dealing with timelessness, but path dependency (Urry 2002), with traces and decay. We are dealing with systems that are far from equilibrium states that nonetheless persist as forms. They maintain their operational closure, that is, their system-ness or form-ness, while being in a disequilibrium state (Varela et al. 1993: 201). They do this through structural coupling with their external and internal environments. Thus, in the organism there is such coupling at levels of generic information, protein, cell, tissue, organ, organism (phenotype or form). The organism draws on cellular and molecular protein and gene networks – as we see in immunology – to reconstitute tissue and to fight viruses or bacteria (Bentley and Corne 2001). Such structural coupling would seem to characterize economies in intensive capitalism.

Value-form is the value of congealed homogeneous labour. Value-form, or the commodity, is the immaterial yet physical bodily extension of Marxian value-substance. The value-form is the commodity in so far as it consists of exchange-value. It is such value-form that generates the superstructures. But exchange-value, the number of units comprised in a commodity that exchanges on markets, is determined not by efficient, or material or formal cause. At stake here is *final cause*. This is not ultimate, but proximate teleological cause. Thus in use-value, the cause and value of the commodity lies in the concrete and singular use of it. It has no measure and cannot be divided into units. The value of labour-power to the capitalist is measurable and consists of units of abstract utility. This is exchange-value. The commodity, in so far as exchange-value, is determined by its purpose, its final cause. The demand-side of markets aggregates such purposes. Thus aggregates demand abstract utility. All four Aristotelian causes are reasons (Witt 1989: 188–91). That is, an individual thing's causes are also its reasons. So the full – all the four causes – cause of the individual is its sufficient reason. In Marx's economic base material, cause and final cause come together. The ultimate cause is thus the economy or congealed abstract labour time in capitalism. But Marx's first cause is material and physical. Today in an age of information and abstract difference, this a first cause that is material and metaphysical.

We introduced the four Aristotelian – material, efficient, formal and final – causes in Chapter 3. In the context of Marxian value and, by extension, value in intensive capitalism, the most important would seem to be material cause and formal cause. We saw in Chapter 3 that the *differentia specifica* of formal and material cause is that these two causes *comprise* the object, comprise the thing under consideration. Efficient cause precedes the object and final cause comes after the object, but material and final cause comprise the object or thing (Hulswit 2005). In Aristotle's *Metaphysics*, none of the causes is the thing's predicate. For Aristotle, these causes determine the substance of this thing that the four causes constitute is substance, in which things are different from each other. This substance, like the grammatical subject, has predicates – eight of Aristotle's ten categories are such predicates. I may be middle-aged, male and Afro-Caribbean. These may be my predicates as a substance (subject). But they are not my causes. Final cause is also not irrelevant here. The 'what-can-I-hope' of religious and messianic critique that was the subject of Chapter 4 has affinities with final cause. And the 'what-can-I-hope' is, for Benjamin, not a predicate of, what for him, is a cultural object. For Marxian and neo-Marxian politics, this utopian dimension is what Ernst Bloch (2004) called *Das Prinzip Hoffnung*. But whereas culture was the object of the last chapter, in this chapter it is the economy. And what we will investigate is not hope but *value*, intensive and intrinsic value.

Let us consider material and formal cause: the *hylomorphism* (*hylo* is matter, *morph* is form) at the centre of Aristotle's – and not Plato's – ontology. Plato, we remember, is interested in neither predication nor matter. Matter only comes into play as a derivative simulacrum of form. There are many critiques of and many problems with hylomorphism. Yet when Aristotle (1998: 21–2) says that substance consists of matter and form, he is giving quite high status to the material. In this same sense, he will want to attribute considerable status not just to substance but also to the material categories that are the predicates of substance. Leibniz, in this sense like Plato, will not give much status at all to matter. He sees matter (see Chapter 3) as derivative of substantial form: of the pure intensity of the monad. In contrast to Spinoza's intensive unity, Leibniz, with his plurality, his infinity of monads, gives us intensive multiplicity. But how can we rescue the material in this? Thinkers like Negri (1999) will rescue the material by reverting to Spinoza and reconceiving Spinoza's monism as material. But let us take a different tack. Leibniz reduces the material to the predicates of what is, for him, substance, i.e. the fully immaterial monad. Leibniz's monad is not purely formal, because the monad is a *substantial* form. Yet it does not comprise matter. In the *Preface* to *The Phenomenology of Mind*, Hegel (1977: 5–6) rejects Romantics like Schelling and his own younger incarnation in his desire to retain the material. Such Romantic Spinozism, in which the divine is immanent in nature as single substance, still conceives matter as derivative. Hegel criticizes these writers for forgetting the material, for forgetting extrinsic predication, and argues instead that reason must work both intensively and extensively. Later, in *The Philosophy of Right*, Hegel (1967: 203–4) is critical of Kant's categorical imperative as not being embedded in the materiality of social life, of what Hegel called *Sittlichkeit*. So Hegel reintroduces a certain hylomorphism, though surely reason, or mind, and not matter is the governing moment. Finally, Hegel wants both intensive and extensive multiplicity to be subsumed by a unity of Spinozist absolute reason. What is compelling about Aristotle is the integral centrality of the material: that matter and form are not at all separate in the sense of Cartesian two-substance notions. It is finally that the material remains part and parcel of and inseparable from a substance. It is that matter and form are not two substances *à la* Descartes, but are active in the same substance. It is that matter is at the core of substances and not a mere external predicate of it.

Let us return to look at Karl Marx. In Marx's dialectical materialism, it would seem that the immaterial superstructure was very much based on the material cause so that superstructures would not have the independent status of another substance. Marx uses the word 'substance' sparingly. He does talk about the twofold nature of the commodity (1967: 41–8). And at many points he equates exchange-value and value-form (*Wertform*). If exchange-value is value-form, then use-value, which is part and parcel of the same commodity as exchange-value, would need to incorporate substance or matter. But there is a major difference between Marx and Aristotle here. A given empirical substance for Aristotle, and, unlike Leibniz's monads, Aristotle's substances are always empirical and comprise form and matter, derives its energy, its dynamic from form and formal cause. The way that form acts for Aristotle is the source not just of change, but of constitution of a given substance in its difference from other substances. In Marx, value-form (or exchange-value) does not comprise an energizing principle at all. It is, for Marx, 'dead labour'. Further, unlike Aristotelian formal cause that engineers difference, the value-form is a destroyer of difference and effaces difference under its own homogeneity. It is comprised not of differences, but identities: by units of equivalence. And it presumes a sort of Newtonian external cause and linearity. This means that, for Marx, the principle of difference of self-cause must come not from form, but from matter itself. Hence use-values, in their production, comprise difference; they entail inequivalence. The engine of change shifts from the formal to the material. The material constitutes the formal, but the formal then – even though it consists of dead labour – becomes itself the engine and dominant moment in the total process of accumulation in the capitalist economy.

In the *Grundrisse* (1973), the notebooks on which Volume I of *Capital* was based, Marx does speak though of *Wertsubstanz*, of value-substance. By this he seems to mean something other than, use-value. Use-value is from the point of view of use, while *Wertsubstanz* is from the point of view of production. In these discussions of four-fold causation and Marxian intensive economy, we need constantly to keep in mind that what we are getting at is not the being of the thing or the object, it is *not* the essence or nature of the thing. This being of the thing is what Heidegger and Husserl, and indeed Leibniz, are in search of as ontological truths. Such ontological truths are what the Western, the Greek tradition are built on. Nonetheless the question we – with Karl Marx – are asking is not about the truth of the thing but about the *value* of the thing. And the value of the thing always has to do with a relation – a relation of production or desire *vis-à-vis* the thing. This relationship of production or desire to the thing, this relation is very different from the truth relation of Heidegger's *Dasein* and Husserl's transcendental ego (Stiegler 2004a: 201–3). The production relation creates the

107

value of the thing. The desire relation evaluates the thing. It is a relation not of knowledge but of evaluation of the thing.

Unlike Aristotle, Marx does not see substance as a hylomorphic combination of matter and form. Indeed, instead he speaks of *Wertsubstanz* in contraposition to *Wertform*, or exchange-value. So exchange-value might comprise half of the twofold nature of the commodity, but this commodity for Marx is not like, for Aristotle, a substance. It is not a substance but precisely a commodity. And this commodity, Marx insists, is not a pure exchange-value: it is only half exchange-value or value-form. The other half is value-substance: the other half is matter. What Marx has done is to recast substance as matter. And the contribution of matter to value is the contribution of its substance to it. This is a very important move. Marx, in talking about the twofold *nature* of the commodity, addresses the *value*-nature of the commodity. This implicitly means that value and matter here are not predicates but enter into the composition of the nature of the commodity. Georg Simmel (1977: 16), for his part, begins his magisterial *Philosophy of Money*, published 45 years after the publication of *Capital, I*, by stating that value is not a predicate; that value is not an object's predicate. Value is much too intrinsic to be a predicate. It is, for Simmel, explicitly about desire for the intrinsic nature of the object. For Marx, too, value is not a predicate.

All of the moderns Nietzsche, Marx and Freud – and Simmel does the same for the social – take the driving force of change, the energetics, the self-causation out of the space of substantial forms, and they re-situate it at the level of the material. Thus energy-forming power or force or *puissance* is displaced from Apollonian formal cause to a rethought Dionysian material cause, to the self-organizing nature of the id in the psyche, in which any hylomorphism is driven by the material. This shift to the material happens in late modernity, not the early modernity of Leibniz, Spinoza, Descartes and even Locke. To ask the question of value, as any economic philosophy or social philosophy of the economy must do, is to make us re-evaluate the four causes. Now efficient cause and final cause take on a far greater importance. Simmel, writing his *Money* book in 1903 some 12 years after Alfred Marshall published *The Principles of Economics* (1890), was always going to share assumptions with neo-classical, marginalism. Simmel could necessarily focus on the demand side, and hence situate value in the space of the desire of the user or consumer. Marx, for his part, writing in the paradigm of classical economics and a tradition from Locke through Smith and Ricardo that saw labour as creating value, looked at the labour side. Marx thus puts value-determination, i.e. the determination of intrinsic (or intensive) value, in the 'hands' of Aristotelian efficient cause and Simmel in the agency of final cause. Here final and efficient cause are much more pivotal in the constitution of the value of the thing than they are in the truth of the thing. At stake is something other than pure ontology, which addresses the truth of the thing. The point, as we said, is that value is much more *relational* than truth. Efficient cause is being the closest to modern physical causation. It is curious in this context that Aristotle's examples – e.g. the sculptor – have a lot more to do with labour and implicitly economics than the physical action of one body. Final cause, for Aristotle, is also closer to the user in economics rather than today's functional (and in this sense final) causation of system needs. Finally, in the Aristotelian truth of a substance, the efficient cause is delimited to motive force and final cause to aim or purpose. Hence both are separate from what constitutes the substance, which is its form and matter. In contrast to questions of truth, in questions of value – in both Marx and Simmel – the efficient and final cause also very much comprise the object: they are not just its motive force and purpose but enter into its composition. Thus for Marx labour, i.e. *Wertsubstanz*, is both efficient and material cause. For Simmel (1977: 14) final-cause as to desire also enters into the content of the object. In Aristotle and the Greeks, matter before any form is chaotic, it is entropic and plastic. Matter is the clay that God or Zeus breathes life into and forms, i.e. to which God gives energy and organization. It is the mother to whose primal and chaotic matter the father gave form. But for our modern materialists – Marx, Nietzsche, Freud, Simmel – there is already an organizing principle and an energetics inside matter. It is more than chaos. It ascends to ever-higher levels of organization, of negentropy. At stake here is the *intensive-material*. This is neither matter as chaos nor even matter as eternally organized into more or less mechanical atoms. It is intensive matter: the intensive-material.

Externalities: intensive capitalism and neo-liberalism

Intensive capitalism is in a very important sense a by-product of extensive capitalism itself. That is, it is in large part generated by what economists call '*externalities*'. These externalities are right at the centre of intensive capitalism. Capital accumulation in intensive capitalism consists of units of information (Castells 1989). In this sense, intensive capitalism is at the same time a *cognitive* capitalism (Moulier Boutang 2007). The financial meltdown of 2008 was due to externalities, a spillover: a set of side-effects from the excess risk-taking of financial transactions. If Nicholas Stern can say that global warming is the greatest market failure in history, then the implosion of finance from the summer of 2008 is (alongside the Great Depression of the 1930s) in the running. In both cases these are questions of externalities. Externalities are especially important in urban and regional economies. Externalities and endogenous growth are central to Paul Krugman's work. Krugman (Fujita, Krugman and Venables 1999) speaks of 'economies of scale', not on the level of the firm but for a region or nation. He notes that unlike the assumptions of classical economics, trade does not typically take place, through competitive advantage between nations producing very different kinds of goods, say on the one hand primary products and on the other high value-added new sector manufacturing, but between regions producing rather similar types of product: say, Volvos for Volkswagens. His argument is basically for specialization in regions. Krugman focuses on 'pecuniary externalities'. Pecuniary externalities have to do with the proximity of suppliers and purchasers as well as with the geographical proximity of final consumer demand. These pecuniary externalities are not just reasons for what Alfred Weber (1909) understood as location decisions. They constitute the economies of scale of an urban locality or a region.

Though Alfred Marshall may have invented the term 'externality', it was A.C. Pigou who first addressed the theme in a sustained way. Pigou was a Cambridge University economist and student of Marshall – both were Professors of Political Economy at Cambridge. Pigou's (1877–1959) work especially covered welfare economics. His most influential book was *The Economics of Welfare* (1929). Here he spoke of 'private' and 'social' 'marginal product'. Pigou (1929) was predominantly concerned with externalities as market failures, i.e. with 'negative externalities'. An externality is defined as an impact on a party that is not directly involved in a transaction. For Pigou: 'A person A, in performing a service, for which a payment is made, to another person B, incidentally brings about either services or causes damages to a third party of such sort that a payment cannot be drawn from those who benefit nor pecuniary compensation made to the profit of those injured' (Pigou 1929: 716–71). So here we begin to get a clue as to what externalities are external to. They are not necessarily external to the firm but to a *transaction*. David Harvey (2005) also understands externalities as external to transactions, to what for him are commoditized transactions. Moulier Boutang (2007, 2008) understands externalities as external to such commoditized transactions. Now Pigou, for his part, very much influenced by Jeremy Bentham, was a utilitarian: a sort of 'social utilitarian', who believed that an increase in welfare would come from a redistribution of property from the rich to the poor, providing it did not diminish national income. So we can add utility and a utilitarian dimension to our idea of the 'internal', to which externalities are external. Subsequently, to correct market failures and negative externalities, economists have spoken of 'Pigovian taxes'. We would want then to define externality as what is external to commoditized and utilitarian or instrumental exchange. This said, we need to be clearer about what a transaction is. The logic, or even dialectic of transactions, on the one hand, and the externalities of such transactions, on the other, is central to our understanding of intensive capitalism and neo-liberalism. The meltdown of 2008 was brought about by neo-liberalism, and it is the meltdown of neo-liberalism itself. Neo-liberalism and intensive capitalism rise together from the end of the 1970s, with the breakdown of the Keynesian Welfare State, but intensive capitalism logic of externalities is the bridge to a post neo-liberal economic and social order.

To come to terms with both what a transaction is and with neo-liberalism we must look to the work of Ronald Harry Coase. Here we can specify that these 'internal' transactions need not be purely market transactions. They can be transactions inside firms. Indeed, perhaps Pigou's most influential critic was Coase, who, among others, contested what they saw as Pigou's statist paternalism. Coase did this in his late work, in an article published in 1960 some 50 years after Pigou's book, called 'The Problem of Social Cost'. Coase thought that more 'efficient outcomes' could be produced, not through state redistribution of 'property' (we note that both Pigou and Coase are addressing the redistribution not of income, nor wealth generally, but *property*), but through clearly defining property rights, so that parties – with the support of courts – could settle disputes regarding negative externalities without government intervention. Coase's very strong notion of property is interesting again in the context of Chinese capitalism and the Chinese city, which is thoroughly 'Uncoasian'. This is important because intensive capitalism emerges alongside neo-liberalism, and Coase is arguably the paradigmatic economist of neo-liberalism. Coase is one of the founders of institutional economics, which we also encounter in Oliver Williamson's work on *The Economic Institutions of Capitalism* (1998) and *Markets and Hierarchies* (1976). Let me reiterate that this is not central to the paradigm of classical liberalism, but to today's neo-liberalism. And it is not just mainstream economics, but overlaps legal studies, organizational studies, business and urban studies. Urban institutionalists in China, for example, insist on clear and distinct Coasean property rights and the principle of one legal person being the owner of any given unit of property. Anne Haila (2007) and Zhiyuan Cui (1998) have argued that it is precisely where rights in property are vague that has given rise to Chinese economic success. Cui, in this context, thus argues for bundles of rights in the same property. Thus the same atelier in Shanghai can be owned by a local state-owned enterprise, a Hong Kong property developer, the district council, Shanghai's municipality and an art dealer. Institutionalists understand such multiple *de facto* ownership in terms of 'rents'. Cui and Haila instead will speak of the desirability of such social and environmental rents. All these are external to the transaction. They are not externalities, generated by the transaction, but they are external to the Coasian neo-liberal transaction indicate.

Coase is the father of transaction-costs theory ('The Nature of the Firm' (1937)). This basically wanted to account for why there were so many firms and not just individuals – as liberal and *laissez-faire* economics might assume – engaged in economic activity. Coase argued that using the firm rather than the market can save on the costs of transacting. These transacting costs included, for example, information costs and bargaining costs. His point was if that if you produce internally to firm – if you 'make' instead of 'buy' – you can reduce these costs. Coase, though a Briton, was an early figure in the Chicago School of Law and Economics. He was Emeritus Professor of Economics in the University of Chicago Law School and mentor of George Stigler, one of Milton Friedman's closest collaborators. Using legal language, Coase talks of the number of 'contractual relations' that there were internal to or outside the firm. In each case in each transaction, then, you are 'contracting'. His paradigm-defining article, on externalities and well-defined property laws, 'The Problem of Social Cost', was published in 1960 in the *Journal of Law and Economics*, of which he later became editor. Coase's argument was that if transaction costs are high in the case of a negative externality, then property rules should be assigned so as to make economically efficient action possible. We need to make a few points in this context. First is this focus on 'economically efficient outcomes' and 'economically efficient action'. Coase is talking about what is internal to a transaction. The assumption is that with poorly defined property rights, situations in which there are bundles of rights and where property rights are boundary objects, in Bruno Latour's (1993) sense, you will get inefficient outcomes. Note the shift in discourse from utility and benefit to that of efficiency. This is part (Davies 2009) of neo-liberal discourse. Indeed, if there are social rights

and environmental rights in a unit of property, it could prove benefi-
cial to the long-term productivity of an economy. Second, we need to
note that the Coase position on hierarchies was a justification of
monopoly and used in the USA during the Reagan administration to
roll back anti-monopoly legislation. The point is that neo-liberalism
(and not liberalism) is defined not by free market competition but by
competition *between* monopolies. This is important because of a possible post neo-liberal economic order, after the 2008 financial meltdown of neo-liberalism's 'excess risk society'. Third, perhaps we can
think of externalities, whether in China or in the West, in a post
neo-liberal economy as also what goes on outside contracting. We
are, with Coase, adding a quasi-legal dimension to the notion of
what is a transaction. Fourth, we see in Coase that an externality
could pertain to the 'spillovers' from a transaction either in a market
or internal to a firm – what Williamson calls a 'hierarchy'. And at the
heart of cognitive capitalism for Moulier Boutang and its externalities is that these are external to both market and hierarchy, but
instead are reabsorbed (*resorber*) in a third mode of economic governance that exists alongside markets and hierarchies. This mode of
governance is *networks*.

This Coasean notion of transactions is central to the neo-liberal
project in three ways. First, in its justification of monopolies and
monopoly competition. In liberalism there is thus market competition; in neo-liberalism the competition is between monopolies. The
rise of intellectual property law from the end of the 1970s has
allowed firms such as Microsoft to secure monopolies of, for example,
operating systems. If modern property law was necessary for liberalism, *intellectual* property law is central to neo-liberalism. If the ownership of land labour and capital is necessary for the market
competition of liberalism, then intellectual property and the ownership of ideas are central to the monopoly competition of neo-liberalism.
In the former, at stake is the ownership of particulars, in the second,
the ownership of universals, or 'virtuals' that can embrace or generate
many particulars. The second aspect of neo-liberalism involved in the
Coasean transaction is public goods, especially welfare goods. With
clearly defined property rights, as Coase says, these can be internalized into the transactions. In a very important sense, it is not just
welfare goods that Coase attacks, but also public space, the public
sphere. What Habermas understood as *Offentlichkeit* itself is absorbed,
swallowed up into the transactions. If modernity's public sphere was
central to the emergence of liberalism and the liberal economy, then
this experiences a certain demise in neo-liberalism. This includes the

anti-commodity nature of modernity's and avant-garde culture as well as a political and legal institutional framework. Legality itself in neo-liberalism is always put at risk in, for example, Guantanamo Bay. Critics are right to say that neo-liberalism gave birth to postmodernism in the arts (Huyssein 1987). In this, the arts themselves become swallowed up into the transactions. Now culture had no external space to move in and could only resort to pastiche and kitsch glosses on the logic of the neo-liberal transactions.

Economics has been mostly concerned with negative externalities. Thus welfare economics deals with what, for Pigou, were the extreme income and wealth inequalities generated by markets and industry. Environmental economics is the other major subdiscipline dealing with negative externalities. For Moulier Boutang, the former type of negative externalities comes from industrial capitalism's main contradiction of capital and labour. In cognitive capitalism, the contradiction is no longer mainly between classes, but involves finance and the environment. Thus negative externalities in industrial capitalism consisted of 'damages to labour', and in cognitive capitalism of 'damages to nature'. If in industrial capitalism nature was an unlimited resource, in cognitive capitalism it is an active, self-organizing and complex system. Welfare economics would then deal with welfare externalities through the creation of public goods. This is of importance for the nature of the city. Notably, Manuel Castells (1977) spoke extensively about public goods in his earlier work in the context of the urban fabric.

Coase and neo-liberalism have been criticized, in their notions of 'internalizing the externalities' in markets and firms through well-defined property laws. One of the classical examples is the case of one farmer using another farmer's meadow to graze his cattle. Critics of Coase say that this does not work when the meadow or the forest does not belong to anyone. This is the question of the commons, and the subject of debates around the 'tragedy of the commons'. The commons is at the core of the open-source and 'copyleft' movement. This is also the critique of neo-liberalism in as much as intellectual property is at the heart of monopoly competition. Moulier Boutang endorses a sort of 'cognitive commons', a 'pollination society'. The classic example of positive externality is pollination, in which the beekeeper's returns from the bees' honey spills over into the pollination of surrounding crops that can create greater value than the harvested honey. The cognitive commons entails knowledge spillover – of inventions and information. Joseph Stiglitz (1999) writes thus on 'Knowledge as a Public Good' in a volume in which health, peace and security, and a clean environment are among the most important global public goods.

In industrial capitalism, externalities, Moulier Boutang observes, were at the margins of the economy, while in cognitive capitalism they become absolutely central, they become the norm. This is a bit like Ulrich Beck's (1992) 'risk society', in which the unintended consequences of actions become no longer the exception but the rule. Norms govern action, sociologically, and actions have unintended consequences, which are more or less contingent. When these become the norm, we have cognitive capitalism. And these go for 'bads' as much as goods. Cognitive capitalism's central issue is about the governance of externalities, both as goods and bads. The emerging environmental sector of the economy works through the conversion of such 'bads' into goods. So at the centre of the post-crisis – yet still intensive capitalist – order will be bad-reducing goods in the environmental sector, and making positive externalities work in the knowledge sector.

Cognitive capitalism works partly through minimizing Coasean transaction costs. In this context, Moulier Boutang draws on Benkler's (2002) open-source critique of Coase. Coase and transaction-costs economics add complexity to the classical economic problem of 'minimizing costs and maximizing the value of output'. Coase thus argues for 'maximizing the volume of *transactions* while minimizing the transaction-costs'. So to start with, you are minimizing your costs for the resources of production – land, labour and capital – and maximizing your output for this. Alongside this, to procure each factor of production entails costs. You may save here, if there are a huge volume of transactions, by bringing labour in-house rather then subcontracting it. Before you incur the transaction costs of price-bargaining, and deciding property rights, contract and form of authority between you and your contracting parties, you must *find* the resources you need (Moulier Boutang 2007: 104). The Internet – 'the network of networks' – cuts down enormously on the transaction costs of finding resources and information (Benkler 2002). The Internet is a network of distributed knowledge, which puts at your 'disposition an unlimited number of economic agents with pertinent information at almost no cost' – only the cost of your monthly broadband subscription. Here, what is external to commoditized transactions of both markets and hierarchies can be internalized in the quasi-commons of the Internet. This is the paradigm 'form of the cognitive division of labour'. These partly compensate for the law of diminishing returns (Moulier Boutang 2007: 106–7) to the factors of production. Endogenous growth theory takes exogenous factors such as human capital and technology – that may counteract diminishing returns – and endogenizes them. Both human capital and technology are factors of invention – are non-linear inputs – and hence are potentially counteracting factors. The same is true of networks.

Moulier Boutang makes a distinction between two types of knowledge involved in new technologies of information and communication. He calls these Level 1 and Level 2 knowledge – if in the industrial revolution machines make calculable repetition in muscular work, the NTICs digitize and make calculable all that is repetitive in mental labour. This depreciates the value of codified knowledge: of Level 1 knowledge (Cyert and March 1992) that enables you to do what you already know how to do; of Level 2 knowledge that allows you to do what you did not already know. This second type of knowledge is an externality that cannot be held within the limits of the commodity. It is a knowledge of attention, care, intelligence (capacity to understand context), learning and, above all, innovation (Stiegler 2004b). It is this that creates the real value-added in cognitive capitalism. This knowledge cannot be exploited directly by capitalists in the commoditized labour process. It cannot be appropriated in industrial capitalism as 'energy by unit of time'. At stake is not Marx's capital as 'dead labour', but instead as the 'activity' of 'living intelligence', that is networked, complex and innovative. Level 2 knowledge is not codifiable because its two main characteristics are (1) singularity, and not a number of cases as in codifiable knowledge, and (2) contextualization. Uncodifiability entails implicit knowledge that cannot be reabsorbed into markets. It can be reabsorbed into capitalism, but into the above-mentioned sort of networked capitalism. Lazzarato (2002), following Gabriel Tarde (1999), has understood this sort of positive-externality innovation-network as a 'collective brain'. In this, Marx's labour-power (*force de travail*) is contrasted with cognitive capitalism's 'force-invention'. Web 2.0 and 3.0 especially 'allow the relational representation of the multitudes, their network-making and the vitality of their proliferation' (Moulier Boutang 2007: 165–6).

Financialization

Let us look at intensive capitalism and neo-liberalism in the context of a periodization of capitalism. In this, 'liberal capitalism' would find its heyday in the 1850–73 long wave of expansion, especially in countries like England, France and Belgium. What Lash and Urry (1987), along with Rudolf Hilferding (1968), called 'organized capitalism', and Hilferding understood also as 'finance capitalism', would date from

1893 to probably the end of the 1970s. This included two massive waves, the first at which capitalism organized 'at the top', with the consolidation of monopolies, of cartels, of the intertwinement of banks and industry and the export of capital in imperialism, whose paradigm cases are Germany and the United States. Organized capitalism falls into initial crisis from the end of the First World War and really only pulls out of it after the Second World War. Capitalism from the 1930s organizes 'at the bottom' through national-level collective bargaining of employers and trade-union confederations, relatively comprehensive trade-union organizations, social-democratic parties and very developed welfare states. *Neo*-liberalism, for its part, begins after the breakdown of Breton Woods, the oil crises of 1973 and 1977. It begins with Thatcher, Reagan and the 'Washington Consensus'. Neo-liberalism is 'financialized' in a very different way from Hilferding's *Finanzkapital*. It is based on competition but this time on *monopoly* competition. It features not 'real' property, but intellectual property, as the basis for monopoly competition. Thus the intensive capitalism of invention, of the intensity of the one-off, of informationalized intellectual property – of copyright, patent and trademark – is also the economy of monopoly competition. It is here that Joseph Schumpeter's innovation economy of creative destruction combines with the hierarchical Coasean firm (Jessop 2007). This is not the cosy age of early twentieth-century cartels but one of megaliths engaged in competition with one another, whose paradigm cases are the likes of Microsoft, Google, Goldman Sachs and Morgan Stanley.

What are the major differences between neo-liberal finance and Hilferding's original finance capital?

1 First, there is not the long-term intertwinement of banks and industry that existed in finance capital. Early 20th century Finanzkapital featured commercial banks with large deposit accounts involved in long-term lending at low interest rates to industry. This normally comprised one particular bank and one particular vertically and horizontally integrated firm, in some ways not entirely different from the Japanese *zaibatsu*.[1] These were not non-performing loans, but in effect they subsidized industry at low rates of interest. The banks were also very large shareholders in these industries. In neo-liberal financialization there is instead an anonymization of finance through capital – stock and corporate bond – markets.

2 The rise of the investment banks. Goldman Sachs, UBS, Credit Suisse, Lehman Brothers, Morgan Stanley and Merrill Lynch have organized and underwritten IPOs (initial public offerings) and

bond issues. They have featured private banking divisions for high net wealth individuals. The investment banks (and hedge funds) become massively involved in very highly leveraged proprietary trading.

3 The lending to states. The Washington Consensus got its name through the conditions that the International Monetary Fund (IMF) imposed on Latin American and other emerging countries for loans (Kuczinski and Williamson 2003). The debt that preceded these loans stemmed from state bond purchases by these Western banks. These banks purchased state debt. With these countries losing their bond ratings, interest payments became higher and they needed to be paid back in dollars, not in the devaluing currencies or the currencies of bond issuers. The payback of such sovereign debt became a priority and considerable resources were transferred from their own spending on public goods for their citizens (Davis 2006).

4 The centrality of funds – of hedge funds, venture capital (VC) and private equity (PE). These funds consist of pooled money from institutional investors and high net worth individuals. The types of funds work differently. Venture capital funds innovation-intensive projects. The VC firm raises these funds to invest in high-tech start-ups, in whose specific technology the VC team will often have expertise. At the very peak of the dot.com bubble in 2000 there was c. $56 billion invested in VC funds. In hedge funds, private equity and VC firms there is a fund manager who manages investor funds (Frush 2007). The investor does not invest directly into the stock or bond markets or in the acquisition of companies to take them private. He or she invests in the fund and is part owner of the fund. The fund manager takes a 1–2% annual fee and on average 30% of the fund's annual profits. The model for this was the older and safer mutual funds which invested in an array of stocks and bonds for institutional and private investors. Compared to the old mutual funds, contemporary investment is in much higher risk vehicles. Hedge funds were originally meant to spread risk. But even short-selling, which is meant to cover bets on the downside, the funds make their money through volume. This entails massive leverage and often the telescoping of risk. For VCs, private equity and hedge funds, the rule is high risk and high return. For the big banks in the 2008–09 crisis, the returns were high, but the taxpayers have borne the costs of the risk.

Private equity entails a strategy of leveraged buyouts (LBO). LBOs have had two big moments, first in the 1980s and second in the 2002–07 financial bubbles. In LBOs the leveraging took place through speculative-grade bonds that were issued in order to acquire majority stakes in firms. Private equity has also worked with funds that are owned by investors.[2] They have used these to organize the issue of such 'junk bonds'. The neo-liberal funds have quite high returns. You own a unit or a share in the fund, which normally is not a publicly quoted but instead a limited liability set-up. The firm (whether hedge fund, or PE or VC) that manages the fund own shares or units in the fund. Private equity and venture capital realize their gains through an exit strategy of either FPO or being acquired. The negative externality of state-issue of bonds to Western investment banks was borne by the populations of the emerging nations. This was the 1980s and 1990s of financialization. From the 2008–09 crisis, these externalities have been borne by the taxpayers of the advanced nations.

In financialization there is a focus not on market share or organic growth, but on share piece. The value of stock market capitalization in the USA as a proportion of GDP increased from a 50% average from 1950–75 to 185% by 1999. In October 2002 the US GDP stood at about $US10 trillion. In the dot.com stock market crash of 2000–2002, US market capitalization lost some $7 trillion. For non-financial corporations the ratio of credit market debt to net worth (Crotty 2005: 83–4) increased from 38% in 1968 to 55% in 2001. The ratio of total profits of financial companies in comparison to non-financials increased from an average of 15% in the 1950s and early 1960s to some 50% in 2001. This entailed a massive increase in leverage, for both households and non-financial companies (NFCs). For NFCs the proportion of investment derived from financial liabilities increased from an average of 7% from 1950–70 to 10–12% from 1980–2000. The ratio of total credit market debt to US GDP increased from an average of 1.5 from 1961–81 to 2.3 in 1989 and 2.8 in 2001. For NFC investors this meant a shift from long- to short-term time horizons: an anonymization of both debt and equity. Financialization differs from the long-termism of Hilferding's *Finanzkapital* and 'Organisierter Kapitalismus' in that: (1) stock share holding, once long term becomes short term; and (2) debt from corporations to financial institutions is transformed from long-term and personalized loans to fungible and anonymized bonds. This is moving from a 'stake-holding' to a shareholding economy (Hutton 1998). The earlier liberal capitalism was neither stake-holding nor share-holding, but outright-owning, in which the family owned the firm and funded growth largely out of profits or arms' length relations with a bank. Organized capitalism was a stake-holding capitalism, in which managers too – unlike neo-liberalism's share-price maximizers – were stake-holders. In organized capitalism, largely to counteract its negative welfare externalities, such stake-holding came to include workers' rights in firms and the firm's responsibilities in the context of a welfare state. The Coasean logic of internalizing the externalities through clear and distinct property rights at the same time disenfranchises workers and public welfare goods, as rights now only reside in the shareholders. Coasean neo-liberalism is a share-holding capitalism.

Hilferding's organized capitalism witnessed a transfer of power in companies from family to management. In neo-liberalism there is a new transfer of power, this time from management to shareholders. Management, themselves previously strongly identified with their firms as stake-holders, now take on the logic of shareholders. By shareholders we mean not long-term committed equity investors but short-term, return-maximizing, footloose investors – that is a shift from a Warren Buffet type to a George Soros type investor. Management are increasingly paid in stock options. The average earnings of the top 100 US CEOs comprised of stock options increased from 22% in 1979 to 63% in 1995–99. This shift of managers from stake-holders to shareholders was paralleled by the telescoping disparity between their and workers' wages. The ratio of top-100 CEO compensation to average workers' wage went from 38 in 1970 to 101 in 1980, 222 in 1990 and 1044 in 1999 (Crotty 2005: 93). The less committed managers were, effectively, rewarded for their very footloose-ness and non-engagement, unlike the workers, whose fortunes rose and fell with their firm's.

In financialization, NFCs pursue a logic not of maximizing revenue growth, market share or asset value, but a financial logic of maximizing their stock share price. This equity price begins to fluctuate in correspondence not with the movement of the income streams of its main operations, but instead along with the financial logic of the NFC's own mergers and acquisitions. These acquisitions, in which NFCs carried out by buying equity in other NFCs, were done through leverage, more through anonymized corporate bond issues than through the long-term stake-holding loans. These were bonds issued by the company that were carrying out the takeover. Thus between 1984 and 1999 $1 trillion was borrowed by NFCs to finance takeovers or to defend against them through purchases of their own stock. From 1995–2001, NFCs contributed to the maintenance of high stock prices through the purchase of $870 billion of their own stock. This peaked in the junk bond movement and the leveraged buyouts (LBOs) of the 1980s. Junk bonds are very high risk, potentially high return, bonds. Specialists like KKR used them in their hostile takeover of RJR Nabisco in 1988. In some cases, the LBO firms used the assets of their target firm for collateral for their bond debt. In such activity the NFC itself becomes 'a portfolio of liquid subunits' (Crotty 2005: 80). The ratio thus of NFC gross portfolio income to cash flow increased from an average of 20% from 1952–79 to 35% from 1980–98. The proportion of cash flow that NFCs paid to financial markets – net interest plus dividends plus net stock purchases – increased from 20% from 1950–66 to 30% from 1966–79 to over 50% from 1984–2000. Thus the already financialized NFCs were also paying out to financial interests: to stockholders, bondholders and to purchase stock shares. From 1995 to 2001 – the Clinton–Rubin–Greenspan boom years of the 'New Economy' – NFCs added some $2.1 trillion in new debt (Crotty 2005: 99).[3]

Neo-liberal financialization is a *traders'* capitalism. From 1960 to 1978, the average turnover per year of all the shares on the New York Stock Exchange was 20%; in the first six months of 2002 it was 100%. That is, in 2002 the average time period for which a given stock was held was one year. This is largely due to the rise of institutional shareholding from the 1980s. In the 1950s US households owned 90% of corporate stock, but by 1970 this had decreased to 68%, by 1979 to 59%, by 1985 to 47% and by 2000 to 42%, while institutions held 46% (Crotty 2005: 91). These institutions, pension funds and insurance companies, but also university endowments, expected very high returns on their investment. They did not stake-hold in any given NFC; instead their relationship was with fund managers. Typically, an NFC's Chief Financial Officer will hire dedicated staff to oversee a company's pension fund. This staff, who can be fired if risk and return objectives are not met, find a consultant to help them choose between funds in which to invest (Parenteau 2005: 120). The consultant is judged on the quarterly performance results of the investment managers they choose. These investors started to expect very high returns on their investments. This is in a real economy growing by an average of about 3% per year. Over the long term in US history the annual average return on equity investment was 9–10%. By 1999 investors were expecting median returns of 15–19%. From 1997–99 mutual funds were earning returns averaging 22.7%. Households too were resorting, as in 1928–29, to leverage. Between 1989 and 1999, the proportion of household financial assets devoted to discretionary equity holding increased from 34% to 60% (Galbraith 1969; Parenteau 2005: 116).

Neo-liberalism began in earnest after the sharp recession of 1979–82. Partly the rebound came through the slashing of labour costs. But most pivotal has been the rise of the investment banks and their effect on state power. First, the equity market – from 1987 – and then investment banks themselves came to be seen as too big and too interconnected with the whole of the financial system to fail. This embodies the chronic moral hazard at the heart of financialization and neo-liberalism more generally. This chronic moral hazard can mean an equally chronic bubble. This new traders' politics surfaced in the conflict between Federal Reserve Chairman Paul Volcker and Ronald Reagan's Treasury Secretary, Donald Regan. Volcker had followed the timeworn tradition of the Fed and other major central banks in supporting the anti-inflationary interests of commercial banks and bondholders by keeping interest rates relatively high and monetary supply under control. Commercial banks and large bondholders (in those days of low corporate leverage, predominantly Treasury Bond holders) were particularly vulnerable to inflation. Volcker was a Democrat, an economist who had moved between Chase Manhattan Bank and the New York Federal Reserve Bank where he had served as economist from 1952–57. Like Barack Obama's Treasury Secretary Timothy Geithner, who ran the New York Fed from 2003–09, Volcker was President of the New York Fed from 1975–79. In 1979 President Jimmy Carter appointed Volcker to Chair the Fed System, where he served until 1987 when he was replaced by Alan Greenspan. Volcker inherited the hyperinflation of the late 1970s, and substantially raised interest rates to bring inflation down: from 13% in 1981 to 3% in 1983 (Morris 2009).

This 1979–82 recession, inaugurated by what investment bankers called Volcker's 'October Massacre', laid the ground for the 25 years of neo-liberal expansion. After 1982 Volcker acted again against financialization in the context of the junk bond and LBO phenomenon. He used the Fed's authority over margin requirements (i.e. the maximum proportion of equity acquisition that could be debt financed) to block buyouts. Target firms had complained that buyout firms were using target firms' shares as collateral for debt to support the buyout. Donald Regan, who was at the Treasury from 1981–85, organized other key players and agencies in the administration to block Volcker. In 1987 Ronald Reagan appointed Greenspan as Fed Chair. Greenspan's first act – though the real economy was strongly expanding – was a liquidity injection of $13 billion to counteract the

October 1987 stock market crash. This was an injection into money markets – as distinct from capital markets, into the financial markets for very short-term borrowing and lending, carried out through reducing the Federal Funds rate. At that point trading volume in equities was far below that of both government securities and foreign exchange, both markets of strong Fed activity. Daily trading on the foreign exchange markets in 1987–88 (Parenteau 2005: 139) was of the order of $130 billion, of Treasuries some $110 billion, of equities some $7–10 billion. So, *pace* Greenspan, the stock market after the crash was not too interconnected or too big to take a hit. The message of this money-market injection was that equity market investors were being protected against a possible down-side. And equity prices correspondingly rose, buoyed by increasing leverage through bond markets. This new centrality of equity markets was underscored in Ronald Reagan's new Working Group on Financial Markets, comprising James Baker, then Treasury Secretary, Greenspan at the Fed, and the Chairs of the Commodity Futures Trading Commission and the Securities and Exchange Commission. This group attained even more power under Bill Clinton and came to include the heads of the New York Fed – responsible for the nation's exchange rate policy, basically through a vast activity of buying and selling foreign currency on the foreign exchange markets – and the National Economic Council. Clinton created the NEC, whose first head in 1993–95 was to be Treasury Secretary Robert Rubin, by executive order (Freeland 2009). The NEC Director under Obama from 2009 is the now converted Keynesian ex-Clinton Treasury Secretary Larry Summers.

The first major act of true financialization, in contradiction to classical *Finanzkapital*, was the Latin-American lending binge of 1982–83. The US banks were attracted by the high interest rates on these bonds issued by Latin-American governments. With yields skyrocketing and the burden of the dollar peg, default seemed likely. In renegotiated payments, the US banks suffered large losses. The banks were more or less rescued by the subsequent LBO lending binge. The investment banks earned enormous fees for IPOs, bond issues and mergers and acquisitions in the LBO binge. They also bought bonds in huge volumes as part of their own proprietary trading. The Savings and Loans bailout was connected to the LBOs. These 745 'thrifts' in the Savings and Loan Association are in the business of accepting savings deposits and making mortgage loans. The thrifts were caught holding large quantities of bad assets: of worthless junk bond LBO debt and of bad loans in the commercial overbuilding bubble. They were subject to a $124 billion federal government bailout during 1986–96. A ubiquitous moral hazard. Investment banks, burnt by LBO defaults on junk bonds that they held, were assuaged by Greenspan's 1991 intervention, in which his lowering of the Fed Funds rate made overnight borrowing very cheap compared to the yield on Treasuries. Now effective arbitraging – the 'carry trade' between the market for overnight inter-bank borrowing and the Treasury bond market could rebuild profits at the banks. These were risk-less returns. Indeed, the Fed Funds rate stayed low during 1990–94 and banks' margins were restored. The result, however, was that a bubble was created in the Treasury bond market. This and fear of an equity bubble alarmed even Greenspan. Consequently the Fed doubled its short-term interest rates from November 1993 to February 1995. This led to a flattening of the bond yield curve and it became more difficult to raise capital through bond issues. This hit the investment banks, especially their proprietary dealing activities, and following 1994 losses even Goldman Sachs needed to be recapitalized (Greenspan 2007).

Enter Robert Rubin, whose own career at Goldman was built on arbitraging skills – the risk-less exploiting of conditions between different markets. In early 1993, Rubin, still at Goldman, was able to lobby Bill Clinton in the White House. Clinton, disturbed by the jobless growth in the Reagan administration, was ready to engage in federal deficit infrastructure spending to create jobs. Rubin helped convince Clinton instead to run budget surpluses, which he did from 1992 to 2000 and to instead create the conditions for private sector – household and corporate – deficit spending. Rubin at the NEC was dismayed by Greenspan's 1994–95 dear money policy. This made restructuring more difficult in the 1994 Mexican crisis and caused banks to repatriate funds from South East Asia, provoking the Asian crisis 2–3 years after. The last gasp of Greenspan's short-lived monetary austerity was seen in his famous 'irrational exuberance' speech in December 1996. Now Rubin had joined him at the Treasury and they had to deal with the Asian Crisis of 1997–98, the Russian bond default of 1998 and the bailout of LCTM (Long-Term Capital Management) – a hedge fund that was involved in telescoped leverage to support microscopic arbitrage positions. Greenspan and Rubin lowered interest rates to try to prevent capital outflows from Asia. The debt/GDP ratio run by ASEAN countries was some 180%. The IMF intervened to attempt to stabilize currencies (Parenteau 2005: 140–1).

This neo-liberal 'shareholder' paradigm is accompanied by chronic bubbles. These are asset price bubbles – equities and house prices. What they entail is a separation of price from value, and especially private sector – both household and corporation – deficit spending. This leads to very large national external debt to finance household, corporation and state deficits – into which China, Japan, Germany and the Gulf States have stepped as creditors. There always was a conflict between the interests of the Fed and of politicians. Richard Nixon was, for example, convinced that he lost the presidential election in 1960 due to Fed high interest rate, anti-inflation policies that had led to increased unemployment. Thus he appointed the malleable Arthur Burns as Fed Chair from 1970 to pursue a fuller employment expansionary monetary policy. Inflation soared to 12.3% by 1974, which Nixon tried to counter with an incomes policy. But what Donald Regan and Greenspan were pursuing was something else. It was not the full employment stake-holder's objectives, but pure shareholders' objective of buoying equity prices. This was government by investment bankers: Donald Regan from Merrill-Lynch, Greenspan from Morgan Stanley and Robert Rubin and Hank Paulson from Goldman (Griffin 2002).

The intensive-material: machines of predication

Gilles Deleuze writes in a great deal of his work in the register of the intensive-material. Leibniz's differential calculus is at the heart of the notion of the virtual, of the 'plane of immanence' in Deleuze's *Difference and Repetition* (1968). For Deleuze, the virtual is difference-in-itself: the virtual is difference's noumenon. This virtual generates the more or less metric world we encounter – this takes place through a process of actualization, which Deleuze (1968: 317) characterizes as differenciation. Differentiation, or virtualization, will bring us back again towards Deleuze's plane of immanence. Differenciation is like integration or integral calculus and differentiation is like the differential calculus. Differenciation is a bit like structural differentiation in the sociology of modernization. But Deleuze's differentiation is like de-differentiation: a move towards indifference or compression. The actual movement of bodies in space, which we can graphically draw on x and y axes, de-differenciates or differentiates to a single point, a non-metric point of instantaneous acceleration. Similarly, a process of differentiation will bring us from the actual level of Euclidean geometry to the non-metric topology of Riemann geometry (Delanda 2001). This differentiated plane of immanence is also the space for non-metric fractals or attractors or the vector plane that differenciates out into solids. This plane of immanence is Deleuze and Guattari's 'body without organs', the de-differentiated and *informe* body which then differenciates into the actual body with organs. The body is the *locus classicus* of the material. Take the organs away, take the parts away, and the body becomes intensive: we are in the space of the intensive-material. This originally Spinozan 'plane of immanence' becomes, at the same time, metaphysical and physical – intensive and extensive – for Deleuze. Deleuze's noumenal difference in-itself is also a physical, a material intensity. For Spinoza, nature/the divine is the generator of all the individuals, of the monads and also of the actual. The single substance of Spinoza's first cause generates the multiplicity of differences, Leibniz's still intensive monads. Deleuze's ontology is the intensive-material: it is hence a 'transcendental empiricism', fusing the empiricism's matter with the transcendents of intensity.

Heidegger spoke of 'ontological difference' – of the difference between Being and beings. Twenty-first century intensive culture is based instead on ontological *indi*fference: it is the fusion of being and beings. Historically, extensity is body or the material (Descartes' *res extensa*) and intensity is mind (*res cogitans*). In contemporary intensive culture, mind and body merge: they fuse. The result is no longer the opposition of the extensive-material and the intensive-spiritual but their fusion in an *intensive-material*. This new intensive-materiality is informational. Information is the materialization of ideas. For Gregory Bateson (2000) information is a difference that makes a difference. That is, informatronics is a noumenal difference that generates phenomenal difference. Information is a difference generator (Mackenzie 2005; Malik 2005). Information is thus comprised of singularities. Information systems are comprised of a multiplicity of singularities. Such information systems are self-organizing, yet operationally closed (Varela et al. 1993). If they were not operationally closed, they could not preserve their haeccity, their this-ness as such a singular system. These information systems work through structural coupling with their environment, or co-evolutionary structural coupling with other such systems. In such structural coupling they exchange information through communications (Spuybroek 2004). At stake in such coupling is not exchange

of equivalents but co-evolution in the exchange of inequivalence, the exchange of difference. Structural coupling of such
systems entails the exchange of difference. Now, with Niklas
Luhmann (1997), we have systems of communication that are
inequivalent and far from equilibrium. We have systems that
are immanently reflexive and generate values and energy from
the inside. In the information economy, capital accumulates as
difference.

Heidegger, in *Being and Time* (1986), speaks of two ways in
which we can engage with objects. Either we can be 'in-the-world'
with these objects or we can have a distanced relation to them. To
be in-the-world with objects is in a very important sense to engage
with them as use-values; to relate to them in a distanced, calculating
mode – as if we were in another world than they – is to engage with
them as exchange-values. Heidegger speaks of these two possible
relations as 'ready-to-hand' (*zuhanden*) and 'present-at-hand'
(*vorhanden*). In this an object's use-value is like Marcel Mauss's gift,
only the gift is primarily symbolic, while use-value is primarily material. Each gift, like each use-value, is concrete and different from
every other. It is of this contrast between gift and commodity that
Arjun Appadurai (1986) speaks in his classic essay on the social life
of things. Appadurai was speaking largely not so much of the economy in general, but of the cultural economy. Lash and Lury, in
Global Culture Industry (2007), argued that contemporary culture
industries do not primarily work, like Adorno and Appadurai main-
tained, through the commodity. They argued that, unlike the commodity, culture industry objects work not through homogeneity but
through heterogeneity or difference (see also Lury 2004). The goods
produced here themselves become generative, become potentials.
Intellectual property, in copyrighted software or metadata systems or
trademarked brands are such goods that are themselves potentials
and generative of value. Hence the brand operates, not like a commodity in terms of homogeneous units of equivalence, but in
their difference to other brands. The brand is effective through its
'difference-value'. This difference, consolidated in intellectual
property, is productive of value. It adds value to a firm's market
capitalization. Where the gift or use-value is concrete difference,
and the commodity abstract equivalence, the brand and intellectual
property is abstract difference. In the 'difference-value' of such a
'neo-commodity' labour and labour-time become heterogeneous. 'Human capital' – if it is a capacity for innovation – has to do
with the accumulation of such difference. Finally, commodities

themselves are linear, with their cause – which is labour – coming from the outside. But the difference-value of the objects in today's culture industries, for example, yields non-linear trajectories with unintended and unpredictable consequences. These products, whether brands in the culture industries or, say, complex products in the finance sector, take on lives of their own, they take on self-organizing properties, whose consequences can go in any direction. They can – as above – generate positive or negative externalities. This is abstract difference. It presumes training not in concrete craft labour but in the uses of abstraction in the accumulation of human capital. These neo-commodities of difference-value are comprised not of the homogeneous units of industrial capitalist exchange-value, but instead of abstract units of information.

We know that Heidegger rejected the notion of substance for several reasons. For one thing, the Aristotelian subject or soul was infinite, whereas Heidegger's (human) being in the world was first and foremost finite. This idea of substantial form is at the core of Aristotle's metaphysics. Thus Heidegger and more contemporary thinkers from Derrida to Deleuze have rejected the notion of substance. Yet all of the classical sociological theorists – Marx, Weber, Durkheim and Simmel – have used a notion of this time fully finite substance. They have used it not in the sense of an infinite soul, but with assumptions of finitude. Serres (1968) describes in Leibniz a distinction between *substance*, on the one hand, and *system*, on the other. This is a distinction between substance, which is metaphysical, and system, which is physical. Here every substance is different from every other and substance is the source of its own internal energy. The units that comprise system, that is atoms, are not different from but identical to one another. In the Lebnizian system, the energy comes from the outside and thus works in terms of causes and effects. The atoms in systems not only cause and affect one another, they collide with one another and are exchanged for one another. These collisions are described in Galileo, and in Hobbes' Galileo-derived war of all against all. The exchanges are also the exchanges of the possessive individuals of the capitalist market. In Leibniz's exchanges, one atom takes the place of another, and at the same time the other atom – which is equivalent to the first atom – takes the place of the first atom. These two atoms change places without any change taking place to the system. The system remains in equilibrium. In substance, a monad, which is different from every other, cannot take the place of another. So there is no exchange. Instead of exchange, there is *change*. If the units of system work in terms of cause and effect, the units of substance do not. Instead of causing, they *perceive*. They perceive and then reflect on this perception in apperception. They perceive, they apperceive (think) and they represent. They represent other substances, first in images and then, once there is culture, in symbols. They represent and they communicate. They communicate these representations to other substances. First, they communicate in signals and images, and then, with culture, they predicate. These substances thus issue as it were their own predicates that may be different from the predicates that we as observing human scientists place on them. Now system, as we noted, is physical and substance metaphysical: system is extensive and substance intensive.

The point in this chapter is that in contemporary capitalism, system and substance come together; they fuse; there is a de-differentiation of extensity and intensity, of the physical and metaphysical. Now system, and captitalism, themselves become monadological. System starts to work from a principle of difference. It is no longer comprised of identical units of time space and value, but of heterogeneous units of information. As such, system starts to self-organize. Moreover, system begins to shift from a governing principle of causation to one of *representation and communication*. Thus industry becomes culture industry. When system takes on the guise of substance, the mechanistic becomes 'machinic'. The id, once part of mind and therefore substance, becomes transformed by system into 'desiring machines'. Phenomenology, with Bernard Stiegler (1998) and Georges Simondon (2007), becomes 'machine phenomenology'. But most of all, mechanism or system that once worked through a logic of cause and effect starts to work like substance or mind had worked – through predication. Sociologists will know that Talcott Parsons' linear social systems worked through a logic of function, while Niklas Luhmann's non-linear systems operate not through function or even action but *semantics* – that is meanings and communications. When substance and system fuse, capitalism – contemporary capitalism – starts to predicate: becomes a set of predicating machines. These are predicating machines that are at the same time material and immaterial: extensive and intensive. These are communication machines that, with Francisco Varela et al. (1993), relate to their environment through structural coupling and through the exchange of information. They couple in relationship of co-evolution with other such machines in their environment. Metaphysics, we observed, has substantial form at its very core. And it is in the materialization of such substantial form and difference in these machines of predication that we can understand contemporary capitalism as metaphysical. Yet this is a materialist metaphysics: an *intensive*-materialism. Thus intensive capitalism entails a different kind of labourpower: such labour-power (or invention-power) would need to be more than an empty Lockean 'capacity', or 'faculty'; labour-power needs to take on substance itself as real potential. Labour-power needs to be not a faculty, working from the outside through mechanistic cause, but a substance, dynamically forming matter and at the same time self-transformative. Labour-power, through what Leibniz understood as desire (appetition) and reflexive intelligence, must become *intensive*.

Notes

1   *Zaibatsu* were the main integrated and cartealized Japanese financial and industrial conglomerates that controlled much of the Japanese economy until World War II. They were succeeded by the less dominated *Keiretsu*.
2   To take private means to buy up all the shares of a company listed on the stock market. Once the company is de-listed it is no longer available for investment by the public. Thus it is 'taken private'.
3   Harold Greenspan was Federal Reserve Chairman and Robert Rubin Secretary of the Treasury.

6

Intensive Politics: Power after Hegemony

Hegemony is a concept that has been around for a long time. From the beginnings of cultural studies in the 1970s, 'hegemony' has been perhaps *the* pivotal concept in this still emerging discipline. Cultural studies has been perhaps primarily concerned from its outset with the question of power, and it is through hegemony – or an equivalent – that its analysts have understood power to be effective. In what follows I do not want to argue that hegemony is a flawed concept. Indeed, I do not want to argue at all against the concept of hegemony. Hegemony as a concept has, I think, great truth-value. What I want to argue instead is that it has had great truth-value for a particular epoch. I want to argue that that epoch is now beginning to draw to a close. Instead, I want to suggest that power is now largely *post-hegemonic*. I want to suggest that cultural studies should perhaps look mostly elsewhere for its core concepts. I should also like to propose what might be some of these alternative concepts. I believe that these are not only concepts but are also the way in which power is beginning to work in a post-hegemonic age. Hegemony was the concept that *de facto* crystallized cultural studies as a discipline. Hegemony means domination through consent as much as coercion. It has meant domination through ideology or discourse. It has meant symbolic power in the sense of the late Pierre Bourdieu. In classical British cultural studies, hegemony has largely been understood in terms of resistance to such symbolic power. 'Disciplinary power' is, for these purposes, a way of understanding hegemonic power. In disciplinary power there is always a discourse (jurisprudence, psychoanalysis, etc.) that lies behind the disciplinary institution it supports. The institution then exercises power in the micro-instances of the capillaries of society. At the root of all this is cultural discourse and legitimate power. In between is a set of disciplinary institutions. Thus hegemony presupposes symbolic domination, legitimate power and viable institutions.[1] Each of these three elements presumes that cultural power is largely addressed to the reproduction of economy, society and polity. This too moves into the background in a post-hegemonic order. If the hegemonic order works through a cultural logic of reproduction, the post-hegemonic power operates through a cultural logic of invention, hence not of reproduction but of chronic production of economic, social and political relations.

The treatment in what follows of the politics of hegemony is not per se one of Gramsci, or Laclau Mouffe or of Stuart Hall's earlier work. At stake is something that encompasses a more general regime of power that will be developed throughout the length of this: what might be called 'extensive politics'. Below, what I will try to show is that such extensive power or such an extensive politics is being progressively displaced by a politics of *intensity*. I will trace the shift from hegemony or extensive politics to such an intensive politics in terms of: (1) a transition to an *ontological* regime of power, from a regime that in important respects is *'epistemological'*; (2) a shift in power from the hegemonic mode of *'power over'* to an intensive notion of *power from within* (including domination from within) and power as generative force; (3) a shift from power and politics in terms of *normativity* to a regime of power much more based in what can be understood as a *'facticity'*. This is a general transition from norm to fact in politics. From hegemonic norm to what we will see are intensive facts. The fourth section will look at this shift through a change from an extensive (and hegemonic) regime of *representation* to an intensive regime of *communications*. The fifth section will look at implications for what might be called 'first-' and 'second–wave' cultural studies.

Language: power become ontological[2]

Hegemony is often understood to work through 'the symbolic order' or *the symbolic*. This presumes a great measure of domination through the unconscious mind. It presumes that when we as children enter the order of language with the resolution of the Oedipus complex, we become subject to the 'law of the father', which actually constitutes us as subjects. This law constitutes the symbolic order of a given society. In this context, some authors advocate resistance to the hegemony of the symbolic through the imaginary. Others, such as Slavoj Žižek, suggest that resistance to the symbolic is situated in 'the real'. The real, unlike the symbolic or the imaginary, escapes the order of representation altogether. We – i.e. those who think that power is largely post-hegemonic – agree with Žižek (see Butler,

Laclau and Žižek 2000). We agree part way. We think that both domination and resistance in the post-hegemonic order takes place through the real. The symbolic, which is structured like a language and whose propositions and judgements contain this 'law', operates through what might be called 'epistemology'. Epistemological power works through logical statements or utterances, through propositions that are predications of a subject. The language of the symbolic through which hegemony is exercised in this sense as a mode of predication is also a mode of judgement. The real in contrast is the unutterable. It is ontological. Power in the post-hegemonic order is becoming ontological.

Let us look into this a bit more closely. What is 'this symbolic' through which hegemony is exercised? What indeed in this context is a symbol? Žižek, like Julia Kristeva (1986), identifies the symbolic order with the law of the father. The symbolic order carries out normalizing functions of domination. Kristeva contrasts the domination of the symbolic with the freedom of the 'semiotic'. Žižek contrasts it with a Marxist politics of the real. This is complex though. In Lacan, there are several different positions. One – which was taken up by screen studies in Britain in the 1970s – pitted a sort of decentred and ambivalent symbolic with the normalization of the imaginary. There is though another Lacan (1998) in, for example, the *Four Fundamental Concepts of Psychoanalysis*, in which the symbolic embodies normalization and law and the real the powers of resistance. And finally and perhaps most interesting is Lacan's mathematization in which the space of number is at the same time the space of jouissance. Kittler (1997) has recently addressed this: he stresses the influence of Alan Turing and non-linear cybernetics on Lacan. One should look here also to the mathematical ontology of Alain Badiou (2005). Staying with the idea of the symbolic, we need to remember – as all of these authors of course are aware – that Freud's notion of symbol ran very opposite to Žižek's and Kristeva's notions of the symbolic as a site of predication. For Freud, symbols worked not in the clear and distinct propositional language of law, judgement or the ego. They worked through the processes of displacement and condensation in the unconscious. Symbols were comprised of figures displaced from the instrumental clear and distinct subject–verb–qualifier temporality of the ego. These figures were condensed and even compressed into symbols. They were very opposite really to the space of judgement and law that is the ego. Now the ego, despite of course working in the idiom of instrumental rationality and the commodity, also works linguistically through predicative statements, through propositional logic: through the clear and distinct succession of subject, verb and object or qualifier. It works through a succession of judgements. Walter Benjamin (Menninghaus 1995) spoke of this kind of language as 'semiotic'. And this is, I think, what Saussure meant by semiotics. The unconscious with its symbols, displacements and condensations works quite opposite to this. In the analytic situation, language does not work in the sense that it does in the real life of the ego. The analytic situation takes place in a room set apart from this world of judgement and logical proposition. It is a 'talking cure' that is profoundly *anti*-semiotic. Its figures are not clear and distinct but as symbols, fuzzy and merging into one another. Freud's idea of symbol is drawn rather uncritically from his contemporaneous anthropology. Yet this is the way in which they have meaning, a way vastly different from the precise imperatives of the law. It was not then a large step for Lévi-Strauss to re-import Freud's idea. Thus myth and *la pensée sauvage* are comprised of symbols built, indeed *bricolé*, through such displacement and condensation. Likewise, the surrealists drew on dreams and Freud's sorts of symbols to counter the propositional language of the ego and the dull commoditization of everyday life. Lévi-Strauss' and the surrealists' pose, against the ego's epistemology, an unconscious in ontological mode. The symbolic, which is at the same time mathematical and linguistic, can relate to objects in either epistemological or ontological mode. In the register of hegemony and classical cultural studies, the symbolic worked epistemologically. In post-hegemonic cultural studies, the stakes are increasingly ontological.

Cultural studies, in its hegemonic paradigm, understood power largely as operating semiotically, through *discourse*. Serious speech acts, or statements, in their systematic articulation, constitute for Foucault a discourse. Such a framework of propositions is pre-eminently epistemological. The heuristic is very much Kant's *Critique of Pure Reason*. Here at stake are cognitive judgements that work through logical statements, or predications, whether the latter are analytic or synthetic. The presumption is that objects, whether physical or mathematical, cannot be known in themselves or in their being. Instead, we can only know things through their predicates, their qualities. For classical cultural studies, both power and resistance work in such a sense epistemologically. On both sides is a semiotics of predication. Ideology works like this just the same as discourse: both capitalist and proletarian ideologies. It is discourse versus discourse. Discursive will formation, and the legitimating arguments for the propositions therein comprised, whether used in domination or resistance, is pre-eminently epistemological.

Post-hegemonic power and cultural studies is less a question of cognitive judgements and more a question of *being*. In this sense that Walter Benjamin, in his essay on language in general and the language of man (see Chapter 4), counters the epistemological and semiotic language of judgement with the ontological and naming language of creation and of criticism. He thus speaks of semiotic versus kabbalistic language, of physical versus metaphysical language, of extensive versus intensive language. It is this sort of ontological language that is at stake in Giorgio Agamben's work. Language is still an important stake in post-hegemonic cultural studies, but it is less semiotic or epistemological language than some dimension of ontological language. In Benjamin's early essay, the language of power would be epistemological: the language of criticism and against power ontological. Similarly, in Agamben (1999), normalizing power is discursive and epistemological, and the language of *homo sacer* ontological. The same would go for Žižek, whose 'real' as site of struggle is surely not at all knowable through cognitive judgements. But ontology now goes much further than this: that is, not just resistance in our post-hegemonic culture, but also domination works ontologically. There are traces of this in Benjamin's somewhat later, more materialist work, like in his essay on Karl Krauss and in *One Way Street* (1977e; 1996a). Here we have a shift from the focus on poetry of the earlier work to the materiality of the street, of adverts, kiosks, dime novels, newspapers, movies, the arcades. We know of course that a politics of critique as well as of invention work through the more material (and less metaphysical) medium of such popular culture for Benjamin. But they also work as part of capitalist power. They do so not just as the simple commodity. And the abstraction of the commodity is very much on the lines of the instrumental reason of predicative judgements and what Benjamin called semiotic language. If the commodity works epistemologically, then the advertisement and the neon sign work for Benjamin on deeper, ontological levels. Thus he speaks of the power of meaning as lying not in the sign but in its 'dark reflection in the pool of water in the street below' (Benjamin 1996a: 476). In post-hegemonic politics, the stakes – whether through the prism of language or adverts or indeed new media – are no longer epistemological, they are instead ontological. Instead of the ontological being only a site of resistance to such abstract power, it now becomes an apparatus of domination itself. Power has become more sinister in a post-hegemonic age. In the age of hegemony, power only appropriated your predicates: in the post-hegemonic present, it penetrates your very being. Power, previously extensive and operating from without, becomes intensive and now works from within.

Two types of power

In the age of hegemony, there was essentially one type of power: power in the sense that it is the power that A has over B. Thus in classical cultural studies, power is seen basically as power over, the fashion in which individuals or collectives or structures made others do what they otherwise would not do. In a post-hegemonic age, a second type of power emerges and comes to the forefront. This is what Antonio Negri (1999), drawing on Spinoza, calls *potentia*, which has more to do with power as force, energy, potential. In French, *potestas* is *pouvoir*, and *potentia* is *puissance*; in German, it is *Macht* versus *Kraft*. What is this *potentia*, this *puissance*? It is connected not so much to domination as to 'invention', as in Maurizio Lazzarato's (2002) seminal work on Gabriel Tarde, whose title is *Puissances de l'invention*. Indeed, in post-hegemonic cultural studies the notion of invention, or 'performing the exceptional', starts to replace resistance, which comes to be rejected for its negative connotations. How can we get a handle on what is meant by this second type of power? *Potestas* or *pouvoir* works through external determination, like mechanism. *Potentia* (*puissance*), in contrast, works less like mechanism than like '*life*' and there is an important neo-vitalist dimension to post-hegemonic cultural studies. Where *pouvoir* (*potestas*) is conceived mainly as epistemological, *potentia* is fully ontological. It is the motive force, the unfolding, the becoming of the thing-itself, whether that thing is human, non-human or some combination thereof.

This *potentia* is at the heart of the theme of ontological plenitude in Heidegger. This is the multiplicity of being that attempts to break through in all its colours through the mechanical greyness of semiotic predication, law/judgement and the commodity. Heidegger's implicit or explicit idea of *potentia* is in his early work featuring *Dasein*, at least residually humanist. Heidegger's notion, further, mostly understands *potentia* as residing in individual beings, in their unfolding. Thus it is strictly ontological or metaphysical as opposed to physical. This is because of the strong doctrine of ontological difference at the heart of Heidegger's work. Now post-hegemonic power works partly through an emergent collapse of metaphysics into physics, or a growing ontological indifference. Thus in Nietzsche, for whom what we just described as *potentia* is indeed life, or will to power, Heidegger's plenitude becomes a much more physical notion of energy. This energy also pervades non-humans and inorganic matter. At the same time, this energy becomes no longer internal to but transversal of all types of material beings (Colebrook 2005). This was perhaps implicit in Spinoza, for whom nature is the divine and thus the physical already metaphysical. Hence the penchant of post-hegemonic cultural studies for the non-human: for the culture of things.

What Hardt and Negri did in *Empire* (2000) was to capture this idea of *potentia*, and read it into contemporary politics. Even in Negri's very early work on the 'labour process' of the early 1970s, he insisted that it was labour as *potentia* that constituted capital as *potestas*. For Spinoza's metaphysics of single substance, it needs always to be *potentia* also that constitutes *potestas*. The *potentia* of concrete labour, which must be labour as difference, in which the labour of each is unique, constitutes capital as abstract homogeneity in which this difference is brought under the sign of equivalence, which then reigns over its constitutive difference. In *Empire* (2000), this position becomes a more literal neo-vitalism, and the production of difference takes place not just through labour but also outside the sphere of work, in 'life' more generally. Here the authors point to an older 'extensive' politics of *le peuple* and the proletariat. *Le peuple* were atomized citizens, each standing before the state and law as equivalents. The proletariat also came together politically as equivalents as abstract homogeneous labour. All this is displaced by an intensive post-hegemonic politics of what Hardt and Negri call the multitudes, in which political individuals are more like monads than atoms, each different from the other. Organization in the older hegemonic politics had to come from the outside, whether it was the proletarian political party or the distanced political representation of classical parliamentarism. In post-hegemonic politics, there is organization from the inside: there is self-organization. It is no longer like *le peuple* or the proletariat-like mechanism with the brain on the outside; now the brain – or something like mind – is immanent in the system itself. Hence the classical Taylorist and Fordist collective labourer becomes the *cerveau collectif*, the collective brain (Lazzarato 2002). The multitudes give self-organization in politics as well as self-organization at work. In both, life is such self-organization.

This is the potentia of post-hegemonic politics. Where then is *potestas*? If this is *puissance*, then where is *pouvoir*? If *potestas* as power-over comes somehow from above, then *potentia* and *potestas* come, not just from within, but 'from below'. In the post-hegemonic order, *potestas* or domination also begins to come from below. *Pouvoir* and *puissance* somehow begin to merge into one another – become somehow fuzzy and indistinct in relation to one another. The hegemon is above. It is outside and over. In the post-hegemonic order, power comes to act from below: it no longer stays outside that which it 'effects'. It becomes instead immanent in its object and its processes. No one describes this better than Michel Foucault. For Foucault there are two modes in which *pouvoir* works. In the first, it normalizes *puissance* from above. In the second, it takes the shape of *puissance*: of life itself. It is power that does not work through normalization. At stake are two modes of power-knowledge. The first is the power-over that Foucault talks about in terms of surveillance and discipline. The second is when power starts in more contemporary times to work from below. When it begins to circulate in the capillaries of society. In the second mode, power enters immanent to life and forms of life themselves. Each of these modes of operation of power is at the same time a mode of knowledge. These are described in the *Order of Things*. In *Les mots et les choses* (1966), Foucault describes one episteme that he understands in terms of classification and representation, in which words are outside and above things and classify these things. These are succeeded by a modern episteme in which knowledge comes to grasp the things from within. In biology there is a shift from the classification in genre, species and order of natural history to a focus on life – physiological explorations of the interior of the organism. In economics there is a shift from the classical understanding of value in mercantilism to the more modern understanding of value in terms of labour, again constituting value from the interior. Classically, language was understood through the classification of subject, verb and object in the *Grammaire générale* while in the modern, language took on its own lifeblood in the national languages and philology studied by the Grimms and Herder. So knowledge and indeed words (discourse), which once acted outside and above in the classical period, now enter the object themselves. As knowledge enters the capillaries, i.e. the life, of language, the body and economic value (thus value of things), so does power. At stake is a shift from mechanistic to vitalist power. Life and *puissance* (*potentia*) now operate not through the equilibria of reproduction, but through chronic far-from-equilibrium production. We are no longer normalized: instead we self-constitute in difference. When power (*potentia*) starts to work immanently, power (*potestas*) enters into difference itself. *Pouvoir* was much easier to unmask when it worked from the outside as power-over. The critique of ideology of left-hegemonic politics could manage this. But when power enters into us and constitutes us from the inside – not through our normalization but through our difference – through partly producing (i.e. not reproducing) this now disequilibrate difference, it becomes far more difficult to unmask. Indeed, working no longer through a visual paradigm, but through the multiplicity of senses, un*mask*ing is no longer at issue.

From norm to fact[3]

The notion of hegemony of course comes from Gramsci, but it presumes a certain normativity. Indeed, Gramsci's idea of the 'organic intellectual' was to provide this sort of normativity for the masses on the left. But ideas of normativity are ubiquitous in the age of hegemonic politics. Ideas, for example of 'civil society' or 'global civil society', often refer to a global normative order that does not yet exist and might never exist. A cultural studies or a sociology that deals in the idiom of such normativity begins to lose track of the *facts*: of social and cultural facts. This can lead to very inaccurate description, so that we really do not get a grasp on what social forces are acting in a given time-space, but instead the state of affairs which we might (or might not) like to bring about. Some analysts, e.g. Habermas, have quite properly spoken of this as dealing in 'counterfactuals'. It seems to me that to understand how global capitalism might work, it is much better to work through facts than counterfactuals. These counterfactuals seem indeed to be norms. And not even actually existing norms, but norms that we might in the best of worlds think it desirable to have. Sociology, it seems to me, can learn a lot more from facts than from counterfactual norms in describing the mechanism by which today's global capitalism works. Cultural studies, for its part, begins to deal with facts as artefacts, as prisms through which to explore the relationships of cultural worlds. Again, this would seem to be much more productive than for cultural studies to focus on counterfactual norms. There is often such a focus on counterfactual norms in studies of global democracy. This is a highly normative notion and often corresponds to states of affairs that are not even realized in the West. Yet such ideas as the norms of global democracy are used as legitimizations by powerful Western states in order to install these norms – sometimes militarily – in far-away cultures. The discourse of global normative democracy is often not realized by the powerful Western states, especially in violating any notion of human rights through such activities as 'rendition'. Not only are the rights of sovereign states overridden, but there is little regard for the already existing facticity of on-the-ground social and cultural relationships in these countries. Universal, abstract norms, especially when they are brought in on the backs of bayonets and tanks and missiles, often tend to violate the grain of the facticity of social relations in that country they are meant to liberate.

Post-hegemonic politics leaves such normativity and enters into the realm of the factual. This does not mean breaking with ethics, though it does mean breaking with abstract ethics.[4] But let us stay with facticity for the moment. What is a fact? For Max Weber it is something that stands in opposition to value. Emile Durkheim as well speaks of 'social facts'. The notion of fact for both Weber and Durkheim refers less to events or things out there in the world than to statements about the world. We recall *Dragnet* – 'I want the facts mam. Nothing but the facts'. Facts are the data that Sergeant Friday in *Dragnet* works with to solve crimes. To put together a case that will in court at a later date come up against the rather more concrete norms or rules of the law. Facts here are such things as 'I saw a man running from the scene of the crime. He was white, in his mid-twenties, with black greasy hair, sunglasses and a "hoodie". He was about six foot and was quite thin'. These facts are not about the being or substance of this man. They are about his qualities, his attributes, his predicates. They are objectively described. The police and the prosecuting attorney will put together a case from a large collection of these predicates, these facts. These facts are knowledge abstracted by our perception and understanding from the being of the man-himself. For Weber, these facts are abstracted by the sociologist from concrete social, political and cultural practices. They then, in their constellations, form ideal types. These ideal types then serve as guides for us to understand other complexes of social phenomena. Again these are objective – surely in the sense that Kant understood objectivity – and we are again dealing with the predicates of individual and collective social beings. These are cognitive judgements. Even though individual subjects make them, to have any validity they need to be objective, and meet a set of logical conditions. In Durkheim we have a similar state of affairs. In *Primitive Classification* we see that facts come from the classifications of those whom anthropologists and sociologists study and from what those sociologists and anthropologists select from all of this (Durkheim and Mauss 2009). There is another side of Durkheim (1982) however. It is where he says that 'social facts' are *things*. Here he instructs sociologists to study social facts as things. The assumption is that everyday social actors also come up against social facts as things. Note that this is a major shift. In this facts are no longer the characteristics, or qualities or predicates of things. They are those things.[5]

Durkheim's thing-like facts are getting closer to what is at stake in post-hegemonic power. That is, facts that once were abstracted as attributes of events and things are now not separable from the things and events themselves. In such a context, architects and urbanists like Rem Koolhaas and Stefano Boeri put strong emphasis on facts. For Koolhaas (Koolhaas and Mau 1995), there seems to be almost an obsession with sociology, and his books, and indeed his pitches in architectural competitions, are pervaded by hordes of facts: about Lagos or Shenzhen or wherever else he is thinking of building, accompanied by bar charts and other graphs of distributions of such facts. But these facts, like Durkheim's, hardly come across as attributes or predicates. They seem to function almost like armies, crushing the reader (viewer or jury) with their omnipresence and sheer mass. The graphics are in compelling colours and shapes, transforming the usual greyness of factual analysis. Stefano Boeri and Multiplicity (Boeri and Bregani 2003) also speak the language of facts. They describe their political interventions into urban timespace in terms of the 'physical facts' of the city. There is a sort of politics in this facticity. This facticity is physical, but it cannot be described as a static 'built environment'. At stake is not the completeness of something that is built, but instead something physical that is in process. There is no fixedness in Boeri's idea of the social and urban fact.

The thinker who introduced the term 'facticity' into modern discussions (*Faktizität*) is of course Heidegger. For Heidegger (1986), when beings, and especially *Dasein*, escape from the confines of technology into the space of existence, they enter at the same time the realm of facticity. This facticity is in the realm not of beings but of being. It is the Kierkegaardian dark night of the soul into which we are thrown, yet into which we must be thrown in order to project our being in its potentialities. Otherwise we are mere beings closed from any possible opening. For Heidegger, in the empirical–transcendental couple of being and beings, facticity is not an empirical but a transcendental. Georg Simmel importantly foreshadowed Heidegger's thoughts, though for Simmel fact was on the side of beings and *value* on the side of being. In the opening paragraphs of *The Philosophy of Money* (1977), Simmel separates value from fact. Facts are qualities of objects for Simmel. Values are not. Value is not a predicate, he says. If facts are qualities, then value has to do with being. If facts have to do with categories, value has to do with life. Thus value = being = life. It follows that use-value and exchange-value are not qualities of things. They are something else. They are not objective, i.e. they are not abstracted from objects. When a subject operates through categories and logically predicates, he is 'objective'. When a subject looks at the thing and views it as a microcosm of the world from the point of view of the thing, then in Simmel's sense he relates to that thing 'subjectively'. Value in this sense is subjective. Value has to do with the resistance of the thing to the subject's desire to have it. To have a thing is to, so to speak, merge with it as content. To use it, to eat it, to have sex with it. When we have a thing, we no longer stand in a distanced or separated relation to it – either objectively or subjectively.

The rise of the money economy brings an objectification of this realm of value. There is a destruction of subjective culture through money. There is a 'factification' of value. What was being gets parcelized and atomized. What was once life turns into mechanism. My subjective use-value becomes anybody's exchange-value. Yet what Simmel noted taking place was still in the age of hegemony. At stake in post-hegemonic power is less a 'factification' of value than, as it were, a 'value-ification' of fact. Fact takes on the logic of value. Money comes alive. Instead of facts being a dead abstraction, the factual comes alive. In the age of hegemony, the concept squeezed the life out of the thing in reducing it to its predicates. In the post-hegemonic age, the concept is dis-intermediated and we come up against facts as raw sense data. In their rawness, facts come very much alive. Thus the 'positivism' of the age of hegemony gives way to post-hegemonic *empiricism*. This is an empirical that is even more immediate than sense data. It is the empiricism of the thing, of the event. Empirical data comes to life as transcendental fact. In this more radical, indeed *extreme* empiricism, the virtual and the actual merge under the sign of life. This is the sort of facticity that is at stake in Koolhaas' and Boeri's urbanism. This is the grain in which post-hegemonic politics needs to work. It will find its ethical moment inside the factual itself. Post-hegemonic politics is a politics not of normativity but of such facticity.

From representation to communication

The psychoanalytic notion of the symbolic has its roots much earlier in the work of Emile Durkheim. For Durkheim, the symbolic is the *conscience collective* (i.e. the collective consciousness, and at the same time the collective conscience). For Durkheim, the conscience collective dealt with deviance or the pathological through its exclusion. The exclusion of the pathological through a healthy conscience collective guaranteed the reproduction of society. Durkheim's most effective critic was Georges Bataille. Bataille was on the side of the pathological. He was on the side of social classes and phenomena that were abjected by the functioning of the normal. This abjected pathological was understood by Bataille as '*excess*'. Today we would understand it as 'the real'. This real of Bataille and, as we saw above, of Slavoj Žižek is a space of frenzy. It is the space not of the sex drive (reproduction), but the death drive. It is the space of the patricide and patrophagy of Freud's primal horde. The symbolic is in effect macro-sociological. It needs a micro-sociological counterpart in order to function. This micro-sociological counterpart is found in Marcel Mauss' notion of the gift. This is a process of reciprocal and obligatory gift-exchange. In gift-exchange is the basis of the social bond. Hegemonic power works through the social bond. Bataille has another notion of the gift. For him, gift-giving has little to do with the reinforcement of the symbolic. It has to do with agon, with waste, burning vast cornucopias of gifts, sacrifice. Bataille's agon of the gift, which has nothing to do with reciprocity, runs counter to the social bond. It instead guarantees the destruction of the social bond.

That this social bond is in decline has been the subject of very large numbers of commentators on both the left and right. In the context of intensive politics, the social bond of the hegemonic order of the national manufacturing society is in decline. In the global information society, the social relation is reduced to the *communication*. Niklas Luhmann has most profoundly understood this. The social relation is longer term, embedded and in proximity. The communication presumes the short term; it is disembedded and is at-a-distance. The social relation operates in the logic of hegemony, in the reproduction of the symbolic. The communication occupies instead the sphere of the real: the space in excess of the symbolic. Bataille's excess is reminiscent of Max Weber's 'charisma'. Weber spoke of the routinization of charisma. In this sense, the communication is the banalization of excess. The communication is at the heart of the post-hegemonic order. The symbolic is somehow national;

the communication is in the first instance generic and global. It may be site-specific, but it is global. The communication is 'lighter' than the symbolic. Hence it can travel faster and further. The communication is immaterial.

In intensive politics, the symbolic – iconic of hegemonic power – is collapsed into the order of communications. Into the profane banality of the everyday. The dualism of the hegemonic order disappears. Hegemony presumes *legitimate domination*. It presumes sovereignty. Sovereignty presumes a dualism of ruler, or mode of rule and ruled. So does legitimation. The global information society is an order of not dualism, but monism, immanence. Now domination is through the communication. The communication is not above us, even as disciplinary power is. It is instead among us. We swim in its ether. When domination is through the communication, sovereignty, indeed democracy, must be rethought. Although it takes place increasingly through the media, domination was never so immediate, so unreflective: so without a separate sphere of discursive legitimation. When there is no separate instance, there is only – as Lyotard (1984) said – legitimation through performance (*Legitimation durch Verfahren*) (Luhmann 2008). This is non-hegemonic. It entails an immediacy to legitimation. Another way in which power is illegitimate follows from the way it works not in terms of reproduction but instead production. This is the chronic decisionism that is called for in intensive politics. Further, reflexive and autopoetic self-production is always more than just reproduction. At stake is not reproduction but the chronic production of society that is necessary in a fluctuating environment. Thus we can understand the contemporary importance of Carl Schmitt and his doctrine of the rise of the executive function and the 'decision'. We live in an age of such chronic decisionism: one in which legality as a mode of legitimation is displaced by performance.[6] Hegemony – and the symbolic – are effective through meaning. Communications work through performativity. Legitimation is no longer separate from what it is meant to legitimate. It becomes automatic.

The symbolic, and our values, were embedded in more or less linear institutions. In this context there has been a general institutional meltdown. This is internal as well as external. Internally there is meltdown of family, church, trade unions, hierarchical firms, institutions of art. Externally there is meltdown of the institutions of international relations. The breakdown of the cold war stability of US–Soviet relations that opened up the anarchic communicational space of international relations, or the replacement of international *relations* per se by the violence of communications. Thus we can understand September 11. The stability of the institutions is displaced by the violence of flows: of flows of communications and finance. The institutions of moderate 'church' and international relations break down. Fundamentalist 'sect' and networked communications rage. Thus a hub of world trade and not the institutions of the state were the focus of attack. In war the hegemon was the leader of a group of states – a *primus inter pares*. Greek city states are for Gramsci the model. This presumes an institutional framework. With institutional meltdown and what Hardt and Negri called Empire, this no longer is the case. America not so much leads. It dictates. It does not act like a hegemon. Post-9/11 US power was well beyond hegemony. In hegemony, there is a leading class or leading state to cement an alliance. Communications do not cement. The USA saw no need to cement.

In this context Stuart Hall has rightly criticized Hardt and Negri for underestimating US power in their notion of Empire.[7] The decline of hegemony and the symbolic makes all this US power possible. It is institutional meltdown both internally (decline of national symbolics) and of international-relations institutions that makes the communications order and hitherto unsurpassed US power possible. Empire is what happens after the modern world system of nation states. It is only after the demise of the modern world system – and of hegemony – that the USA as sole hyper-power emerges. The Roman Empire worked first through a coordinated bureaucracy which became the basis for a symbolic and institutionalized church. The American Empire is based less on institutions (and representations) and takes place more on the violence of communications. The social bond of Marcel Mauss' gift is the micro-sociological face of Emile Durkheim's macro-sociological collective representations. As the social bond attenuates, the collectivity fragments and so do its representations. Collective representations, once giving solidity to the social formation from the heights of the superstructure, fragment and recombine in the infrastructure as communications. Unlike the serious speech acts of an earlier politics, which needed to be legitimated through reasoned discourse, communications carry their legitimations inside them in their very performance.

Communications are extraparliamentary. They don't need a social contract. They are what Max Weber called *nicht-legitime Herrschaft*. Domination in the global communications order is, many argue, not through discipline but control. The communication order's non-linear systems are such apparatuses of control. In the communication order, power is not just in the flows: it is in the emergent non-linear socio-technical systems that channel, block and connect the flows. Hence literally power through control. Cybernetic power works through command, control, communications and intelligence. Here intelligence scans the system's borders. It processes the rather amorphous stuff out there, the already somewhat patterned noise out there into information. Guy Debord (1993) already understood in the 1960s this new power of control through cybernetic-like mechanisms. They are military mechanisms. They are a question of force and strategy. They have nothing to do with ideology or culture or hegemony or meaning. At stake is not meaning from the order of representation (and hegemony), but instead non-representational 'operations'. Debord already gave us the way out. Not to resist but to *dérive*. 'Lines of flight' are the *dérive*. But the *dérive* is site-specific. It is site-specific and generic at the same time. To *dérive* is not exactly to resist. It is to evade. It is an 'exit', not a 'voice' strategy. The *dérive* moves slower than lines of flight. It moves from engagement to engagement.[8] *Dérive* says I don't like your logic: I won't contest in a class-versus-class struggle or through rituals of resistance. Those are voice. Instead *dérive* says: I'll drift. Is *dérive* the heart of twenty-first century critique? The response to domination through interactivity is the 'interpassivity' of drifting. In the hegemonic order, we challenge power through contesting domination through discursive argument. Or through symbolic struggles. To *dérive* is to do none of the above. It is to slip out. It is strategy through movement.

Cultural studies: first and second wave

The observations above do not really do justice to the power-as-hegemony position. Hegemony was a powerful concept, and still is in the analyses of a great number of phenomena. The concept arose in the context of 1970s' Marxism. This was in the context, indeed, of certain Althusserian Marxism, as instantiated in the work of Jacques Texier and Christine Buci-Glucksmann and fundamentally Nicos Poulantzas in France, and especially Ernesto Laclau and then Laclau and Mouffe in the UK. At the heart of all this is the phenomenon of *social class*. This was particularly important in Britain, in which the phenomenon of social class, and a certain power of the English working class, was experienced with a depth, on the level of everyday life, that was infrequently found elsewhere. Hence a generation of British sociologists, writing before the 1970s, already based their work in a sort of empirical – what was called 'Weberian' or what was later called 'neo–Weberian' – notion of class. The generation of their students were, in their aggregate, largely Marxist, and the fundamental text in regard to social class was here Nicos Poulantzas' *Classes in Contemporary Capitalism* (1978). Other major texts that were of greatest influence at this point in time were Harry Braverman's *Labor and Monopoly Capital* (1974) and Eric Olin Wright's more empirical early work on social class (1983). At stake was not yet a power-as-hegemony position, but more arguments that were directly about class power. And what really counted was what workers did in factories and the centrality of trade unions. Now cultural studies work, from the 'Birmingham School', was appearing in publications from the mid-1970s, but attained much wider recognition from the end of the 1970s. This was at the same time that Laclau wrote his early book on ideology (Laclau 1977) and Paul Hirst his famous piece on the 'Ideological Apparatuses of the State' (1979). This was the context of the power-as-hegemony position. It was one in which there was a shift from a focus on the economy and the factory to ideology and especially *culture*. The idea was that power was not just economic but also cultural. That capitalist state power was not just a question of coercion but of consent, again of ideology. In the work of Hall, Hebdige and McRobbie, popular culture came to the fore (see CCCS 2006). The purveyors may have been of working-class origins, but this was not the space of the factory, but the streets or indeed often the art schools. And these kids were probably not going to work in factories, even if their parents did. So the idea of hegemony becomes prominent with the decline of a more fundamental Marxism, and indeed a decline in the importance of the working class and the factory. What Gramsci gave to this was the importance of consent, on the one hand, and culture, on the other. If the fundamental Marxists saw power in terms of class versus class, then Gramsci gave to us a question of *class alliance*. The rise of cultural studies itself was based on the decline of the prominence of fundamental class versus class politics: an abeyance of the fundamental structuring of society, economy, ideology and politics by the opposition of capitalist class and working class. Gramsci spoke of alliances of the working class with sections of the middle classes, under the umbrella of a sort of counter-hegemonic culture that opposed the dominant culture and could potentially aggregate the alliance of different classes. Later, from the early 1980s, cultural studies would be influenced by Lacan and semiotics. With the accession of Margaret Thatcher to power, cultural studies gave us powerful analyses of her regime under the idea of authoritarian populism. But at the same time as the British working class was numerically in fast decline, with factory closures everywhere and trade unions being decimated, social class began to decline at the same time in cultural studies analyses. The power-as-hegemony position began to talk less of socialism than 'democracy', and in many cases Marxism, any kind of Marxism, was left behind altogether, often rejected for a general notion of antagonism, which has owed more to Carl Schmitt than to Karl Marx.

Yet in its heyday the notion of hegemony had a great deal to do with social class. Post-hegemonic cultural studies much less to do with social class. Its analyses may be much the poorer for this. Post-hegemonic cultural studies may be less political. It is more oriented to art, science and technology. Yet phenomena of inequality and class disparities, especially on a global level, have worsened over these decades. Cultural studies needs to be able to address these phenomena. It does so now not at all sufficiently. Class is still with us, more than ever. Yet, no longer being concentrated so much inside single nations and in concentrated places like factories, class has reconfigured, or more or less fragmented. Some global movements have attempted to remedy this. But the obstacles are major. Attention has, unhappily for social inequalities, largely turned elsewhere. This is mostly because of globalization and also information-alization. Thus technology and media have become much more central to social and cultural life. This is something that the power-as-hegemony position did not sufficiently address. More recent tendencies in cultural studies are much more attuned to what seems to be a more generalized vitalization of social and cultural, indeed of natural life. On the one hand, there is a vitalization of power, which I tried to address above in discussions of power as *potentia*. *Potentia* here is at the same time life. Thus can be understood the rise of a sort of neo-vitalism in the work of Delanda (2001), Massumi (2002) and, as I mentioned, Negri Hardt (2000). The point I wanted to make in this context was that not just resistance but domination itself works through such life or *potentia*. This is very different from a previously existing power that works through the dead labour of the commodity. Classical, hegemonic power worked through the abstract homogeneous and dead labour of the commodity. Indeed, 'the *thing*' in the hegemonic order was paradigmatically the commodity's dead labour. But things – in the global and informational order – and the power-as-hegemony position dealt basically with a national and manufacturing society – are now no longer dead and mechanical. They have, as Arjun Appadurai

(1986) noted, taken on their own social life. They have come alive, they come alive and move, not 'mechanically' – in terms of external causation – as the commodity, but 'vitally'. They flow in their logic and indeterminately in their unintended consequences. These are the 'neo-commodities' of the post-hegemonic order. These neo-commodities are in the information order things that think – in the words of the MIT Media Lab. The old *res extensa* of the commodity becomes at the same time thinking substance, substance that thinks. Capitalist power itself, though – indeed, global capitalist power – works through such thinking and in an important sense living matter, rather than the solely extensive matter of the commodity.

As important as the 'vitalization' of power is this just-mentioned mediatization of life. These are two interweaving processes. At the same time as power is being 'vitalized', life is being mediatized. Hence there is a new importance in cultural studies of media theory: from Friedrich Kittler (1997) to Katharine Hayles (1999), from Stiegler (1998) to Sloterdijk (2004). I tried to address this above partly in what I argued was the rise of communications in the post-hegemonic regime of power. This includes a mediatized social life. Thus Ken Sakamura of Tokyo University has spoken of 'ubiquitous computing'. This needs to be taken one step further and we need to speak of ubiquitous media. Here at stake is not just technological forms of life (Lash 2002), in which forms of social life are technologically mediated. At stake is the technologization of life itself, the mediatization of life itself. Once we make the step from computing or technology to media, the question also of content comes to take centre-stage, as does that of communication. When media are ubiquitous, interfaces are everywhere. The actual becomes an interface. People and other interfaces are connected by protocols that connect an ever-greater variety of interfaces with one another. It is such protocols that make communication possible. Most important is the ubiquity of code, of mediatic code pervading more and more regions of beings. First, the communication codes of human beings on the level of mind or the metaphysical level, the neural codes and network of biological human brains; then the genetic codes, of bio-media; and finally, the coding in nanotechnology of inorganic matter. There is further the importance even in the generation of content and perhaps especially interactive content of coding itself, of the algorithm. Computer scientists understand algorithms in terms of 'rules'. But these rules are far different from the sorts of rules that human scientists have dealt with over the decades. Two types of rules have long structured the human sciences and human societies: on the one hand, what amount to constitutive rules and, on the other, by regulative rules. The first type of rules is found in the constitutions of states or in the rules of games. Without them the game cannot exit. They let you enter the playing field of the game and a nation. Such rules are effectively a passport. Regulative rules are entities that regulate your activity once you are on the playing field. They address at the same time how you play the game once you are there. But in a society of pervasive media and ubiquitous coding, at stake is a third type of rule, algorithmic, *generative* rules. 'Generative' rules are, as it were, virtuals that generate a whole variety of actuals. They are compressed and hidden and we do not encounter them in the way that we encounter constitutive and regulative rules. Yet this third type of generative rules is more and more pervasive in our social and cultural life of the post-hegemonic order. However, they do not merely open up opportunity for invention. They are also pathways through which capitalist *power* works, in, for example, biotechnology companies and software giants more generally. Power through the algorithm is increasingly important for media companies in digital rights management. A society of ubiquitous media means a society in which power is increasingly in the algorithm.

This leads us back to questions of ontology that have been so central to this chapter. I have spoken of a shift as we moved to the post-hegemonic power regime as hegemony from the symbolic to the real, from semiotics to intensive language, and most of all from epistemology to ontology. Here I have understood the symbolic, semiotics, representation as basically epistemological and the real, intensive language, and the communication as basically ontological. Epistemology has to do with the understanding of the things we encounter, while ontology and the real have to do with the thing-itself that is never encountered. The thing-itself, and the real, is never encountered; it is a virtual, a generative force; it is metaphysical rather than physical. I understand the epistemological order of power-as-hegemony to be fundamentally Kantian. For Kant, knowledge and experience are much more than a question of sensation, as they were for the empiricism of Locke and Hume. Knowledge and experience also entail another faculty than the faculty of perception: the faculty of the understanding. The understanding consists of categories. These categories deal with sensation in terms of predication. Perception or sensation is not enough. We experience and know only through predication.

For Kant, sense perception or sensation were not sufficient for knowledge – either for philosophical, scientific or social scientific knowledge. Sense perception had to be brought under the orderings of the categories or classifications, which functioned through making predications about a substance or a subject. The point is that a transcendental is necessary for these predications. This transcendental has two sides. For Kant, looking outward – in science it works through categories and is epistemological. Kant's transcendental is reason. And as reason, it is two-sided: looking outwards, reason is what Kant calls the understanding (*Verstand*) and science: it is epistemological. Looking-inwards reason is what Kant calls 'Reason' or *Vernunft*. *Vernunft* is ontological. Reason as the understanding works through categories and predication: reason as *Vernunft* works not through categories but ideas. These ideas do not predicate because they work with what we do not encounter. They operate in the ether of the metaphysical. Looking, as it were, inwards – in terms of ethics, religion and art – it is ontological. Looking inwards, it is being that is at stake rather than knowledge of the outside world. The Kantian philosopher looks at both sides – the metaphysical inside and the physical outside. Kant's critique of metaphysics preserves a great deal of the metaphysical and the ontological. The same thing needs to take place in discursive thought, and in particular in the human or social sciences, for which again empiricism is not enough. Social science must work through transcendental categories to classify social sense material. The social sciences must identify the subject and then discover and, indeed, attribute these predicates. These predicates are not, as in metaphysics, included in the subject. They are attributed by the social scientist. The condition of possibility, again of this social epistemology, is a social ontology that structures the moral life of modern society and its social scientists.

As Foucault understood in *The Order of Things* (1966), and Max Weber had already addressed in his methodological argument on the explanatory adequacy of causality and meaning, man is an empirical-transcendental double. This empirical-transcendental double is the subject or substance that cultural studies and sociology must deal with. Unlike, classically, in the natural sciences, in which the subject or substance is merely extensive, the subjects that the social sciences must predicate about are both extended and intensive, or thinking substance. We are metaphysical-physical doubles. Once we are aware of the dual nature of the subject, we are aware of the fact that his or her predicates are often less a question of what we as social scientists attribute than intrinsic to the intentions of the subject. To the extent that those who social scientists study are metaphysical, the predicates are included in this human subject. Once we, as human scientists, are there, we can decide to deal with this human double either through classifications, as Durkheim and Weber chose to, or through values, ideas and interpretation, as Simmel and later the phenomenological tradition chose to. There is a third methodological choice for todays post-human and also post-hegemonic cultural sciences. This third choice is neither classification nor interpretation. It is a method of tracking or mapping – it is also topological in that it deals with virtuals as much as actuals[9]. Or, more precisely, it deals with actuals as virtuals. It entails entering into the world of cultural things as a human thing, whose difference is that we may be marginally more reflexive than other things.

This excursus was necessary in the sense to set up again the counterposition of what we have been discussing as hegemonic versus post hegemonic, or 'first-wave' and 'second-wave' cultural studies. First-wave cultural studies – whether Marxist or not – with its assumptions of representation and Saussurean semiotics, stayed very much within the epistemological realm. Typically, this epistemology was decentred from positivism, as knowledge was contingent and indefinitely delayed. If there was an ontology, it was understood in an aporetic relation to the epistemological. This aporia was the unbridgeable chasm between the epistemological and the ontological that could not be sublated in Hegel's sense. This was an aporia – of freedom on the one hand, and necessity on the other – with which we were condemned to live. Now what much of second-wave cultural studies do – and the first three sections of this chapter try to exemplify this – is to collapse the epistemological into the ontological. This is why writers like the early Lyotard and Deleuze have been so influential in recent years. Lyotard and Deleuze destroy the categories, destroy the predications, destroy centred and decentred positivism and go back to the original empiricism of Hume in their philosophy of 'sensation'. Traditional empiricism of course rejects – as we – any notion of a transcendental. But for today's philosophy of sensation, the transcendental is already there in the empirical. It is immanent in the empirical. So we have here an empiricism that is already ontological, in which empirical substance is not extended, as in Descartes, but is intensive substance. The other side of ontology in such a philosophy of sensation is a reconfigured epistemology that is now inseparable and fused with the ontological. This is epistemological and in this sense a question of logic. But this logic is neither that of deductivist predication nor of inductivist empiricism, nor even a combination thereof. The logic is not something that is applied, as in Kant and Durkheim,[10] to sense material. The logic, as broadcast in the titles of two of Deleuze's (1993b, 2003) books, is there already in the sense material: the logic is immanent to sensation. In this 'transcendental empiricism', the transcendental is collapsed into the empirical.

Why is this second-wave cultural studies, this post-hegemonic cultural studies, so suggestive to today's generation of students? Because it speaks to the world that they encounter. If the empirical is informational, then it is already knowledge: it is already transcendental. If the empirical we encounter is mediatized, then it is already transcendental. If an earlier sociology and cultural studies – as we saw above in Durkheim, Weber and Foucault – saw man as an empirical-transcendental double, second-wave cultural studies also understands *things* as such doubles. An empirical that is already transcendental is what we deal with at work, at play, in science and in art. Second-wave cultural studies and its transcendental empiricism speaks to us because we encounter a world of transcendental-empiricals. Thus science encounters a world of bio-media. And art deals in (video and information) materials that are already mediated in addressing a transcendental that is equally mediatized. In all these cases it is a question of both ontology and epistemology. Being is mediatized, as is knowledge. The two stand less in a relation of radical separation than of fusion.

Conclusions

If power has become ontological, intensive, factical and communicational, then what are the implications for cultural studies? Culture – that was previously somehow outside the profane everyday now – is now inside it. Culture, previously in the realm of value, was a place from which critique could be launched. Culture was a site for critique of the commodity and indeed of industry. But as culture comes no longer to have that separation as it becomes itself part of the realm of fact, as it enters the profane order of communications, then what was cultural studies is no longer easily separable from industry (McRobbie 1998). Cultural studies and what many of us now call cultural research come in many ways to be indistinct from culture industry. Horkheimer and Adorno (1972) of course foresaw the rise of culture industry many years ago as the final twist in the tail of the dialectic of enlightenment and triumph of commodification. Yet the increasing overlap of the cultural and industrial principles – as we saw above, of fact and of value – is not necessarily, as Adorno said, the industrialization of culture: it is at the same time the 'cultur-ification' of industry. On the one hand, the deadening abstract homogeneity of industry suffocates the being, the life of culture. On the other, culturification brings life and indeed ontology to the mechanism of industry. What this means in practice is an engagement of cultural studies with the culture industries: with art, the media, architecture, design, information and communications technology, software and protocol design and urbanism.[11] It must engage with the sciences and technosciences as well. This is partly because these sectors are expanding and are increasingly destinations for our students, but also because of the critical interventions that need to be made there.

Notes

1 Ernesto Laclau and Chantal Mouffe's (2001) idea of hegemony is specifically not a theory of institutions. Laclau's idea and indeed Stuart Hall's use of the concept in the context of Margaret Thatcher's political power in Britain is not institutional. They presume already the decline of the classical institutions of working-class politics. The influence of Laclau here of Peronism in his discussions of populism and also institutions is striking. In many ways Laclau and Mouffe's work describes a transition from hegemonic to post-hegemonic power. Indeed, cultural studies itself – and Hall's work – needs to be seen as situated in this transition. What this chapter is arguing is that 25–30 years on, this transition has gone a lot further.
2 I am indebted to Sebastian Olma for this idea.
3 I am indebted in this to discussions with Jeff Alexander and Francisco Carballo.
4 Spinoza's ethics work through this sort of facticity.
5 Predicates may be connected to the things – we don't most likely encounter things without predicates any more than we have ever encountered men without qualities.
6 *Legitimität und Legalität* is from Carl Schmitt (1998). *Legitimation durch Verfahren* is Luhmann's (2008) Schmittianism that Lyotard picked up on in *The Postmodern Condition* (1984).
7 From Hall's Commentary on Michael Hardt's lecture at Goldsmiths in April 2001. This chapter was drafted as an article in 2006. Subsequently, the rise of China and BRIC has complicated things further. Yet a new set of symbolically bound institutions of international relations has yet to emerge.
8 See Lyotard's *Dérive à partir de Marx et Freud* (1991).
9 This sort of method is introduced in the work of Appadurai and Latour. Celia Lury and I have attempted to develop it in our *Global Culture Industry: The Mediation of Things* (Lash and Lury 2007).
10 In his case of course a 'socio-logic'.
11 Stuart Hall's work in the 1990s and first years of the new millennium, with INIVA and the Stephen Lawrence Foundation, exemplify this.

7

Intensive Religion: Emile Durkheim's Elementary Forms

This chapter is devoted to the study of Emile Durkheim's *Formes élémentaires de la vie réligieuse* (1968). This book is about the origins of religion. It is about the most *elementary* forms of religion. Sociologists will know that for Durkheim religion was society itself. Religion was society in the sense that religion was the social group's collective self-representation. What is somewhat less well known is that *Elementary Forms* describes a transition from some sort of pre-social 'nature' to the birth of society and religion. The book describes, in other words, the transition from nature to culture. Thus, in a very important way, *The Elementary Forms* is about the origins of culture. What we will see in this chapter is that the origins of culture that Durkheim describes in *Elementary Forms* are at the same time the origins of *intensive* culture. What Durkheim shows us is that culture is originally intensive. This was already hinted at above in Chapter 4 on Walter Benjamin and intensive language. Here Benjamin starts from the *Genesis* of the Old Testament. Durkheim reaches back behind Judaism, back beyond all transcendental religions, to original immanent religion. In such primordial religion, unlike in Judaeo-Christianity, the sacred is not personified. The sacred does not take the form of a god on the model of the human person. A second major difference between Benjamin and Durkheim concerns the relationship between intensive and extensive culture. Benjamin sees the birth of intensive language – the language of the name – in Paradise. Extensive language – the language of logic and judgement and classification – is a phenomenon of the Fall. For Benjamin, there is a chasm, an aporia, between intensive and extensive language. For Durkheim, the relation between intensive and extensive culture is much more integrally intertwined.

For Durkheim, intensity is the sacred and extensity the profane. Durkheim takes this dialectic of intensity and extensity further back than Aristotle and Plato, back to the origins of being and of thought. Being is, for Durkheim, in the first instance sacred, spiritual or ideal being. This ontological being is at the same time cultural and social being. Knowing is a question of the objects involved in sacred substance, this sacred effervescence: these objects are in the sacred *symbols*. These symbols, once constituted, then turn outward into the profane and become the basis of modes of classification and the categories of thought. Durkheim insists that he is on the side not of the nominalists but of the realists. At stake is networks of these symbols in various combinations with one another. This *combinatoire* of sacred being is energized by the *mana* of a generalized vitalism or effervescence. Durkheim's more or less vitalist symbol-systems are religious substance: religious substance made up of these constellations of totemic objects. This is Durkheim's vitalist metaphysics. Yet these same symbols then turn outward and become the categories of profane knowledge. That is, knowledge through predicates that is more or less nominalist or 'epistemological'. For Durkheim as for Kant, we can know only the predicates of things. For Durkheim, the original intensity is the totem and the totemic system that make up tribal religion. In the daylight of the profane, this same totemic system becomes our everyday system of classifications: the origins of the categories of knowledge. This totemic system as both intensity and extensity is on the lines of Kant's transcendental a priori. This becomes for Durkheim, and now generations of social scientists, the sociological a priori. This a priori is collective religious assembly: it is the condition of possibility of both society and knowledge. Durkheim establishes his great book's central thesis – as he founds the mature discipline of sociology – in a debate with empiricist anthropology. To understand Durkheim's foundational case for the *sui generis* character of both society and the categories of the intellect, we need to understand his debate with these empiricists. It follows from the logic of these empiricists, in terms of the a posteriori nature of knowledge, that society itself is no more than a collection of individuals: that sociology is no more than a collection of psychologies. Durkheim shows that society is not just an accumulation of individuals, but is *sui generis* and exists simultaneously with totemic beliefs and practices. Thus also are the categories of the intellect more than an accumulation of sense impressions.

Against empiricism: a sociological a priori

In the introduction to *Elementary Forms*, Durkheim identifies the enemy. It is *utilitarianism*. The origins of culture are anything but utilitarian (Durkheim 1995: 5). Yet Durkheim criticizes the utilitarians, not so much for their psychologism as for their *empiricism*. Durkheim's positivism is fully opposed to empiricism. Durkheim is a sociological rationalist in a lifelong search for the social basis of our categories of thought. These are, as he states (1968: 13), the Aristotelian categories of the understanding (*entendement*) – that is, for Durkheim, most importantly, time, space, number, genre, cause, substance and personality. He says that the principal categories grow from religious belief and 'mythology'. For example, Kantian empty space grows out of a more 'primordial, social ordering of space'. For Herbert Spencer, famously Durkheim's main antagonist, the categories are 'made of the same elements' as sense impressions and constituted a posteriori from these 'sense impressions'. Durkheim maintains instead that the categories and reason itself are both 'external' to the psyche and *prior* to (sense) experience. This categorial a priori for Durkheim comes not from sense experience, but social collectivity. For empiricists, the categories are constituted from sense impressions but by the individual subject (1968: 15). Durkheim argues less against the psychologism than this individualism of the empiricists. For the British anthropologists E.B. Tylor and James Frazer, the categories derives from the 'accumulation' of sense impressions, which are 'individual representations'. Sense impressions, through their 'accumulation', lead to a certain 'generalization' and thus abstraction. It is the representations of things that are impressed on the senses. And those representations are 'images'. The things and empiricist sense impressions or 'images' are, notes Durkheim, not at all cultural but instead natural and material. Durkheim contrasts his collective representations with such individual representations. Collective representations are not sense impressions but blurred and indistinct precursors of a priori ideas. They have to do not with sense, but 'the intellect'. These Durkheimian representations are not material but ideal; not individual but social; and are most importantly not images but *symbols*. Images are material and from the body. Symbols are immaterial and of the mind.

Durkheim believes this cultural and symbolic order comes with the full entry into language. Language does not just mirror nature in isolated words but comes to form an independent system. Durkheim says that language is a creature not of imaging, or imagining, but a collective symbolic system of the mind. Categories, Durkheim says in the introduction to *Formes*, 'express the most general relations between things'. Without them not just intellectual knowledge would be impossible, so would 'common life'. These categories are, on the one hand, 'tools' (1968: 18). They are also moral guides (1968: 26). To live together requires minimal moral and minimal logical consensus (1968: 16–17). As logical categories, collective representations are tools; they are knowledge as applied to nature. This is the external side or outside of collective representations. On the other hand, these representations, looking inside, are moral. Ethos and ethics and morality have to do primarily not with knowledge but with conduct. They have to do with what Durkheim understood as non-material, anti-utilitarian and hence ideal 'needs'. Thus Durkheim wrote: 'religion responds to a fully other needs than those which adapt us to sensory things' (1968: 118).

Durkheim argues further against the necessity of an individualized and thus personalized divinity. Religion needs neither, he insists, a divinity nor a doctrine of creation. There is, he notes, no notion of divinity in Buddhism and no interest in the creation of this world – which is a world 'of suffering and becoming'. Salvation has less to do with goal-oriented prayer and more with goal-less meditation. The Buddha is a saint, not a god, but the wisest of men. The Buddha has entered Nirvana and can do no more in the course of human events, unlike the 'ever living Christ', who is 'daily sacrificed', as the 'community of faithful' go on 'communicating with its supreme source of its spiritual life' (1968: 30). For Buddhism, salvation has little to do with personal faith in the Buddha and more with 'the knowledge and practice of doctrine'. Buddhism and Jainism reject the idea of a creator – for them the world is eternal. Confucianism, Buddhism and Jainism had gods, had divinities, but they more or less disappeared. 'Religion and cult give primary importance not to deities, but to symbolic and at the same time material ceremonies' (1968: 33). It is these *rites* from which the gods – the 'divine personalities' – derive. Rites, as symbolically mediated collective assembly, come before beliefs for Durkheim.

Durkheim's most fundamental classification is of the two 'classes' of the sacred and profane. At stake here are two types of '*chose*' (thing): *les choses réeles* and *les choses idéeles*. The sacred comprises 'the beliefs, myths, legends' 'that express the nature of sacred things', as well as the virtues and powers they have, their relations with one another and with profane things' (1968: 51). In the more modern and 'idealistic' religions, such as Judaeo-Christianity, 'concepts' are at the centre and 'sensation and images' are in the background. In elementary forms of religious life, the concepts are immanent in the sensations and images. Alongside these sacred beliefs are the rites: 'rites of conduct with sacred things (*les choses sacrées*)' (1968: 56). Durkheim is very concerned about *things*. He often refers to the totemic animals and plants as things. *The Elementary Forms* is fundamentally about symbols and things.

Religion is above all 'a system of cults' (1995: 39): a system of cults that will tend to form an institution, which Durkheim calls a 'church' (1968: 60). Against the English anthropologists of magic, Durkheim says: 'Il n'ya pas d'église magique'. Witches and magicians might form a brotherhood (*confrérie*) to pursue their material interests as collections of individuals. But a church is not 'simply a *confrérie sacerdotale*', it is a 'moral community' (1968: 61). These collections of individuals are, for Durkheim, not fundamentally different from 'animal societies'. It is the 'institution [that] is the defining characteristic of human societies: there are no institutions in animal societies' (1968: 523, note). Animal societies are based in the individual and the transitory. In contrast, institutions fix: they give duration. The performative repetition of rites also gives collective assembly fixity in institutions.[1] Magical prohibitions like religious prohibitions work through the separation of things and taboo. The difference is that magic separates things not because they are sacred and not because of social approbation, but because they are dangerous, because they are not spiritually but instead physically harmful. At stake for magic is not a sacred intensive object but a dangerous extensive object. Prohibitions are only observed because of this danger. In this sense we observe the law very often for transitory reasons. In magic, Durkheim notes there is a 'secular notion of property'. Observance of prohibitions has to do with questions of 'transitory utility'. At stake in these utilitarian maxims are not social facts but instead physical facts (1968: 430). Observing prohibitions between sacred and profane things would presume an intensive and not *laïque* notion of property. At stake would be 'non-utilitarian maxims' that are social and metaphysical. Observance of prohibitions comes, not from physical fear or utilitarian calculations but from *respect* for the sacred object. Law is transitory and based on external rules. Respect is enduring and comes from the inside. Respect has to do with value. I respect something or someone because I value it or her. I value her/it because I have an investment of mental energy in it that is not a question of utility or what it/he/she will fetch on the market place. Durkheim writes, 'a respected being … is always expressed in consciousness [*la conscience*] by a representation, which because of the emotion that it inspires is charged with a high degree of mental energy' (1968: 453).

Durkheim looks at accounts of the origins of religion in debate with Tylor (1873) and Spencer's (1896) 'animism'. 'Animism's focus is on spiritual beings – on genies, souls, demons, spirits, deities. These souls animate the body during life'. These start from ideas of the soul that occurred to individual men in dreams as man's more or less spiritual double. Focus was on the soul as separated from the body after death, which then is extended to the ancestors' souls. Durkheim's problem is with the individualism of these explanations, which begin from souls of men and then move to souls of things. Durkheim understands the origins of the souls of individual people to derive from the collective things that are totems. Against Tylor and Spencer's dualist assumptions of soul and body, in Durkheim's Australian tribes 'the soul is seared intimately in the body' (1968: 86). The empiricists treat these primitive cultures in terms of what Durkheim would have seen as 'natural facts'. Nothing could be further from Durkheimian 'social facts'. Social facts, unlike natural facts, come from extraordinary, i.e. transcendental, experience. Durkheim, in search of collective origins, will focus not on souls but instead on *totems*. Thus not ancestor worship but totemism is the 'elementary religion'. Here the focus is the clan (1968: 86).

Durkheim cites with approval the British anthropologist Robertson Smith, whose *Religion of the Semites* (2002) was so central to Freud's *Totem and Taboo* (2001). Robertson Smith spoke not of the dualism of soul and body, but of the 'consubstantiality of man and animal' (plant) (1968: 87). The Australian tribes featured such totemism in comparison with the ancestor worship of the more advanced Native American tribes. The Native Americans had a complex system of differentiated and hierarchically ordered classes. For the Australians, social organization is segmental, with the same segments, even the same names, repeating themselves. The Native Americans had social stability; Australian institutions were changeable, protean. There was no centralization among Australian tribes, for the Native Americans there were confederations under central authority (1968: 93).

The soul: from rite and totem to myth and ancestor

In the soul and gods, the sacred leaves the space of collectivity and immanence to become individual and transcendental. Durkheim will see society as emerging out of a logic of intensity as opposed to the extensity arguments of the empiricists. So the soul and gods, which bear individual representations, meaning not just the representations of individuals but the representations *as* individuals, need to be secondary and derivative. And the totemic system as collective representations – again as representations both of a collectivity and as a collectivity – are primary. We originally encounter the soul in myths of the founding ancestors. For Durkheim, myths which feature individual ancestors are derivative of rites that feature the totem. For him, the practice of collective assembly comes before belief in myths. In such collective assembly, the primordial symbol is the totem: myths are in this context an evolutionary step in the development of symbols. Because they are only created in myths, the founding ancestors are referred to as the 'uncreated ones' (*l'incrée*) (1968: 353). The religious idea of the soul presumes that 'men think there are two beings in him' (1995: 249). The soul is indeed individual: each individual has a soul. For Durkheim, the soul has nothing to do with the immortality of the individual. It has to do not with the individual but with the collective eternal. It has not to do with an individual's afterlife, but with the reproduction of the collective. It has not to do with death, but with birth and indeed with rebirth. This can be reincarnation and transmigration also in a very biological sense. It is literally often a question of pregnancy. Reincarnation of souls often takes place through the mythic ancestral soul entering a clan woman. The ancestors themselves are joint human-animals. The kangaroo clan mythic ancestor is at once kangaroo and man. This joint character of the soul, Durkheim insists, is under the primacy of the animal (1968: 354–5) and the human ancestors are secondary. For Durkheim, 'the soul is the totemic principle incarnated in each individual' (1968: 357). This soul is more bodily than spiritual. The soul passes the spiritual substance of the clan – as collective memory – from generation to generation. The soul is the totemic principle of the clan 'subdivided among individuals'. Just as the individual souls are the fragments of the totemic principle, so are 'the ancestors the totem divided into parts' (1995: 258). Cultic instruments unite the ancestor, the actual individual and the totemic animal. For Durkheim, it is less that the man has his soul, and more that the soul (which incarnates the collective) has its man. Thus he writes that 'this double (of man) can only be the soul, because the soul is already by itself a double of the subject that it animates' (1968: 371).

The soul is much more incarnate in totemism than in Western religion. It needs, says Durkheim, an 'organ' (*organe*) to incarnate the totemic principle. This organ is often the blood, commonly the soul's residence in totemic ceremonies (1968: 371). Christianity also incarnates spirit in the bodily – and bleeding – individual of the Christ. The totemic soul has its carnate side not in a being but in the flow of blood. If the soul as seen from the inside is 'divine substance'

(1995: 265), then the blood is 'the soul as seen from the outside' (1968: 374). When blood flows, life slips away and the soul escapes. The soul is made of 'much more fluid material than the body' (1968: 375). The blood, as spiritual substance, is society itself – as it moves us from the inside. For Durkheim, society moves us from the outside in norms and laws that are transitory. Society moves us, in contrast, from the inside, eternally through the soul, through what we would call values. Thus there is also the difference between laws and norms on the one hand, and ethics, the moral or the ethos on the other. The immanent soul of elementary religion – unlike the energy-less soul of Buddhism and Christianity – is a seat of vitality and energy. The soul is, for Durkheim, 'anonymous force': it is *'mana individualized'*. It is not just through negative prohibitions but positively as force that the soul guides our conduct. The soul is very much 'like a germinative plasma of a mystic order. That transmits itself from generation to generation and constitutes the spiritual unity of the clan across the winds of time [*à travers la durée*]' (1968: 385). This very secondary nature of the soul underscores the extent to which Durkheim's ontological account of the origins of culture is *not* a theory of difference. At centre for Durkheim is the collective group, the clan, and not the difference of every individual. Not for Durkheim the Judaeo-Christian proper name of Leibniz and Benjamin: for him, the (proper) name is the name of the clan. And this clan is also immanent and bodily. As bodily it appears as image: as spiritual as symbol. Bodily representations are made from 'impressions' that literally impress, which are 'images' that 'se dégagent' from all points of the 'organism': from all the senses. Standing against this are representations, 'ideas' and sentiments (not sensations) that 'come from society and express it' (1968: 388–9). The totem is the fusion of the bodily and the spiritual: its representations are at once *im*pressions from nature and *ex*pressions from culture.

There is no radical break in tribal religion between ancestral souls and gods/spirits. The gods/spirits are more transcendental and less bodily. The ancestor as tutelary genie is already on the way to being god or spirit. And at the heart of the notion genie or genius is 'he who engenders, a generative force'. This generative force is periodically re-enacted not just in myths but also in rites. The ancestor is literally a spiritual father 'as the group of mythic ancestors becomes attached to the society of the living through a moral bond [*lien moral*]' (1968: 397). The father, the generative father is thus central to the original social bond. This social bond is older even than the gift. To move, then, from soul to spirit or god is one step further in the individualization of religious evolution. The spirit will not be of the clan, but of the more universal level of the tribe or phratry. Also, the spirit takes on quasi-transcendental qualities, no longer attached to animal or plant, but raised to the stars and the heavens. Thus the god 'Amatu is born in the sky, named himself with the stars as his wives' (1995: 288); or the god Bunjil, the father of men who made a statue from clay and breathed life into it. The more individual and otherworldly the god is, the more it takes on creationist powers and actually creates the world. Only then does god also create man.

Intensive religion: the totem and ontology

The totem: clan and emblem

Unlike the ancestor cult's individualism, the totem is collective: it embodies communion and consubstantiality. The totem is the symbol of the *clan*. The individuals in the clan consider themselves to have a 'kinship bond' (*lien de parenté*). Yet this is not because they share the same blood but because they bear the same name (1968: 142). This is the name of the totemic species. The totemic species is a material thing – either animal or plant – with which the clan has certain relations of kinship (1995: 99–100). Let us reflect a moment on this bond (*lien*). Marcel Mauss (2001) spoke about the 'gift' as the original social bond. The gift is about exchanges between tribes. The intra-tribal totemic bond is more primordial than the gift bond. Before the gift, the totemic bond is the acknowledgement of reciprocal obligations: help, vengeance and exogamy. What cements these obligations, what guides this conduct is the bond with the totemic animal or plant. The bond is one of consubstantiality: of the sharing of substance. This sharing not of material substance like blood: it is the sharing of spiritual substance. The clan shares spiritual substance with the totemic animal and therefore with one another. This substance constitutes a *lien de parenté*. Durkheim's elementary forms of religious life are indeed what Claude Lévi-Strauss later would call the elementary structures of kinship. The totem is not an individual but a variety, a species (Durkheim 1995: 103) that brings together not the tribe, nor even the phratry, but the clan. 'Phratries' are classes within a tribe united by particular bonds of fraternity: they regulate interconnubium, which along with intercommensality entails shared substance. Phratries may have originated from dispersed clans. Australian tribes are very unstable, comprising often 50–60 clans in a tribe of a few hundred individuals. North American tribes, which

Durkheim frequently compares with the more elementary religion of the Australians, comprised fewer large and more stable clans.

This shared spiritual substance had less to do with a clan's individuals or designated animal than with the totem's 'emblem'. 'The totem' itself *is* 'an emblem'. The designated plant or animal is the 'crest', the 'sign', the 'badge' of the group. These signs sometimes mapped out sanctuaries where the sacred objects were kept. The sacred objects, such as the *churinga*, were liturgical or cultic instruments made of wood or stone engraved with a totemic sign and making a noise. Australian tribes featured inscriptions of totems on bodies: in masks and feathers in hair. These were often gashes or incisions, especially in initiation rites, for example, in the sub-incision of penises. For Native Americans and Scots, warrior coats of arms were important totemic signs. Religion is, for Durkheim, on the level of the tribe, not the clan. The clan has its cult: the more institutionalized religion is a 'system of cults'. Things were classified as sacred or profane with regard to the totemic mark (1968: 188; 1995: 121). The animal is sacred only in so far as it incorporates the social substance of the emblem. As a sign, the emblem is not metaphoric in that it does not *stand for* the animal – or even stand for the sacred in the animal. The sign is instead metonymic: it is a part, the sacred part, the sacred essence of the thing. In Chapter 4 with Walter Benjamin we saw how the language of paradise is emblematic and metonymic, while extensive language after the Fall is metaphoric. Here we see in Durkheim that before spiritual substance came to inhere in language, in God's words, it inhered in godless and totemic things. The order of things preceded the order of words.

Totemic man and animal are brought together in myths. Though myths are central to systems of beliefs, they are for Durkheim secondary, derivative. Myths do not commemorate past events: their object instead is 'to interpret existing rites' (1995: 185). Myths are about ancestors and ancestors are derivative of the totem. The man bears the name. Less of his ancestors than of the totemic animal. This name is not nominal, arbitrary or metaphoric of the man: the man instead *is* that name. This name is not a word, but an essential part of his being. Now myths, Durkheim insists, are conceived of by the phratries to account for this dual nature of what is at the same time animal and man. Again the animal is not metaphoric but partakes of the man's being. The myth gives this partaking intelligibility. What myths do is to 'diminish the *scandale logique*' of this (1968: 190). Myths gain in importance with evolution from elementary religion towards the universalism of more advanced forms of religious life. Indeed, myths reverse the hierarchy of thing and man in order to 'establish genealogical relations between man and the totemic animal which make the former the parent of the latter' (1968: 190).

Alimentary communion

Perhaps most important for Durkheim are relations of communing and especially of eating. Thus cults feature narratives of mythic ancestors eating the totemic animal, and, consequently, themselves becoming sacred (1995: 129). At the centre of all this are relations of 'communing'. In initiation ceremonies the initiate has his first access to the ritual instruments as he begins to 'commune' (*communie*) with the totemic substance (1968: 189). In eating, the human eats the spiritual nature of the animal, and thus becomes that sacred animal essence. Because the animal's profane role is to be food, sacredness is operative through eating prohibitions. In Christian communion, sacredness passes into worshippers (communicants). The bread and wine is body and blood and this reinforces the power of the sacred. For the Roman Catholic Church, the Eucharist is the most important of the sacraments. The bread and wine is consecrated in the Eucharist. The priest, partaking of the sacred, carries out this consecration. The wheaten bread and grape wine – that then become the body and blood of Christ – is the host. The communicant receives the host. In doing so he/she receives Christ. This is 'trans-substantiation' which entails the consubstantiality of Durkheim's totem. The Jew and some Protestants pray to God. They don't need a sacrifice. The Jewish ceremony is such a set of prayers. The Eucharist is not prayer at all, but a reception into one's own body – it is the commemoration or anamnesis of the Passion, Death and Resurrection of Jesus. It makes the event truly present. It is a participation in the sacrifice of Christ. Participation in the sacrifice of Christ is the fulfilment of God's plan for the salvation of humanity from sin. Christ is the Head of the Church. The priest and the victim of sacrifices (Jesus) are one and the same. The Mass is the sacrifice at Calvary made present in an unbloody manner.[2] The Eucharist, which comes from the Lord's Supper, brings the communicant into a special relation with Christ. At the Last Supper Jesus says to his disciples: 'this is my body; this is my blood'. So not just the sacred or the spiritual, but Christ himself is present in the wine and bread. The Eucharist is part of the 'divine economy' that makes present the crucifixion and the resurrection. In the words of the institution of the Eucharist spoken by

Jesus at the Last Supper, 'the communicant abides in me and I in him'. So for Durkheim it is the totemic cult and alimentary communion that is constitutive of the man–animal relation. The cult is the totality of religious practice and observance, whose neglect is impiety.

Sacrifice is a rite, which institutionalizes communion. Durkheim opposes empiricist/utilitarian theories of sacrifice as tribute or homage, in terms of 'what the subjects owe their prince' (1968: 481). For Durkheim, 'it is not just an offering to a god but instead the use of the sacrificial animal to remake man's own substance' (1968: 391). He endorses Hubert and Mauss, for whom sacrificial rites as an institution can have functions of communion, expiation, oaths or contract. Durkheim follows Robertson Smith, for whom sacrifice is not primarily an act of renunciation (cf. expiation) but of such alimentary communion. Sacrifice is above all a *meal*. And 'ce sont les aliments qui en sont la matière'. It is a meal first and foremost of the faithful and only secondarily an offering to a god. Even the biblical Old Testament sacrifice was a meal prepared before Yahweh. In Robertson Smith (2002), as Freud drew on him in *Totem and Taboo* (2001), the Semitic tribe's eating of the camel was their ritual meal. At stake is *ritual* eating. Ritual consumption of the totemic animal or plant by the head or elders of a clan will confer 'virtues' on the celebrant or communicant from the totemic plant or animal (Durkheim 1968: 480). What is being eaten in the ritual meal is the sacred: the sacrificed animal is immolated into 'une chose sainte', after which 'la sanctité se communiqué' to the 'fidèle' who eats it. Thus the meal taken in common 'creates a bond of "artificial kinship" among participants'. Kin are beings 'naturellement fait du même chair et même sang', and the food 'sans cesse' remakes 'la substance de l'organisme' (1968: 481). Thus shared food creates the same effects as shared origin. Sacrifice is for Durkheim, and for our purposes, one of many practices (rites) of alimentary communion. And communion itself is at the basis of the cultic institution. With evolution to what Weber called the 'world religions' (religions of India, China the Middle East), sacrifice does primarily become an offering to the now transcendental God or the gods: 'when the gods were separated from the things with which they were originally merged' (1995: 345). When sacrifice becomes more a gift to the gods, more an act of renunciation, the worshipper is connecting as much with the gods as with his fellows. Here *la fidèle* relinquishes a part of his own substance, his goods and/or his blood in offerings to his god. Durkheim stresses the *fidèle* is giving his god not so much his blood or his food as 'his thought', his mental substance. Thus the 'do et des', I give in order that you might give. The cult meets in rites specifically to regenerate 'its moral being' (1995: 352).

These ideas of communicant, alimentary communion, consubstantiality and substance-sharing is, at the same time, a question of *communication*. The point is that communication is not just extensive, but also intensive. Marshal McLuhan (2001) was of course well aware of this. But the cybernetics literature's exclusively physical – featuring sender, channel and receiver – notion of communication is still prevalent today (Hörl 2005). In Chapter 4 we studied Benjamin's idea of intensive communication. In Durkheim's elementary religion, thus negative rites (and ascetic rites) are 'to prevent all communication between' the sacred and the profane. This will prevent contamination or pollution of the sacred by the profane. Thus only the already initiated can touch ritual instruments. And prior to initiation there are rituals of washing, and anointing and fasting to avoid contamination of the sacred by the profane. The neophyte is to talk not at all or even to look tribal elders in the eye. Even 'le souffle expiré etablit la communication' (1968: 435). In sacred places we talk in a low voice, we observe silence. We avoid the noisiness, the chatter (Heidegger's *Geschwätz*) of the profane. Thus Jews cannot utter the name of the Lord without profaning him. And initiates are given a secret proper name which becomes the sacred element of the person who bears it, 'associés dans les esprits a l'idée de cette personne'. This name is unknown to women and children and cannot be uttered (1968: 436). 'Work', in contrast, 'is the pre-eminent form of profane activity' (1968: 439). If utilitarian eating is based on physical needs, fasting raises alimenation to the sphere of the sacred. In initiation rites the youth must separate himself from women and children, go into the bush and have a temporarily monk-like existence (1968: 449). The initiation rites, Durkheim notes, 'communicate' to the novice the 'virtues (*vertus*)' that 'bring him into the world of sacred things'. It is 'the sanctifying virtues of a sacred object' (1968: 460), its spiritual substance, that are being communicated to the novitiate. These virtues are at the same time powers – sub-incision and circumcision give special powers (*pouvoirs*) to the genital organs (1968: 434). Such virtues are not physical but metaphysical. Negative cult treats matters of 'consecration' and 'profanation'. This is a question of the contagiousness of 'religious force' (1968: 459), not just in regard to the profane but inside the sacred itself. Thus, in perception, in the profane we tend to think in terms of clear and distinct images. In the sacred, in 'la pensée religieuse', there is instead between images 'contagion', a contagion 'of similitudes, of touch and nearness'. These are 'the fusions and confusions of *la pensée religieuse*'. It is 'religious force' – which 'radiates and diffuses' – that is contagious. These are 'emotions' that spread 'like an oil slick' to other mental states. Thus rocks and bodies may begin as clear and distinct images but when infused by the sacred they become confused and indistinct symbols. This force of contagion is a precursor of modern scientific cause (1995: 329). For Durkheim, 'the contagiousness of the sacred is affirmed a priori and not on the basis of improperly interpreted experience' (1995: 326). Religious thought more generally is based always on first principles. It is never a question of empirical generalizations from a series of sense impressions. It is necessarily more a priori than secular thought.

Totemic vitalism: Durkheim and Freud

The totem thus comprises 'an anonymous and impersonal *force*' (1995: 191): a force that animates and generates. This 'essence', shared by animal, man and totemic emblem, is an 'intangible substance' (*substance immaterielle*) that is represented 'in the imagination as a tangible form' (1968: 270). This 'is alone the veritable object of the cult'. The metaphysical and vital force is immanent to totemic substance: it is its 'life principle' and 'essence'. These are moral and, secondly, physical forces. In moral life, the forces that reside in totemic beings constitute a sort of power that binds obligations of assistance and vengeance, that binds kinship relations. It is the force, the power of God the Father as legislator and judge of human conduct (1995: 192–3). The force has not just moral but 'cosmic functions' that are at the origins of physical effects like sickness and death but especially play the role of life principle to ensure the reproduction of the totemic species (1968: 272). This 'impersonal religious force' is called *mana* in Melanesia, and in North America *wakan* and *orenda*. For the Sioux, 'all life is *wakan* – the principle of all that lives, acts, moves'. *Wakan* is not god as a supreme being 'with attributes or characters': it has undefined power (1968: 275), which itself is the source of 'diverse divine power [*puissance*]'. This is metaphysical force that reveals itself in the totem.[3] For the Boruh American Indians, if a totem has powers (*pouvoirs*) it is because it incarnates *wakan*. (1968: 279). There could not be such a general notion of energy in Australia because of the very primacy of the clan and totem. The primacy not of the clan, but the more universal tribe in North America and Melanesia allows a notion of force above the particular totem to emerge (1995: 198–9). *Mana* is a spiritual thing not yet soul or spirit: 'it is protean, has extreme plasticity [*protéomorphe*]' (1968: 288).

We see such immaterial energy in Freudian libido – which is immaterial in contrast to the physical and utilitarian characteristics of drive (Stiegler 2004a). Both Freud – in *Totem and Taboo* (2001) – and Durkheim were influenced by William Robertson Smith. The totem and alimentary communion was the basis of the latter's thesis in *Religion of the Semites* (2002), in which the Semitic clan fell upon the sacred camel in an orgiastic rite of consumption and ate it, bones and all. Thus also did the band of brothers consume Freud's primal father who dared to have *all* the women. *Totem and Taboo* is Freud's narrative of the transition from nature to culture. Here the totemic meal is nature and taboo, i.e. the principle of exogamy, the origins of culture – and indeed of Freud's symbolic.

For Durkheim and Robertson Smith, however, this alimentary communion already was culture. In Freud, we enter into culture with the family, in Durkheim and Robertson Smith through the tribe and collective representations. For Durkheim we enter into the symbolic as soon as we have symbols. For Freud it is only with taboo, law and family that there is a symbolic. Man collectively needs to symbolize to survive, to keep his place in the food chain. Like animals, man's sense impressions tell him what to flee from and what to pursue. It is his collectively developed ideas that let him dominate nature. Man's long period of attachment to and dependence on the mother conditions his non-utilitarian imaginary and symbolic. Here the individual human baby's 'lack' or disconnection to the mother corresponds to a similar lack in collective man. Arnold Gehlen (1997) and Peter Berger (1990) have compared animals' full plenitude of instincts to man's instinctual poverty (*Instinktarmut*), to a chronic lack in his system of instincts. To cover up this gap, man learns to symbolize. Thus for both Freud and Durkheim, utilitarian animals – who have no lack – have no need to symbolize. And it is just where man is not utilitarian, the space of this lack, in which symbolizing emerges.

Both of Jacques Lacan's (1998) real and symbolic emerge in this instinctual void: the symbolic separating from the real as the child becomes separate from the mother. Sense impressions come to man and to animals from the beginning. They become less amorphous: become increasingly clear and distinct. Animal senses may be – and often need to be – sharper than humans. Human senses have less to do with the sharpness of an outer nature of predators and prey. Man's individual *conscience* and *inconscient* are structured by this symbolic. Durkheim's man is further immersed in the symbolic order through initiation rites, before, analytically, he encounters nature. If the imaginary represents through sense impressions, and the symbolic reworks these through the mediation of culture, then the real is unmediated. Animals represent nature straightforwardly in sense impressions. Human *concepts*, however, for Durkheim, have already represented society before they represent nature: they come from 'the idea that society has of itself' (1995: 425). This is the *conscience collective*, which is the faculty of idealization ('faculté d'idéaliser') (1968: 604). Symbolic systems are effective on the level of Freud's individual unconscious. For both Durkheim and Freud, these systems work initially through 'primary process', in which they are charged with surplus quantities of energy. Freud's 'over-determination' (*Überbestimmung*) comes from such a surplus of 'mental' energy, often via symbol-condensation.[4] For Durkheim this process is 'a whole world' of 'sentiments, ideas, of images' that obey their own laws. They attract and repel (*repoussent*), fuse, segment, proliferate in a panoply of combinations not dictated by the underlying reality. This is a world 'without end, without utility of any kind, for the sole pleasure of self-affirmation' (1968: 605). From this symbolic unconscious thought, the ego is formed: its thought is not overdetermined, but thinks through what is necessary and sufficient determination. In its economy, symbols are no longer sites of surplus cathection but lose intensity of energy-investment to the point at which they become concepts. As concepts they work through processes of non-contradiction and logic in combination with clear and distinct sense impressions from the imaginary. Freud's imaginary and symbolic are operative in both conscious and unconscious mind: the one clear and distinct, the other, as it were, dazed and confused. At the basis of the utilitarian ego is the anti-utilitarian unconscious.

For Durkheim there is a 'low intensity of investment of (moral or cultural) energy in physical facts', in their 'representation' as in the 'everyday economic activity of the family [*oikos*]' (1968: 217). In Freud, the minimal investment of psychic energy in the ego's utilitarian life stands in contrast to the id – and indeed the superego's (*Über-Ich*) high levels of energy-investment in their objects. The clearness and distinctness of the representations we make with our egos – a combination of intellect and perception – allow rational and utilitarian action and thought. Thus the mind's logical categories entail lower levels of energy investment in comparison to the tribal categories of primitive classifications. Similarly, a God who is a supreme being with attributes is less over-invested than the protean totem. Also, the protean nature of the superego parallels religious representations. The superego also comprises energy *surajouté*: it is not an energizer, is not a source of *puissance* like the id, but only a governing *pouvoir*.

Like the animist anthropologists, Freud theorized in the register of dreams. The animists saw 'sacred beings as constructed from sensations that physical and biological phenomena evoke in us through dreaming' (1995: 226). Durkheim says this sort of thinking can never give us anything that goes beyond the merely physical. The sensory thus yields only the sensory, extensity only extensity (1968: 321–2). But Freud's dreams stand as polar opposite to Frazer's and Tylor's. Freud's dreams are shot through with symbols and not just images. Freud's dreams are not just biological and physical: are not just brain but are also mind. Dreams start out as perception: the images of the dream material are literally *material*. But these are reworked and re-ordered symbolically by other symbols emerging from a complex Oedipal dynamics. The result is a process, the primary process, that though symbolic and not physical but mental are not in the register of the clear and distinct. Primary process works through condensation and overdetermination: thus through a surplus of determination; not indeterminately but through too much determination. This mental energy comes not from the collective, but the individual mind. It is as though the collective *mana* were divided and distributed among all individuals to constitute their protean id, the seat of energy of the psychic economy. Then mediated through the family, a part of this energy is distributed to the governing power of the superego. This id works like the ecstatic *corroborées* Durkheim describes, the orgiastic and sexual rites – dependent on 'ecstatic states like the states of the prophets, excitable' (1968: 325), 'what we call "delirium", any state where there is *l'esprit surajouté* to the immediate data of sensory intuition' (1968: 325). Such states 'project these sentiments onto things'. Collective representations thus are 'delirious'.

The id is over-invested with energy: it is overcharged. It and Freud's world of dreams is more a set of becomings than beings. 'In the beginning all the kingdoms – animal, vegetable and mineral – are confused among one another.' 'Rocks have a gender, the stars are men and women who suffer human sentiments, while humans are conceived as animals and plants. This state of indistinction is found at the basis of all mythologies' (1968: 337). Like in Freud's dreamworlds, here the social symbolic has reworked the imaginary's sense impressions. At the heart of this is the *symbol*, the system of half-material, half-ideal totemic symbols. Symbols are needed in order to fix ideas to 'material things' (1968: 326). These collective sentiments constitute what Durkheim understands as the ideal (1968: 326). But the ideal as collective sentiments is not yet the symbol. For there to be symbols, the ideal must be fixed to signs. These sentiments, unlike material sensations, are ideas. The sentiments and the symbols that fix them have a *sui generis* character. They are not reducible to the parts that make them up. No accumulation of parts of empirical sense impressions will add up to this sacred and *sui generis* whole. If you are a Lockean or Humean, the empirical thing is the cause of sense impressions. If you are a Kantian, the empirical thing is the sum of its properties or qualities. We cannot know it in itself. We can know it through our categories that are its predicates, its properties, its qualities, its attributes. But the categories are not symbols in that they are not laden with the surplus energy of the sacred, libidual investment of Durkheim: 'The sacred character of the thing is not comprised in its intrinsic properties. It is in the surplus [*surajouté*] of these. The world of the religious is not a particular aspect of empirical nature: it is superposed [*superposé*]' (1968: 328). The symbol not only reworks the images from the imaginary: it is a supplement to the categories of the understanding. This superposed entity is not a part of the empirical thing, but a new and ideal thing. Thus the totemic animal is unlike the empirical thing in which the (categorial) parts add up to the whole. In 'religion the part *equals* [*vaut*] the whole. It has the same powers. Subdivide a soul and it is again the whole soul' (1968: 328). This ideal essence of the social thing is a new thing: a thing that represents the social. The symbols, though they make signs possible, are not mere signs. 'Individual consciousnesses by themselves are closed to one another'; and can 'only communicate via means of signs, which translate interior individual states. For this communication to end in communion, i.e. a fusion of all the particular sentiments in a common sentiment, these signs must fuse in a unique and singular resultant' (1968: 329). This resultant is the system of symbols: the social symbolic. 'Without symbols social sentiments can only have a precarious existence' (1968: 330). For there to be duration of this emergent social, there need to be symbols and there needs to be *cult*. Cult gives institutional form to collective assembly. Cult is the institutionalization of collective assembly. Cult presumes the regularity of rites. The rites must be performed indeed regularly for there to be society (Alexander 1990: 11).

Extensive religion: *sociological* categories

Durkheim, like William James, addressed religious *experience*.[5] Unlike empirical experience, religious experience is a priori and transcendental. It presumes transcendental ideas working not on empirical, but on transcendental, objects. Religious experience is experience of the sacred. Here 'religious sensations' (which are also symbolic) are '*sui generis*' (Durkheim 1968: 597). Religious experience is about 'sanctification and contamination': its sacred is 'intense and contagious'. For Durkheim, the individual is naturally utilitarian in regard to individual impulses. In contrast, religious life 'always lifts man above this' 'and makes him live a higher life'. Religious life comprises beliefs and rites. 'Beliefs express the sacred through representations, and rites organise and regulate its functioning'. The source of all this is different from merely sensory animal experience. 'The animal knows only one world: that which it *per*ceives through external and internal experience'. Only man knows two worlds: 'only man has the faculty to *con*ceive the ideal and add it to the real'. The ideal world is born in the intensity of the collective 'state of effervescence' – which comes from the very 'concentration' of collective assembly (1968: 603). This, Durkheim observes, alters man's 'psychic activity' so that he 'no longer recognizes his empirical self' (1968: 603). When consciousnesses are alone they perceive. The collective consciousness *con*ceives. It is a '*sui generis* synthesis of particular consciousness' (1968: 605). It is *sui generis* in the way that a chemical compound is *sui generis* in comparison to its parts or elements. Thus the conscience collective is fully different in character from the individual consciousnesses. This sacred symbolic, though in the register of what we saw above is the dazed and confused, is the source of the clear and distinct: whether in science, logic or law. 'The only form of activity', Durkheim notes, 'not attached to religion is economic activity'. 'Yet', he writes, 'economic value is a sort of power of efficacy'. 'Wealth [*richesse*] can confer a sort of *mana*'. Wealth comprises *mana*. Thus there is a 'rapport of "economic value" and religious value'. Now we understand the traditional place of the *oikos* in the Greek *polis* – that of the profane or 'nature' of the family and economic activity, dedicated to natural needs like eating and shelter. But Durkheim begins to turn this round, as does Marcel Mauss in *The Gift* (2001), in which the cultural value of the gift precedes and is the basis of the economic value of the commodity. That is, the profane of commodity exchange develops out of the sacred logic of gift exchange.

Religion's collective assembly entails symbols and institution-alized regularity, which give duration to the conscience collec-tive. The rites constitute this world: the representations express this world in a cosmology. Rites through their repetition and symbols through their fixity give duration to this cosmology. Durkheim speaks of *'pensée religieuse'* and the *'faculté d'idéaliser'* and mind (*ésprit*) but the governing notion here is *conscience*. Why? Because of all of the above only consciousness, as Durkheim's contemporary Edmund Husserl (1993) uncovered, must be *of something*. Of all of the above it is consciousness that has an object. This object is material (the animal) and also mate-rial in its being painted or written. But mostly this object is ideal and symbolic. Science does the same: it fixes the flux in concepts that last a very long time. Science thus reworks religious cosmol-ogy on 'a critical basis' (1995: 431). Science may be less about empirical experience than reworking religious notions critically. Of course, evidence and sense impressions are a basis for this. Thus religion, science and even 'vulgar knowledge' 'express' an 'aspect of the real'. The aspect they express depends on their 'method' (1968: 612). For science, this is first the 'ésprit critique'; second, it leaves out the passions; and third, it avoids haste and subjective influences (1995: 431). But science is very incomplete and frag-mentary. Religion cannot be so because its theories are at the ori-gins of ethics. They tell man how to live and conduct himself and thus 'cannot wait': they need completion and thus must speculate where science will not. The perhaps most major difference is that science and religion concern themselves with very different sys-tems of facts. For Durkheim these facts are 'life'. Whereas science expresses life, religion creates life. Science expresses first natural and then social facts. Religion creates social facts. If society became conscious of itself in religion, in elementary religious life, then logical life became conscious of itself with Plato and the Greeks. This, notes Durkheim, brought a sense of 'émerveillement' (wonder). Yet this clarity of philosophy grew from 'obscurity': from an 'état de sentiment obscur'. In such *sentiments obscurs* we have the rev-elation of the impersonality of religious thought. It is in the eluci-dation of such collective representations that philosophy – which never created these sentiments – was the source of Plato's 'pro-priétés merveilleuses' (1968: 623–4). This reveals also the very opposition of positivism and empiricism. Positivism grew from rationalist metaphysics and originally religion – as August Comte understood only too clearly (Levy-Bruhl 2009). Empiricism has little truck with ideas at all. When science grows from metaphysics we have rationalism with facts. We have (Kant's) 'synthetic a priori judgements'.

Durkheim first distinguishes concepts from percepts. Concepts are much more (*sui generis*) than generalized percepts. They are much more than the individual comparing his perceptions or images, finding what they have in common and generalizing (1968: 617). They are a different mode of representation from this. Concepts, he argues, don't need to be general. They can have individual objects like, for example, the individual totem. Yet these representations with individual objects are 'conçus, pas perçus' (1968: 618). Concepts are not – like sensations, images, percepts – '*representations sensibles*' (1968: 618). 'Sense representations' are in 'perpetual flux': they 'don't stay semblable to themselves', they are effective only for an instant; and even if the reality stays the same the 'empirical body' that senses them has changed. To 'conceptualise is thus not to generalise: it is to subsume the variable under the permanent, the individual under the social' (1995: 440). 'Concepts', in contrast to percepts, are 'outside of time and of *devenir* (becoming)'. Concepts are, as it were, 'subtracted [*soustraire*] from this agitation' and situated in a different region of the mind: they are 'more calm and serene'. They resist change and are not 'self-changing' like sense-impressions. Concepts – like the religious symbols we have discussed at length – are a 'crystallized' and 'fixed' 'mode of thinking'. Language – as a system of symbols – is 'also fixed'. Here 'every word must translate' (not a thing, nor a sense impression) but 'a concept'. Language as a whole 'expresses a conceptual organization'. Science, like language, is very slow to change. Such change does 'violence' to 'existing ways of thinking'. Concepts are impersonal while sense impressions are personal. Sense impressions therefore cannot be communicated, as can concepts. It is 'impossible to faire passer une sensation de ma conscience dans la conscience de l'autrui' because the sensation is personal: it connects 'directly to my body and my personality'. This stands in contrast to 'the conversation. The intellectual connections between men consist in the exchange of concepts. Concepts are *im*personal representations'. Through concepts, 'les intelligences humaines communient' (1968: 619). Thus the universality of a concept is not the coverage of an ever-widening scope of things and events by generalized sense impressions. It is instead 'its property of being (in principle) communicated to a plurality of minds, in principle to all minds. This is independent of its degree of extension' (1968: 619, footnote). In this sense we can speak of intensive versus extensive universality. For empiricism, he continues, sense impressions are ideas: particular sense impressions are specific ideas. Concepts are general ideas. For empiricism to think via concepts is merely to see the real by its most general aspect (*coté*). For Durkheim, to think via concepts is instead 'to project on to the sensation a light that illuminates (*éclaire*) it, penetrates it and transforms it' (1968: 622). To think conceptually, and Durkheim quotes Spinoza, is to think 'sub specie aeternitatis'. It is to think under the aspect of eternity. This and not sense impressions are at the basis of what 'truth' is. '[L]ogical life presupposes that man knows, however confused, that there is a truth, distinct from sense appearances.'

Categories

As for *categories*, they are the concepts most strongly linked to collective representations. They are the most stable, the most impersonal: the most immutable, eternal and absolutely universal of concepts. They are the 'permanent framework [*cadre*] of mental life'. Categories are not about the coverage of all the things; nor of all the sense impressions. 'They express the fundamental conditions of the *entente* [understanding] between minds.' Categories' provenance and their content – i.e. the things they express – are social. For Durkheim, beliefs in a religion always include a cosmology, that is, a 'conception of the universe': a system of ideas that tends to embrace 'the universality of things and give us representations of the world'. This cosmology, says Durkheim, is the tribe writ large, in which the things that make up the universe are the parts of the tribe (1968: 242). 'The universe is a large tribe, to one of whose divisions' the individual belongs. All 'things that are classified in the same group as he – both animate and inanimate – are parts of the body of which he himself is a part'. In his discussion of cosmology, Durkheim is working towards a notion of genre or genus: one that has obsessed him since Marcel Mauss and he wrote *Primitive Classification* (2009). These facts, he writes, throw light on the origins of genus and class (1968: 206). Cosmology here is based in the framework of the society. The phratries are the genera and the clans species. Here all 'men did was to make room for things in the groups they had already formed'. And because 'men were grouped, they could group things' (1968: 145). The groups themselves then are unified in the 'organic whole of the tribe'. Thus more generally 'the fundamental notions of the mind – the essential categories of thought – are a product of this social framework. The categories, for Durkheim, express the principal aspects of the social. In this there are four main categories: genus, time, space and cause, whose unity of the four categories is found under genus. Genus will be Durkheim's equivalent of Kant's transcendental unity of apperception. Genus or genre was once the same thing as the social group itself. Time is at the basis of the 'rhythms of social life' and especially ritual. Space is the 'space occupied by society – it is gridded so that household units could occupy bits of it and everyone would know this and why'. And the 'prototype' of causality is 'collective force', as introduced above.

Genus is the queen of the categories as it is the social totality itself. For the empiricist, similar representations come together within individuals, which lead to a new representation formed by their coming together that seems to have a 'generic character'. But nothing here, Durkheim insists, 'can give me the *idea* of "class", i.e. a "framework capable of grasping the total group of all the objects that satisfy the same condition"'. No experience can be so *étendue* and *prolongé* so as to 'give the idea of a total genre' (1968: 629). The 'genre total' contains all the 'particular extended things' and 'coordinates them in regard to impersonal criteria'. The animal, and by extension the empiricist, gives us 'sense that guides dogs back home at the right time and are enough to satisfy man's individual (and utilitarian) needs'. We share with the animal the natural, individual need: the need to 'differentiate between things we must seek after and things we must flee. We have no need to join the effects of things to their causes with a logical link if individual conscience alone is at stake'. The logical categories instead come from social and very much non-utilitarian needs. These and their counterparts in the moral imperative are needed to raise us above our own individual point of view. At the bottom of all of this is society. 'Society disposes of a creative power [*puissance*] that no observable being can equal'. This *puissance* collective is 'not a nominal being or an objective mode of reason, but a system of active forces' (1968: 638). For Durkheim, 'the sentiment of resemblances is other than the notion of genus (genre). The genre is the exterior cadre of which objects perceived as similar form in part the content'. 'The content cannot provide the framework in which it is placed.' The content – supported by the empiricists – is made up of 'images, vague, floating' and the 'partial fusion of a determinate number of individual images that have common elements'. The cadre or frame, in contrast, is 'a definite form with fixed contours' to be applied to 'a determinate number of things, perceived or not, actual or possible'. 'Tout genre' is a 'field of extension' that 'infinitely exceeds' the 'circle of objects', which 'we have witnessed by direct experience to resemble one another'. Thus genre is very much the opposite of 'generic image', which is only a 'vague compilation' of 'similar representations' (1968: 209). A whole accumulation of vague and confused particulars do not add up to a clear and distinct frame. The 'genre is a logical symbol' which enables us to 'distinctly think' similarities. 'Animals are capable of generic images but only man can think in terms of genus and species. Yet genre, *pace* Kant, is not given to us a priori. It comes from a "spectacle de la vie collective".' A genre is an ideal grouping, though clearly defined, 'a grouping of things amongst which there exist an internal bond [*lien*] analogous to the bonds of kinship' (1968: 209). So genus presumes not so much material things, but rather ideal groupings. The former can form collections 'without internal unity'. 'We would never have brought together the being of the universe into genera – if we had not before our eyes the society of men where at first human groups and logical groupings were not distinguished.' What is classified together in totemism is 'not merely (*pace* empiricism) conventional; it is "real" and works from "liens internes"' (1968: 211). These are bonds of 'mystical sympathy'.

Cause

Durkheim particularly obsesses with 'cause'. Cause needs to be more than the Humean association of two phenomena and their sense impressions in time: it needs to be more than just the habit of this and its repetition. For there to be cause, it is generally accepted, there needs to be *explanation* of why the two phenomena appear regularly together in succession (Keat and Urry 1975). But for Durkheim much more is at stake than explanation. His cause is much stronger and more profound. He does start from the fact that 'sense perception alone can never give us explanation'. Sense perception is indeed 'resistant [*refractaire*] to all explanations [*explication*]' (1968: 339). My sense perception may well 'notice that A regularly follows B', but my '*intelligence*' (italics added) is not satisfied. 'Intelligence is not satisfied with (sense perception's) observation that does not carry within it its *reason*' (1968: 340). Only mind, and not 'sensation which sees nothing but the exterior surface' can give us this. By 'reason', Durkheim means not just *a* reason but indeed reason itself. And the origins of reason, like logic's and science's notion of cause, are not physical and empirical; they are instead *metaphysical*. To think cause we need to think how A and B 'vibrate sympathetically through a law internal to their nature'. This law internal to their nature can only be at its origin some sort of C encompassing things A and B in terms of their 'shared essence'. The progenitor of such shared essence is the primordial shared essence of clan, animal and emblem (1968: 338). This essence is vital; it is the *'grande effervescence mentale'* – and again we need to stress, not material or physical, but mental – that becomes causal force. These first forces are necessarily religious forces. To sense habitually and to expect that B regularly follows A is not to understand the connection of A and B. In this sense we see also that the Kantian understanding is much more than sense impression. It is first to understand that A and B stand in some sort of *relation*. This relation is, for Durkheim, a 'kinship relation' (1968: 340). You can reason a posteriori until the end of time and you will never get to this. Durkheim's *sui generis* is the a priori: it is necessarily, as any a priori must be, transcendental. The a priori, the *sui generis*, is the undetermined and transcendental. It is intensive. Sense impressions will never accumulate to the point of constituting the idea. Thus in regard to the origins of thought 'the essential thing is not to let our minds be subjugated to sensory appearances but, on the contrary, to grasp and dominate these sense impressions and for the mind to bring together what the senses hold apart'. And it is 'at the moment of this sentiment that internal connections exist between things that science and philosophy become possible'. Here the world of sensed realities is transformed by this second 'ideal world'. Thus the individual thought of sense perception is transformed by 'collective thought' ... from a *'surexcitation des forces intellectuelles'*. When we explain in science we find something that is internal to two other things. Thus to 'explain is to show how one thing participates in one or several others' (1968: 341).

Durkheim uses an examination of mimetic rites to further open up this notion of causality. He notes that scientific causality emerges from the ideas of power (*pouvoir*) and contagion in elementary religion (1968: 518). This causality again is not about the succession of events but about the causal logic of wholes and parts. Our notion of scientific causality presumes, first, the efficacy of power or force: this is present already in everyday notions of causality. Everyday notions of causality comprise a dimension of efficacy, presume a 'pouvoir productif' of an 'active force'. Everyday notions presume a 'causal relation', and not just the two closed individuals of Newtonian or Humean causality. Further, a cause can 'produce a determinate change' (1968: 519). Apart from power, causality presumes first cause and second effect. Here the cause embodies *potentia*: it is 'a force before it is manifest'. The effect, on the other hand, is the 'same power, but actualized'. Cause is dynamic. Its origins in totemism as force are *'mana* or *wakan'*, that is the 'totemic principle'. Force as *mana* is 'objectified collective force, collectively projected in things' (1968: 519, footnote). Cause thus is collective energy that is objectified and then projected into symbolic things.

Therefore, at the bottom of cause is necessarily the thing – the totemic thing. Durkheim stresses once more that none of this can 'be furnished by external experience'. Our 'senses only see phenomena that co-exist or follow one another', but nothing 'they perceive can give us the *idea* (italics added) of this constraining or determinant action' (1968: 519–20) that we call a 'pouvoir' or force. The senses can 'only grasp realized states, exterior to one another' but 'miss the internal processes on which these states rely'. The origins of cause are thus not extensive but *intensive*. Nothing in the 'senses' can suggest the 'idea' of 'that which is an influence or an efficacy'. Cause is thus something that is to do with reasons and reason. When empiricist philosophy sees causality as a 'mythological aberration', they are indeed, observes Durkheim, 'close to the truth'. Durkheim continues: 'if external experience cannot generate these ideas then they must come from internal experience'. The notion of force thus 'is pregnant with spiritual elements' which can only come – not from external life – but from 'psychic life'.

Empiricist anthropology argued that the origins of epistemological cause were in individual moral behaviour: in individual experience and the individual will's powers of self-control. Thus the animists understood the self in terms of a soul in charge of a body, in which the soul 'sets itself off in distinction from its physical double' (1968: 523). For Durkheim, the origins of cause are in collective, moral activity. He speaks of the 'axiom' of cause, because it is an axiom, not to be doubted. It is a first principle of thought: without cause, rational thought is impossible. Durkheim says that the 'thought axiom comes from the obligation': that is 'the imperatives of thought are really nothing other than the other side of the imperatives of the will' (1968: 527). This is the link between what Max Weber called 'substantive' – which always comes first – and 'formal' (or 'instrumental') rationalization. Durkheim notes in the very last lines of the conclusion of *Formes* that there is 'not an antinomy' between science and religion/morality. He notes that Kant understood this and 'saw speculative and practical reason as two aspects of the same faculty' (*Verstand* and *Vernunft*) and that 'both were oriented to the universal'.

To 'think rationally is (thus) to think following laws that impose their universality on rational beings: to act morally is to conduct oneself following maxims, which could, without contradiction, be extended to the universality of wills'. The difference is that the animists saw this moral-cognitive conjunction as individualist, whereas Durkheim saw it as collective. In both cases of rationality, we need, he says, to 'raise ourselves above our own individual point of view' (1968: 635). Michel Foucault in, for example, his *Order of Things* (1966) and books on sexuality (1998a, 1998b), is with Durkheim on this. Foucault's focus is on the double relation of individual soul and body born in the Christian confessional. This for him is paradigmatic of two thousand subsequent years of Western discursive practice embracing the logical discourses of the natural sciences to the Freudian discourse of sexuality. Foucault himself saw a connection here to the work of Max Weber.[6] In Foucault's last published volumes on sexuality, he effectively counterposed to para-Christian otherworldly ethics and epistemology a much more this-worldly, immanent and less individualist notion of conduct in a society of divine plurality.

'[T]he notion of force', writes Durkheim, 'is of religious origin. It is from religion that philosophy and subsequently science have borrowed (the idea of force)' (1968: 292). Durkheim, like sociology's great positivist ancestor Auguste Comte, conceived of a progression of thought from religion to metaphysics and then to science. His idea of force is integral to such a progression. For Durkheim, the origins of causality are at once irreducibly collective and linked to communication (see Hörl 2005). Force in totemism was conceived as 'communicable'. The individualist assumptions – indeed the methodological individualist assumptions – of empiricism cannot deal with this because 'the "I" is incommunicable'. It cannot spread or transfer: it 'cannot suggest an energy that is communicable'. Understanding cause in terms of communication and the inverse is very central to the much more consistently vitalist theories of Durkheim's rival and progenitor Gabriel Tarde (1999) as well as more contemporary non-linear theorists of the natural sciences such as Ilya Prigogine (Prigogine and Stengers 1984). For Durkheim, the logical idea of force not only stems from the power of the collective, but from collective relations of social subordination and domination, that is social 'pouvoir'. Previous to the mind's conception of logical force, power was experienced as 'organized by societies'. It is in this social image that the 'puissances' of the physical world were conceived (1968: 522–3). Causality presupposes not just a 'principle of force', but also a 'principle of judgement', whose object is the development of the force – the state of the force at each moment predetermining the next. Such force, such causal force, is culturally constituted perhaps first as a potential but then also as a 'constraint'. It is a constraint that 'the mind' sets up a priori, 'before any proof'. It is a 'rule': an 'imperative'. No notion of cause is possible without the totemic thing. Yet it is not the thing that is cause and effect; instead two states of the force (that the thing incorporates) that is the causal relation. Empiricism, Durkheim repeats, cannot deal with this a priori: for empiricism, cause is an a posteriori association of ideas reinforced by habit. It is a strong predisposition of ideas (which are abstract or generalized sense impressions) to call themselves to mind in a definite order. Yet causality's a priori is a 'norm', superior to the flow of sense representations that it rules and regulates. 'It binds the intellect and goes beyond the intellect'. Empiricist cause is based on an a posteriori judgement. In contrast, a priorism's idea of cause is 'pre-judicial and necessary' (1968: 526). Cause is the a priori 'framework' applied to the empirical 'content'. It is 'not without relation to the material it contains'. But it is not this content: it 'transcends and dominates' this content. At stake for Durkheim, is not a logical and epistemological a priori, but a *social and ontological* a priori.

The social fact: metaphysical things

No matter how modern religion is, Durkheim understands, there will always – unlike in science – be 'incomplete personification'. It is in 'the nature of religious force never to be a well-defined number of discrete beings'. There is always the possibility of recombination. It is only philosophy, as Hegel noted, that brings together the moral forces of ontology and the full clarity and distinction of logic and science. Only philosophy can bring together the two sides of reason: the cultural – that is religious, moral and aesthetic side – and the logical, scientific side. Durkheim pauses for a moment in his chapter on totemic force to reconsider his notion of the 'social fact'. The social fact, he notes, grows from the 'religious fact'. And the 'religious fact' first and foremost 'does not presuppose mystical personality'. 'Force', for Durkheim, is at the core of the social fact: at stake are forces like *mana*, especially the initial *mana* of the particular totems. In the context of totemic religion, Durkheim shows (1) that such facts are not personal but impersonal, (2) that they are forces, and (3) that these forces may act either from the inside or from the outside of the human group. The totem is clearly the elementary social fact: it is not a physical but instead a metaphysical fact. There are, on the one hand, the physical facts of nature and what are the metaphysical facts of religion and society. These metaphysical (social) facts are Durkheim's forces. Humans and animals, but especially the totem, are the material embodiments of this metaphysical force. The same metaphysical facts turn around and later are used to classify physical nature. In one of Durkheim's most famous formulations, he writes that social facts are external constraints, yet they are moral and not physical: these constraints are 'exterior signs' – they are signs of what are moral or immaterial forces. The sign (i.e. the emblem or totem) is more highly charged with these forces than is the clan-man or totemic animal. The social fact is thus both the sign and the force. The exterior sign is a 'material expression' of 'an interior and deep-lying (profound) fact' that is 'ideal' (1968: 298).

The social fact itself has a two-sided nature: first, as moral or ideal force and, second, as material expression. Thus Durkheim defines what is for him 'the sociological problem'. It is 'to search *à travers* the different forms of exterior constraint, the different sorts of moral authority that correspond to these and to discover the causes that determine the latter'. These facts are not only things 'that we yield to' ... but 'are forces that buttress our own (energies)' (1968: 211). This is *mana* or religious force not as *pouvoir* but as *puissance*, and it comes not from the constraints but the 'general effervescence' (1968: 217) of religious forces. Here they *surajouté* 'a sense of heightened energy in individual minds': they are a force that uplifts us as part of our individual beings. These forces 'are fixed in the techniques and traditions we utilize, [in] the language that we speak yet have not made', in 'instruments we haven't invented, in rights [we have inherited], in a treasure gleaned from previous generations' (1968: 302). Social facts are thus things: things that incorporate energy. Social facts are on the one side extensive, on the other side intensive. Physical facts are solely *choses sensibles*. They are the 'objective causes of our sensations'. We represent them in images of perception. Social facts are *'choses morales'* (moral things) (1968: 303). As *choses* they have a physical side – be it sign or norm. Yet a sign that *means* nothing to me remains a physical fact. Facts may 'remain perceptions that we experience only as empirical characteristics'. But we only feel 'respect' for 'them (physical facts) after the religious imagination has metamorphosed them'; only then can they 'lift us above ourselves' (1968: 304). They lift us above ourselves as if there were a sociological, libidinal economy in which energy that is constituted through collective assembly is then pumped, as it were, through the totemic man and animal, through the emblem and again back into the individual mind. We must not forget here the importance of symbols and the symbolic. At the risk of repetition: physical facts work only empirically, through perception, the image and the imaginary. Social facts work always via a transcendental, through thought and the symbolic. Social facts entail necessarily a symbolic reworking of what was previously only in the imaginary, only a question of perception.

Notes

1 I am indebted to discussions with Jeff Alexander on this topic. In this chapter most citations are my translations of the French Presses Universitaires de France edition of *Les formes élémentaires de la vie religieuse* (1968: 430). However, some citations are from the Free Press English language edition translated by Karen Fields (Durkheim 1995: 212). Fields' introduction to the book is first rate. Its translation is a free translation, as is best for the undergraduate reader. The Carol Cosman translation is even more inadequate to the advanced student. The more advanced student of Durkheim with insufficient French should refer to the original 1915 Allen & Unwin translation by Joseph W. Swain (Durkheim 1947). It is a quite literal translation, which preserves the philosophical basis of Durkheim's concepts. I am indebited to discussions with Andrew Benjamin on Aristotle and Plato, that persuaded me to write this chapter.
2 Thus Mel Gibson's *Passion of the Christ* (2004) makes the sacrifice present in a *bloody* manner.
3 The totem is indeed a transcendental–empirical double, as are Christ, man and information as we will see in the concluding chapter.
4 In *The Interpretation of Dreams* (1991: 284ff.), where Freud introduces the topographic model, overdetermination comes from a surplus of dream thoughts in relation to dream content. My reading here imports the later Freud's economic and energetic model into such overdetermination.
5 Durkheim cites James, *The Varieties of Religious Experience* (1983), often. See especially pp. 596ff.
6 From personal correspondence with the author in 1984.

8

Information Theology: Philip K. Dick's
Will to Knowledge

Angel Archer is the narrator of *The Transmigration of Timothy Archer*, Philip K. Dick's last novel. This is the final novel of the trilogy provoked by Dick's encounter with the religious. Angel was married to Jefferson Archer, the Damascus-like son of the novel's protagonist Timothy. Angel tells the story in 1980 and the book was published the year of Dick's death, 1982. *Valis*, the first and central book of the trilogy, was published in 1980. *Transmigration*, however, can serve as a frame for the information theory that *Valis* gives us. In *Valis*, God or the sacred is a Vast Active Living Intelligence System (VALIS).[1]

These Philip K. Dick novels are important for us in a number of senses. First, his 'information theology', based on this 'living intelligence system', is a continuation of our investigations into intensive capitalism. Chapter 5 understands economic value in terms of the shift from value-form to value-substance. This chapter does the same for information. Intensity is understood along the course of the book in terms of the transmutations of substance. Thus we understand the origins of culture as the origins of intensive culture in terms of Durkheim's elementary *substance* of religious life. At the core of Simmel's vitalist sociology and theory of value in Chapter 2 is his notion of life-substance.

In today's informational capitalism, substance enters the commodity itself. At the heart of both domination and invention in today's capitalism is information. And what Dick gives us in his late work is an information theology. Here God is divine substance: He is a living information system. Dick's protagonists are driven by a will to know God in his substance, to know God ontologically as a thing-in-itself. They are driven to know God through a literal transubstantiation – through the sharing of substance with God. God as living information system literally enters, surges up into and constitutes the subject in Dick's protagonists. It does so through alimentary communion with God's real for Timothy Archer. In Valis it is through a divine invasion of the subject through laser beams from a distant galaxy.

Transmigration

Timothy Archer is Episcopalian Bishop of the California Archdiocese. He marched with Martin Luther King and is a hero to America's liberal left. The Episcopalian Church is Catholic, Tim Archer notes: the Pope a bishop among bishops, the Bishop of Rome. The book opens in a seminar on a houseboat in Sausalito in 1980, just after John Lennon's death. A sense of loss is in the air. We learn shortly that Jeff Archer as well as Timothy and Timothy's wife Kirsten are dead. Edgar Barefoot, a Bay Area alternative religion radio figure, runs the seminar. This seminar is on Arab mysticism and the Sufis. Sole survivor Angel Archer seems to be just going through the motions. She says she knows now 'why we are on this Earth: it is to find out that what you love most will be taken away from you'. She continues: 'this is probably due to an error in high places rather than by design'. For the Sufis, we hear 'the essence of God is not power or love but beauty'. Yet at the heart of this novel and of Dick's *Valis* is not beauty, but *knowledge*. It is wisdom. It is the knowledge of God, the intimate knowledge of God. It is a Gnosticism in the sense also of esoteric knowledge. The protagonist of *Transmigration*, Timothy Archer, needs to *know*.

Faith versus knowledge

Both Timothy and Horselover Fat, the protagonist of *Valis* are driven by the need to have a Christ-like intimate communication with God. In *Jesus of Nazareth*, Pope Benedict XVI (2007: 5–6) speaks of God's communication with Abraham as a covenant between God and Abraham's descendants. There is, second, the communication with Moses on the Mount: the Ten Commandments and the covenant with the Jewish people. The third communication is between God and Jesus. In each case, communication works through revelation. In each, the profane interlocutor prays. Faced with Abraham and Moses, the sacred interlocutor commands. Faced with Jesus, He is also saying 'you're the Son'. 'You are in effect me.' 'Go out and spread this gospel: this good news. Do this in your public ministry.' And the good news of course is that you no longer need to wait until the end of time to be saved. Paradise will be yours not in a future redemption, but right now – in the present time – in salvation. God is saying to Jesus that salvation is here. It is here already and it is here through you. We need not wait for a messianic age. You are the messiah and it is now that salvation is possible. The Garden of Eden is to be regained not at the end of time for a *collective* of a *particular* chosen people, but in historical time for the *individual* souls of *everyone*. Jesus was already – before the Revelation – the Son of God and the son of Man. He was the Son of God in that he was imbued with grace and holy substance from birth. And it is this that is revealed by God: it is communicated to Jesus.

As Benedict (2007: 236) pronounces, Abraham and Moses stood towards God as friends, in the intimacy of friends. Yet they did not see God face to face as Jesus did. Jesus partook of God and *knew* God. Jesus knew God in himself. Knew God in his being. Man is not meant to have such knowledge. Man's relation to God is a matter of not knowledge, but *faith*. God is beyond knowledge: beyond both epistemological and especially ontological knowledge. For Kant, we can epistemologically know things through the concepts of the understanding. Beyond the concepts of the understanding are the substantive ideas, the Ideas of Reason: ethics, infinity, and freedom, the thing-in-itself and God. For Kant, as in Kierkegaard, God is beyond the ontological knowledge of the thing-itself. For Kierkegaard especially, God is a question not of knowledge but of faith. In what Derrida called the 'Jew-Greek', the Greek is ontological; the Jew is beyond ontology in faith. Only Jesus, and not the Messianic Jew, can know God in himself. It is this that is the stake in Dick's novels: the ontological knowledge of God. It is to know the sacred in-itself. To do this you must not just be a communicant at a distance from God. You must be intimate with Him: almost totemically, and indeed through alimentary communion. There is, there was, a price to pay for this. And Timothy Archer, Horselover Fat and in another sense Dick himself paid this price with their lives. Not the modesty of Emmanuel Levinas before the Lord thy God. But the desire to know and possess God: to connect to God, not as Jew but as Greek. Timothy Archer died, notes the firmly secular Angel, 'because he mistrusted Jesus'. Timothy Archer, instead of faith and trust in Jesus, needed to *know* God the Son. It was this that brought his downfall.

The critique of law is important for Dick as it is for much of contemporary cultural theory that has addressed the religious. In most of these cases the critique of law is carried out from the standpoint of justice. Walter Benjamin's 'Critique of Violence' (1977d) does this from the standpoint of the Messianic, as does – to a lesser extent – Jacques Derrida's *Force of Law* (1992). Some of these texts revolve around the figure of Saint Paul, and Dick was very importantly a Pauline. Jakob Taubes' (2004) and Giorgio Agamben's (2006) books in this context give a messianic reading of Paul. The messianic puts redemption not in history or in time, but at the end of time. For the Christian or Christian-influenced writings of Benedict, Badiou (2003) and John Milbank (2008), it is again justice versus law. But now justice is based in a universalistic community of the gift, trust and faith in the here and now, grounded in the doctrine of the Son, the Crucifixion and Resurrection of Christ. For Badiou it is the event, the event as a truth procedure, whose highest incarnation is found in mathematics, in set theory. For James Burton (2008a, 2008b), in his work on Bergson and Dick – as for Edgar Barefoot in Dick's novel – it is more aesthetic, in a process of fabulation. Dick also obsessively opposed the Law of both Pharisaic Judaism and Roman nomos. Yet his solution, which is not all messianic, still stands in contrast to Benedict, Milbank and Badiou. This is because, for Dick, the religious is neither a question of faith nor of community, but one of *cognition* and the individual.

Timothy Archer thus was driven to pursue knowledge of God to his eventual death in the desert of Syria in pursuit of the artefacts of the 'Zadokite' sect. Opposed to Tim's and Dick's fascination with the esoteric, daughter-in-law and narrator Angel counterposes a non-religious ethics of the concrete and of everyday life infused by love. She reproaches Tim for living with his 'mind' 'on what Kirsten had called "the Other Side"'. 'Like the medieval realists', Angel notes, 'Tim believed words were actual things. This is what cost him his life'. And we will see throughout this novel that Tim will always reject the metaphor, reject the symbol or symbolic for the real. Indeed, Tim's search for the Zadokites was of literally the real Zadokite mushroom, through which the sacred is ingested. The Eucharist, here in which the body and blood of Christ is symbolically ingested, is not enough.

Tim wanted instead to eat the *real*. Tim is with Emile Durkheim on the centrality of alimentary communion. Eating here is a mode of communication, of intensive communication. Tim's pursuit of the Zadokites' artefacts – the documents and mushroom – is what drives the novel's narrative.

Dick's St Paul: against law and the messianic

We move to the early 1970s where Tim's story, Tim's 'transmigration' took place. Enter Tim's lover-to-be Kirsten Lundborg, of Norwegian origin, an American feminist in her mid-forties, a high-ranking figure in a national women's organization. Lundborg and the organization want to have Tim Archer as speaker at their conference. Angel, a friend of Kirsten, arranges dinner for all four at the Bad Luck restaurant, in Berkeley. Tim and Kirsten have sexual chemistry: they have an affair and he sets her up in a flat in San Francisco using the Discretionary Funds of the Archdiocese. This affair will eventually cost Tim his post as Archbishop. Bishop Archer is stationed at Grace Cathedral, the head office of the diocese. He was about to undergo a 'heresy trial', though, because of his voicing his doubts in regard to the Holy Ghost. He reasoned that 'if the Holy Ghost were a form of God equal to Yahweh and Jesus, he would still be with us'. The Holy Spirit is essential to the Episcopal Church's Trinitarianism, their 'Nicene Creed', in which the 'Ghost, the Lord and giver of Life, proceedeth from the Father and the Son', was 'to be worshipped and glorified' (*Transmigration* 1991: 23). The proof of this absence is for Tim in language. The Holy Ghost is encountered speaking in tongues: yet in *Acts* we see that at stake is not glossalalia but xenoglossy. In *Acts* at Pentecost the Holy Ghost descended upon the Disciples giving them 'the gift of speech'. This rush, this *ruah*, caused all the Disciples to start speaking in tongues: yet each of them heard this as if it were in his own language. This 'gift of speech', Archer observes, is 'meant to reverse the unity of language lost with the construction of the Tower of Babel'. This has not happened. Hence the *ruah* (Hebrew for the Holy Spirit) is not a reality but a messianic expectation. And Archer's (and Dick's) Gnostic and ultra-Pauline position lines up against messianism. For them the Christian (and thus Catholic) Church is not not Jewish enough, but instead too Jewish. The Holy Spirit – and the author of *Acts*, who Tim suspects is not Paul but probably the author of Luke's Gospel – makes sense to 'only Jews

189

and not to Greek converts'. This sort of 'dogma', says Archer, 'strickens the creative spirit in man'. Tim here is an explicit partisan of Alfred North Whitehead's 'process theology'. If God is process, observes Tim, He is not actual.[2] VALIS as God, as Vast Active Living Intelligence System, is not actual: it is God as process. But it is the affair with Kirsten that will be Tim's undoing as Bishop. Kirsten is 'inhabited by an evil spirit' like 'the pig that Jesus had cast evil spirits into'. Her son Bill – a psychological cripple, in and out of institutions – inherited this from her. Tim, says the pragmatic Angel, is 'just a fool' (the reference is to Wagner's Parsifal) for getting caught.

Archer (and Dick) begins their most sustained disquisition on St Paul. Tim says he has, so to speak, 'no religious inclination'. Instead, as Malebranche said, 'it is not I who breathe but God who breathes in me'. Both the Catholic and the Episcopal Churches 'breathe only through the living power of Christ: who is the head of which we are the body'. Thus Paul: 'Now the Church is his body. He [Jesus] is the head'. Thus Tim: 'we have our life though Jesus Christ'. 'He is the image of the unseen (by us) God and the first born of all creation.' Why Paul? What Dick is interested in is not so much literal salvation but its perhaps equivalent, man's partaking of the divine. This has to do with first wisdom and then love. It has to do with the creative impulse: with God as process. This cannot be a Jewish doctrine or primarily a messianic doctrine in Benjamin's sense. This cannot be held out to a messianic age, a promise, an age to come. It is less a coming community than a community that is already here. In Christianity this is a state of grace. Judaism does not have such a notion of grace. This is the substance sharing of Benjamin's Adamic Paradise. Only man must share this intensive substance and he must share it now.

Dick and Archer pursue this first in the importance of love in Paul, who in *Corinthians* states, 'faith moves mountains, love moves human hearts'. Paul, Dick notes, started as Saul, the Pharisee with a concern for the minutiae of the law. The Pharisees are the forbearers of Rabbinic Judaism after the destruction of the Second Temple. After the conversion on the Road to Damascus, Paul comes to see salvation not in the law of the Torah but in '*zagidah*, the state of righteousness that Jesus Christ brings'. Salvation through 'works' – which entails following a rule – is much the equivalent of following the law. Hence, unlike Luther or Max

Weber's Protestant, for Paul it is not works, law-following, but righteousness that saves. Archer/Dick cite Paul: 'But now we are rid of the Law, freed by death [Christ's] from our imprisonment, free to serve in the new spiritual way and not the old way by written law' (1991: 47). What a vastly different way to serve God! – on the one hand, by the chosen people who do not partake of God's spirit (because He is too sacred while we are too profane) but have enacted with him into a particular covenant. And, on the other hand, to serve God while in a state of grace, partaking of God's spirit.

So Paul, who once saw redemption as a promise for a future age achieved by a law-following collective Jewish people, now sees salvation in the here and now as achieved through righteousness. This is through a particular '*state* of righteousness Jesus Christ brings'. This state of righteousness is grace. In it we partake of God as the 'Father, the Son and the Holy Spirit'. Though God is in all three of these, we partake of God through the *Son*. The Christian partakes of God through re-living the Resurrection of the Son. There is no resurrection without death. We attain salvation on the one hand through re-living the death of Christ for our sins. We attain it on the other hand through partaking in the Resurrection. Our salvation is the resurrection of our individual souls. We live and re-live the death and Resurrection of the Son. John Milbank (2008) understands this rightly in terms of 'trauma': as symbolically re-living the trauma of the Son's death and Resurrection: as the chronic repetition of the re-living of this trauma[3]. You achieve this state of grace and righteousness through not works but faith. Hence Paul, in *Romans* 4: 8 and 5: 'Through our Lord, Jesus Christ, by faith we are judged righteous and at peace with God.' And 'since it is by faith and through Jesus Christ we have entered this state of grace in which we can look forward to God's glory'. Thus 'divine grace coming through one man, Jesus Christ, came to so many as an abundant free gift'.

Dick identifies Pharisaic Law with pagan astral determinism: that is with causation and death. He cites Paul: 'the law of the spirit of life in Jesus Christ has set you free from the law of sin and death'. Man needs righteousness not rule-following to be set free from sin and death. It is faith (*pistis*) that can do this. There is 'righteousness through grace and grace through faith'. Love (*agape*) is a key to this. Love as *caritas*, as caring. Love in your relationships is inseparable from faith. Through love in the everyday and faith you attain grace. And grace brings you righteousness. 'We are judged righteous.' By our faith we are so judged. Here righteousness is equivalent to salvation itself. And you attain righteousness and salvation through grace. Righteousness is something that is in the Old Testament as an *attribute* of God. God, the just God, is righteous when He fulfils the Covenant. We speak about righteousness in man in terms of ethical conduct. A righteous man is a just man. But we attain righteousness for Tim Archer and Paul not through secular ethical conduct but through faith and grace. That is, man through faith attains righteousness and then he acts justly. Grace is this gift we get, not through being ethically just: it is instead an abundant free gift through Jesus.

Ultra-Pauline Tim Archer is searching for the Zadokite documents. With the Gospel Matthew, Tim sees Jesus' ministry as a 'fulfilment of Old Testament prophecies'.[4] Zadok was a priest, in Israel from the priestly house of Eleazer, who anointed Saul in 950 BC at the First Temple's founding. The Zadokites were the Sadducees who emerged at the time of the Second Temple and fought pitched battles with the legalistic Pharisees. Tim Archer and Kirsten will go to London to scrutinize the documents for Q, 'the hypothetical Aramaic source of the Synoptic Gospels' (1991: 60). Two of the documents focused on the Hebrew noun 'anokhi'. The anokhi is the 'I', in the 'I am the Lord thy God': in the 'I am that which I am'. To say 'I am I' is to say that I exist without predicates. I exist indeed without conditions. This is God, in which 'God is the I, the Existing One' (1991: 63). This 'I', a personal force, is the source of power, life and consciousness. Man rules over the animals by this 'I's will and self-conscious action. God's 'I' is the 'absolutely free personality' that allots to earth its existence and purpose. The Zadokites, Tim realizes, possessed the 'I'-embedded anokhi. And he had to get it.

All this is of great interest to Tim's son and Angel's young husband Jeff. Jeff is constantly playing *c.* 1970 Beatles and Stones records. Jeff, like Tim, takes up a special interest in Albrecht Wenzel von Wallenstein, whose irrationalism and obsession with the occult was the ruin of Germany in the Thirty Years' War and allowed the triumph of Gustavus Adolphus. Once Gustavus Adolphus crushed Wallenstein in 1632, the Catholics no longer had hope of defeating the Protestant cause. Jeff and Tim were reading Friedrich Schiller on Wallenstein, featuring his encounters with astrology. This foresees the sort of Parsifal fool that Tim will become. Schiller's three plays on Wallenstein were written at the end of the Enlightenment thinker's life. This and his letters to Wilhelm von Humboldt evidence Schiller's freedom-based idealism that contrasted with Wallenstein's collusion with fate. This was the 'greatest sin of all' for Schiller, for whom freedom was 'the will to overcome fate'. For Tim Archer, freedom meant the Christian/Zadokite will to overcome fate, *avanke*. Tim, however, is rather indifferent to his son's fate and death. Kirsten also takes an interest in her fellow Scandinavian Adolphus and Jeff falls in love with her. Tim decides to go to London with Kirsten and not take Jeff along. When they are away, Jeff takes his own life. Tim puts on Jeff's gravestone the statement from Heraclitus's school: 'no single thing abides, but all things flow'. Jeff's death occasions Angel, in 1980 at the time of John Lennon's death, to reflect on Sri Krishna's dictum that 'all hosts must die'. Yet this is also pointing towards Tim's absolute will to knowledge. Angel obsesses that Sri Krishna, when he assumes his true form, says all hosts must die.[5] Here he becomes Vishnu 'licking with your burning tongues, devouring all the world'. Sri Krishna appeared initially to Arjuna as a friendly character. When Arjuna asks the forbidden question of Sri Krishna's true form, the latter becomes universal destroyer.

Christ's mushroom: salvation by eating

Tim and Kirsten, now back from London and mourning Jeff's death, are with Angel at their flat in San Francisco's Tenderloin District. Tim speaks of the Satanic desire to know God fully, which is only possible by becoming God. Satan accepts eternal punishment for this. Thus also Prometheus' punishment for stealing fire from the gods and giving it to man. We find out now that Kirsten is ill. Tim and Angel converse on knowledge and the Zadokite mystery. Tim speaks of 'knowing God', of discerning 'the Absolute Essence'. The anokhi, this 'I am', is the thing itself. Tim is certain that 'the anokhi is not the divine intellect', because the Zadokites 'speak of having it literally'. It is real, very real. 'The anokhi dies each year and is re-born each year.' And each year 'the anokhi is more'. In the 200 BC documents many of the Logia, later attributed to Jesus, are attributed to 'The Expositor'. In these scrolls are a number of the parables attributed to Jesus in the Gospels. There is the doctrine of resurrection as well as the Eucharist. Here are found the 'I am' statements of Jesus. 'I am the bread of life.' 'Anyone who does eat my flesh and drink my blood has eternal life, and I shall raise him up on the last day' (1991: 79). 'For my flesh is real food and my blood is real drink. He who eats my flesh and drinks my blood lives in me and I live in him.' This is the source of Q. At stake is the body and blood of the anokhi that is destroyed and then grows to be more each year (1991: 79). This questions the divinity of Christ. In his place steps the 'Expositor', who will also return in the 'Final Days' and act as an 'Eschatological Judge'. Tim Archer is starting to break more fundamentally with the Church. Tim opposes the old more Jewish problematique of unknowability. Archer wants a doctrine that is *so* Christian that even Christ cannot give it. A becoming-God not just in the realm of symbols or of ideas, but in reality. In the realm of ideas (or spirit), the sacraments 'homologize' the Christian communicant to God as represented in Christ Becoming God, that is assimilated to God. 'This is more literal in the Zadokite banquet in which the Zadokites ate and drank anochi and thus became anokhi, became God himself' (1991: 80). 'With bread and wine derived from anokhi' there is 'apotheosis'. Anokhi thus is 'self awareness', the 'pure self-consciousness of Yahweh': it confirms immortality. Whereas Jesus spoke 'metaphorically of bread' the Zadokites spoke metonymically (1991: 83). Dionysus, unlike Jesus, was more than a metaphoric vine. 'His worshippers drank and Dionysus possessed them and they ran over hills and fields and bit cows to death: devoured whole animals alive.'

Kirsten is ill with peritonitis and in hospital. Angel visits her and Kirsten reveals that the anokhi was a mushroom the Zadokites grew in caves. When detoxified, the mushrooms made them hallucinate. Jesus and the disciples smuggled anokhi into Jerusalem, confirming biblical scholar John Allegro's contention – official translator of the Qumran scrolls – that the early Christians were a secret mushroom cult. If you ate the anokhi you were eating God. When Angel returns home there was Kirsten's son Bill crouching on the porch. Bill, recently released from prison and then Napa State mental hospital, was unable to abstract, and could only reason in the concrete, having the 'classic schizophrenic cognitive impairment'. They talk about Jeff's suicide. Bill asks if Jeff was mentally ill. Jeff was full of anger towards Tim, Angel says, and then admits to Bill's questioning that she is hostile to Kirsten. Bill, wondering what sort of vocation Jeff would have taken, says he is taking a course in computer programming, studying algorithms. These are 'nothing but a recipe', a 'sequence of incremental steps', sometimes utilizing 'built-in repeats'. Angel retreats to a corner and secretly weeps over Jeff. She is not sure there is 'any sense in the world' that primarily 'takes away from you'.

Soon after, Bill is back in prison and Kirsten out of hospital. Tim and Kirsten are off again to England for more Zadokite research. Back from this trip, Kirsten tells Angel that 'Jeff has come back': that Jeff is speaking to them, come back from the 'other world'. Tim will write a book on this. Kirsten experiences Jeff sticking needles under her fingernails and setting the clocks to 6:30, the time at which he died. This leads Angel in 1980, and in the context of the Edgar Barefoot seminar on Hindu logic, to digress on the forms of reasoning. She notes Tim's reasoning from seeing needles on his mistress's bed sheets to Jeff's return from the dead, to his immortality. She thinks this is inductive reasoning, that is reasoning from effect back to cause. 'In the West logicians saw deductive reasoning – from premises to conclusions – to be more reliable.' In contrast to both, Barefoot spoke of a Hindu inferential logic, of a Hindu school called anumana, which was in part inductive but you needed 'invariable concomitance', as a 'sufficient ground' for a claim. That is no concomitance can be assumed that 'fails to be exemplified' in 'actual observation'. This was a complex five-step check on inductive reasoning, one that Tim's thesis, in regard to Jeff's immortality, failed to exemplify. Angel compares Tim to Wallenstein's astrology charts in the Thirty Years' War, and not for the first time Wallenstein to Hitler – for Wallenstein, Hitler and Tim the overvalent idea is a problem, not a solution. Thus in his drive to know and be God, in his ultra-rationalism, Tim was under the grip of fate. Here the overvalent idea, Angel observes, 'slides over into the otherworldly orientation of revealed religion', 'of wish-fulfilment rather than reality testing'. Yet Angel goes along with Tim's folly, to be Tim's public folly, in order 'not to lose his friendship' (1991: 116–17). They all know on some level that Tim's pursuit of ontological reason to the heart of God Himself is fatefully leading to its opposite, to a Wallenstein irrationality, to folly and madness. Yet Tim, like P.K. Dick, seems fated to this pursuit.

Bill returns, out of jail, and Angel sees him on a visit to Kirsten and Tim's San Francisco Tenderloin flat. Bill dialogues with Angel about the concrete again: about cars, and about the safety superiority of the Honda or VW on wheel-base, suspension and engine. Tim is there, again with no interest in the exoteric. Bill argues with Tim and Kirsten saying they were 'just assuming Jeff caused all those things'. Tim secretly informs Angel that he is taking amphetamines and Kirsten is developing a heavy barbiturate problem. Tim questions Bill's scepticism of Jeff's immorality: Tim's book is to provide comfort for lost loved ones. The book and Jeff's return is of a piece with the incipient ontological realism of Tim's Christianity. Says Tim, the 'afterlife awaits us: on this the whole promise of salvation depends'. That 'Paul is in no way speaking metaphorically: man literally rises from the dead' (1991: 131). This is the 'kerygma' (i.e. the preached good news) of early Christianity seen in *Corinthians*. 'If there is no resurrection of the dead, then Jesus Christ cannot have been raised and we have committed perjury before God.' This is 'because we swore in evidence before God that he had raised Christ to life' and 'if Christ has not been raised then you are still in your sins and all who have died in Christ have perished'.

Tim steps down as Bishop, losing faith in 'the reality of Christ'. Christ, he says (1991: 139), is just a mistranslation from the Hebrew 'Messiah', the Anointed One, the Chosen One; the Messiah is meant to come instead at the end of the world, in which, as in Virgil's *Eclogues*, the Age of Gold replaces the Age of Iron. Tim continues to believe in resurrection, both of Jeff and in Zadokite Eucharist religion. Angel cannot bear that Tim has reduced Jeff's reality to a book, to an intellectual matter. For Tim, 'books are real and alive as is language'. Jeff is the answer to my (theological and intellectual) problems says Tim. But, Angel observes, 'Jeff does not exist' (1991: 149). And 'that left only Tim'. Thus Angel agrees to go with Tim and Kirsten to Santa Barbara to visit a medium. For the medium, Jeff 'coming back' is inextricably linked with the imminent deaths of Kirsten and Tim. Kirsten does have cancer. Leaving the medium, Kirsten asks Angel if she will sleep with Tim when she dies. Tim blames the medium for taking advantage of a sick woman. He no longer believes in Jeff's return.

Kirsten and Angel go for a drink in a Santa Barbara bar. They, both secular sceptics, are opposed to the 'predestination doctrine of the Church based on Augustine and Paul'. Tim too opposes predestination notions. And bemoans the ignominy of 'Christianity as a Mystery religion, come into existence as a means of abolishing the tyranny of fate, only to reintroduce it as predestination'. Kirsten buckled under the Christian doctrine of original sin and especially Tim's weekly confessions of guilt for sleeping with her (1991: 170). She previously had no idea of the 'destructiveness of Christianity'. She 'didn't know a rat's ass about Christianity' until 'the damned stuff oozed out all over me, that Pauline doctrine of Original Sin. What a demented doctrine, that man is born evil; how cruel it is. It's not found in Judaism; Paul made it up to explaining the Crucifixion. To make sense out of Christ's death, which in fact makes no sense. Death is for nothing, unless you believe in Original Sin'. Later, Angel, who works in a Berkeley record store, receives Tim's phone call reporting Kirsten's suicide. She drives over to Tim and Kirsten's flat and then on to Grace Cathedral. First Tim says 'that's what Jeff said [to the medium]. First she will die and then me'. But he says 'I will fight'. 'I am not going to follow them.' 'This is what Christ came to the world to save man from, this sort of determinism. The future can be changed.' He then begins to question: he starts thinking that the medium and Jeff's return are nonsense. Yet the worldly cold Tim destroys Kirsten's suicide note to hide their affair. He asks Angel which were Kirsten's favourite poems so he can read them at her Grace Cathedral funeral.

Angel reflects on Tim: on the Wallensteinian fool he had become, on the affair with Kirsten and his obstinacy in Church dogmatics. Yet the Church had meant freedom to Tim. He saw the Renaissance not as a reaction against medieval unreason, but as the fulfilment of the kernel of reason in Augustine and Aquinas. He pointed to Dante's Comedy and Michelangelo's Sistine Chapel. For Tim, Christianity reached a climax in the Renaissance, which is 'not the triumph of the old pagan world over faith, but the fullest flowering of faith'. Renaissance man was literally a polymath; the ideal Christian 'at home in this world and the next; a perfect blend of matter and spirit, matter divinized'. The two realms, this and the next, were in the Renaissance 'brought back together, as they had been joined before the Fall' (1991: 190). Christianity rose against the 'astral determinism' of the Greco-Roman world. The need was for 'a god beyond the planetary spheres, a god capable of short-circuiting the astral influences' (1991: 191). Thus Luther 'gazed at fate and is supposed to have said, "Hier steh' ich; Ich kann nicht anders"'.

Angel began to drift away from Tim. Tim resigned as Bishop of California and went to work in a Santa Barbara think tank. His book, which Angel tried to stop, had branded him a fool; his affair with Kirsten exposed in the media. Meanwhile Angel is promoted in the record shop. She moves a guy called Hampton in with her. She is ensconced into the concrete. But then Tim rings her out of the blue. He announces he will go to Israel, to the Dead Sea Desert, next month (we are in 1978) 'to visit the wadi'. He wants Angel to come with him. Tim 'needs to find the anokhi, the mushroom'; 'that mushroom is Christ' and 'Christ has the power to break the hold of fate' (1991: 206). Paul 'mentions in his Captivity letters' that 'Christ unseats the ancient planetary powers; Christ rises from sphere to sphere': this 'power of fate is the power of the world'. The Zadokite documents speak of a book 'in which the power of the world', in which the future of 'every human being is written from before Creation'. This is the Book of the Spinners, 'something like the (Pharisee's) Torah'. The Spinners were 'fate personified. They weave men's fortunes'. Here 'Christ alone, acting for God on Earth, seized the Book of the Spinners, read it, and carries the information to the person. Christ's absolute wisdom instructs the person to avoid fate' (1991: 207). This is, Angel notes, like 'Prometheus stealing for man the secret of fire'. It is this that, for Tim, is salvation, 'salvation from fate'. When Tim says 'Christ really exists', he means in the mushroom. 'It is not the idea of Christ that will save me [Tim] from the Spinners', but 'Christ's flesh and blood will save me'. This is God's wisdom as material information. It is God as reason, as wisdom – that has been absent for the world for almost 2000 years. This material information is there in a mushroom, in a drug. And Tim was a notorious amphetamine user. Tim implores Angel to come with him. He says to her 'you are not genuinely alive. This is what Jesus meant by Second Birth: The Birth from above' (1991: 211). Angel declines, afraid she will die out there. And indeed Tim does die in Israel; of thirst in the desert. He never even brought a professional driver to the Dead Sea: only soft drinks.

The novel's Afterword puts us back to its beginning in 1980 at an Edgar Barefoot seminar. Angel had become friends with Barefoot. Bill Lundborg resurfaces. He has now left the concrete life to become a sort of 'bodhisattva', one who has refused 'Nirvana to come back and help others' (1991: 221). Edgar himself had a bodhisattva experience, in which he could have attained Nirvana as wisdom. Edgar, previously a philosophy student at Berkeley, knew the Kantian categories, 'by which the human mind structures experience – time, space and causation'. But all of a sudden one day 'a satori' – Barefoot comprehended the world not through the categories but as the thing-in-itself. He 'comprehended a world conceptually arranged, a world not arranged by the time, space and causation – but as an idea conceived in a great mind, the way the mind stores memories'. This is a glimpse of the world 'not as my own arrangement, but as it in itself is arranged': 'a great reticulated, arborising structure of interrelationships, everything organised according to its meaning, with all new events entering as accretions' (1991: 222). Edgar was about to turn this Nirvana into text but he saw two children playing dangerously in the street, and spent the next period of time looking after them rather than writing it down. In this sense he too was a bodhisattva. Tim and indeed Jeff and Kirsten were trying to escape fate. Fate as what? For Edgar Barefoot, 'the fate of meaningless words'. Bill believes he is Tim, come back from 'the next world'. Bill is Tim, who could have attained Nirvana in the desert, come back 'out of *compassion*'. To Angel, still mourning the death of 'three good people', Bill says Jesus said 'your fathers ate manna in the desert and they are all dead'. Tim – and the others as consequence – died of the search for Nirvana as wisdom: the intellect degenerated into nonsense, the wise fool's paradox. Angel (1991: 237) laments this intellect-become-nonsense 'to languish without a trace of anything redemptive'. Redemption instead would be through rejecting Nirvana-wisdom and reconnecting through compassion. Bill, familiar with Claude Shannon's information theory, saw such wisdom become foolishness to be 'like transmitted information'. It 'degenerates'; 'becomes finally noise; and the signal that is intellect fades out'. Bill-become-Tim had 'sought holy wisdom and equated it with the anokhi, God's pure consciousness'. But when Parousia (the Second Coming: literally beyond substance) entered him, he, now as bodhisattva, realized it was not wisdom but compassion that he wanted. Bill is then re-hospitalized, thinking he is Tim, and hopelessly out of touch. Edgar wants to take Bill in to live with him, yet Angel is worried. Edgar slips back into the wisdom as Nirvana-thinking: he had veered back from compassion to absolute knowledge. Barefoot notes Tim said 'one of the early church fathers believed in the Resurrection, not despite the fact that it was impossible, but *because* it was impossible'. Similarly, Edgar believes that

Tim has come back in Bill: a final transmigration of Timothy Archer. The proof for Edgar is that 'he talks in languages he doesn't know' – xenoglossy, the 'sign of presence of the Holy Spirit'. Edgar says he will take Bill in. Angel says 'not if you believe in that stuff'.

Tim wanted to *really* know God, to really know divine substance in itself. Tim Archer understands this as constitutive of his free subjectivity. This is where redemption or salvation will come from. Tim's daughter-in-law and best friend Angel (and the novel is about the tension between Tim and Angel) contests this and says we need to renounce divine knowledge because its logic turns into foolishness – and worse, its quest leads to irreplaceable loss. It leads to loss on the part of those who love those possessed with the divine will to knowledge. Angel proposes redemption, not through knowledge of the transcendental but instead through love in the concrete. The strongest love of anyone for anyone in *The Transmigration* of Angel's loving friendship for Tim. But Philip K. Dick, like Tim, is obsessed with knowing the divine.

Vast active living intelligence system

The Gnosticism of Philip K. Dick

In *Transmigration* the divine as substance is in the real of the mushroom, in *Valis*, substance becomes information.

Horselover Fat, the protagonist of *Valis*, has been destroyed by shipwrecked relationships with women: with his wife, Beth, who took away their child Christopher; with Gloria, who took her own life; with Sherri, who willed herself to die by cancer. Fat is so depleted, he tries to take his own life and is committed to Orange County mental hospital, his 'soul' destroyed by these women who wanted to take everyone close down with them. This destructiveness wounded Fat, not through hate but through its very irrationality/ insanity. Fat, suicidal and insane, was invaded in February–March 1974 by a laser beam of pink light. The light carried a signal and a plasmate into Fat's brain. Against insanity and ignorance, this was a beam of reason, of wisdom as information. It was also Jesus Christ. With this beam Fat became at the same time another person, Thomas, a first-century Christian.[6]

The beam, and indeed God, is VALIS – Vast Active Living Intelligence System. VALIS is the true God in what is Dick's Gnostic Christianity. Dick's version is the sort of Valentinan Gnosticism of the second century AD suppressed as a dualist heresy by the Roman Empire when Christianity became the official religion in the fourth century. In Gnosticism, humans are divine souls, trapped in an imperfect world created by a demiurge identical with the Abrahamic God. This blind, mechanical, irrational God creates an irrational and imperfect world. He exists alongside a remote and unknowable supreme being that embodies good. The relation to this good God, who is VALIS for Dick, is not through faith but through gnosis, through knowing. Through a knowledge, an intimate knowledge, more like *kennen* than *wissen*, more like *connaître* than *savoir*. This is a spiritual knowledge only accessible to a learned elite – modern Gnostics numbered William Blake, Schopenhauer, Carl Jung, Hermann Hesse and Hans Jonas. In Gnosticism, redemption is achieved through the intimate knowledge of God: not of God's properties, but of God-in-himself.

The Valentinians and some other Gnostic sects see Jesus of Nazareth as the embodiment of this Supreme Being: superior to the blind, mechanical Abrahamic God.[7] Dick and other Gnostics were influenced by the discovery of the Nag Hammadi Library in Egypt in 1945, where local peasants found 13 leather-bound papyrus codices. The writings dating back to the second century AD are some 50, mostly Gnostic, treatises or tracts. These were written in Coptic, though translated from the Greek. Most famous of these is the Gospel of Thomas. This is knowledge not of appearances but esoteric mysteries. It is a sort of Enlightenment through anamnesis: it is redemption by anamnesis. Anamnesis works not through gaining wisdom but through remembering what had been forgotten. Plato's anamnesis was a development of Socrates' teachings on the immortality of the soul. If the soul is immortal, it is reincarnated. In this doctrine knowledge can never be gained. According to the Socratic paradox of knowledge, if you don't know what you're looking for, you cannot find it, but if you do know it, then you cannot gain – but only remember – it. Thus knowledge depends on reincarnation, dear to some Gnostics. The Abrahamic God of creation destroys the knowledge of this primordial Supreme Being. The Gnostic, through not faith but perception, sees through the illusion of the Cretan God's mechanical world.

The Supreme Being is a 'transcendentally rational mind'. Fat/ Dick receives this vision as laser beams and geometric graphic patterns of Jesus Christ. This, unlike biblical Revelation, came to

Fat not via communication or covenant but via 'divine invasion'. This divine invasion replaces Dick's previous irrationality/insanity with perspicuous vision. The triumph of the Abrahamic God had instituted a regime of law that Horselover Fat and his alter ego, Thomas, experience as the 'Black Iron Prison' of the Roman Empire. Fat keeps repeating, 'the Empire never ended'. Rome was the ultimate denial of the spiritual as its materialism and despotism forced the Gnostics and Thomas underground. Apostolic Christians wore a fish sign as a means of communicating – for fear of being caught – through cryptic figures. In February–March 1974 a girl bearing such a fish sign knocked on Fat's door triggering this Gnostic anamnesis. The anamnesis opened up a reality a bit like Plato's archetypal world, a trans-temporal constancy. This world was the dynamic and mythological dreamtime of the deeds of heroes: the reality a mind, a trans-glossal mind that spoke Greek, Sanskrit and Hebrew. It brought into Fat's mind a 'tremendous technical knowledge', for example information about his small son's birth defect that he could not have otherwise known. This beam that entered his brain, Dick said in a 1981 interview, thought not through digital or syntactical or verbal means but without words, in pure concepts. This beam was also the spirit of Elijah the Prophet, who entered Dick in 1974 'and I uttered prophecies'. Elijah left Dick in 1976, the year of his attempted suicide.

Horselover Fat: healing the subject

We discover Horselover Fat in the opening pages experiencing a new breakdown after a phone call from his friend and love-interest Gloria asking Fat for sleeping pills in order to kill herself. This was 1971 and catalyzed Fat's entropic decline – in 1972 and 1976 suicide attempts. Gloria, who had been hospitalized in San Francisco for her suicide attempt, was at her parents' home in Modesto. A few days later she did take her life, jumping from the Synanon building in Oakland. 'I' the narrator, who is Phil, a science fiction writer, could not help Fat's disintegration into madness. What happened though is that Gloria died and Fat did not die. 'Where Gloria got death, Fat got God'. He got Him in a clay pot found by 18-year-old drug dealer Stephanie. In Stephanie's pot 'slumbered God … for a long time'. 'Fat was in a hunger for God', who 'fired a beam of pink light directly at him'. 'Fat was 'illuminated by holy light fired at me from another world'. His 'brain had trapped information from a beam of pink light'. This 'information fired at him, progressively crammed into his head in successive waves had a holy origin', was 'a form of scripture'. Fat translated these holy information beams into exegeses. Fat's 'world was turning into information'. What appears to be 'rearrangements in a physical universe' in fact is 'information and information-processing which we substantialise' (*Valis*, 2001: 21–30). Fat, traumatized by Gloria's suicide and by ex-wife Beth's taking their son away from him, attempts suicide and is hospitalized.

Against the material world of Rome and the Abrahamic Creator-God, stood Fat's informational world from the Gnostic Supreme Being. In Heraclitus, for whom we use '*noos* to interpret evidence', we see that 'men like Homer were the victims of illusion'. Heraclitus wrote that latent structure is the master of obvious structure; that we must interpret, 'guess the riddle' of latent structure; that the reality of *noos*, or latent structure, is hidden. Fat's information came in 'tight energy beams'. These produce hallucinations: of the 'words, figures, that is the logos'. This energy is 'healing' Fat. This divine information invasion is quintessentially *material*. It addresses not just Fat's mind, but his '*brain*'. At stake is material and physical energy. It fires signals at neurons, which themselves fire in relaying these signals. We are in a world at once intensive and material; a world of intelligent matter. Timothy Archer, we just saw, was looking for the sacred in a mushroom: through Durkheimian alimentary communion with the physical blood and body of Christ. In *Valis* this energy, this information is *fired* at Fat. Its origins, 'another planet', are also material. Light itself is material. Otherwise there would be no 'speed of light'. We have here a coming together of the intensive and the extensive: a non-predicative and non-metric materiality. The object too is unlike Aristotle's object, not filled with solid matter (Kittler 2006), but with information. Alimentary communion is through drugs. In *Transmigration* Kirsten was always on downers; Gloria had lots of Nembutals, downers; Tim and Fat do speed. Downers lead you into entropy, into a dull determinism. Speed takes your self-organization, the unit of energy that Fat is, your information, to higher levels. Indeed, back in 1964 Fat had taken an acid trip and for eight hours he thought in Latin without ever having learnt Latin. In the Old Testament messianic age people would all know the Torah without ever having studied it (*Jeremiah* 31: 33). Now Fat had knowledge in St Luke's and Paul's

Koine Greek, which had replaced the modulated Hebrew of Jesus' Aramaic. Paul wrote (and later Richard Wagner echoed) *'here time turns into space'*.

For Fat, real time had stopped from 70 CE with the Second Temple's fall to the Romans, only to begin again in 1974. In Fat's dreamtime, when the heroes blew up the Roman Black Iron Prison, time did turn into space, into the measureless void that in 1974 once again opened up for Fat. The void (of time-turned-into-space) communicated to Fat (2001: 50): 'You of all people. Out of everyone I love you the most.' Fat made sense of these two modes of time through Parmenides' theory of Forms. Here Parmenides' Form II 'is the lower realm driven by efficient cause, deterministic, without intelligence: emanating from a dead source', an astral determinism. Parmenides Form I, in contrast, is 'sentient and volitional': it is live and its own cause. In Form I, Fat experiences resurrection: 'from God we are born, in Jesus we die, by the Holy Spirit we live again'. Jesus breathes life into us and resurrects us in Jesus. The Forms are carried in the plasmate. Through 'the sacraments, by means of the plasmate, we are extricated'. The plasmate carries blood cells: germ plasma fills up the cells. For Fat there is but one Mind – and this is Form I – with two contending principles. Form II does not in fact exist. Indeed *'time* does not exist' (2001: 59). When St Paul says time turns into space, he means that with the Holy Spirit, which Jesus bequeaths to man, time ceases to exist. It is the very material plasmate that counts. Mind as real mind or Form I is in the 'plasmate'. The plasmate 'slumbered' as a 'dormant seed in the buried library of codices'. It slumbered as 'living information', that is, as the Logos. This very material, living information is 'capable of replicating': it cross-bonds with humans, creating 'homoplasmates'. 'As living information, the plasmate travels up the optic nerve of a human to the pineal body. It uses the human brain as a female host' and replicates there (2001: 61). The original homoplasmates were killed by the Romans: buried for centuries in the codices at Nag Hammadi: they are now back.

It is written that before the blind creator God Samael, there was 'an enlightened immortal man', 'who will topple the blind God' like a 'potter's clay'. Thus Stephanie's little ceramic pot is given to Fat as a 'gift of love'. Love gives and saves; and love takes away. Both Gloria and Sherri – a devout Roman Catholic friend dying of cancer – want to take Fat, who loved them, down with them. Unlike Stephanie's gift, Gloria 'paid back those who loved her with the irrational'. In *John*, the Fourth Gospel, Fat and Gnostics find that man (immortal man) and the true God are identical. It is the 'lunatic blind creator' that separated man from God. The rational. Plasmate will save Fat. Like Jesus (2001: 66), only the proximity of death could bring Fat physical healing and salvation. In John's Gospel we read, 'kai theos en ho logos': and the word was God. For Gnostics, this means that the Word is Reason and Reason is God. Only Christ has seen God, has known God, known the Logos, so for Fat's Gnosticism, 'Jesus Christ is the logos of the Fourth Gospel'. To 'experience Christ' is to experience God and in *1 John*, 'we are already the children of God' and thus can embody God's logos. In the Nag Hammadi codices is written 'man and the true god are identical'. In this very immanent theology the logos had 'broken into the universe' from Sirius, another star system. It camouflaged itself through its code name 'Zebra'. Zebra blends in with its environment through mimicry. Its name is also mimicry, sentient mimicry. Revelation comes when it discloses itself in theophany. Through transubstantiation, Zebra mimics objects and causal processes. Zebra fired the beams of 'information-rich coloured light at Fat's brain'. Paul of Tarsus also had such 'information fired at his head – right between the eyes, on his trip to Damascus – [though it] lies with him unsaid' (2001: 71).

Of the four Evangelists, John is the 'ontological' one (Benedict 2007: 218f) – the most centred around 'Christology'. The three synoptic Gospels focus on miracles and what Jesus did (i.e. Jesus' *works*): John more on the debates with the Pharisees and doctrinal issues. In John, there is focus on the Death and the Resurrection. John's Christology is based on (1) that Jesus Christ is the Logos (Word) and has existed from the beginning, (2) Jesus is the only saviour, and (3) Jesus Christ is God, an aspect of the Godhead. The purpose of this gospel is so that 'you may come to believe that Jesus Christ is the Messiah, the Son of God, and that through this belief you may have life in his name'. John, much more than the synoptic Gospels, focuses on Jesus' 'cosmic, God-commissioned, mission to redeem humanity'. The difference with Judaism is in love. You get love because Jesus is the Son of the Father, a relation based on love, cemented by love, primordial as social bond. God also commissions Moses, once as a young man on Mount Horeb, to take the Jews out of slavery. Here, in the burning bush, God reveals his name to Moses. God commissions Moses a second time – this time with instructions – on Mount Sinai, towards the end of *Exodus*. But God's commissioning of Moses is not primarily about love. Moses is no relation of God. God is too transcendent and Moses not significant enough for this. In Christianity – between the Father and the Holy Spirit, between the Father and the Disciples – the Son is at the centre. As God the Father loves Jesus, Jesus loves the Disciples: they are a tight community, a proselytizing community. As God the Father commissions Jesus, Jesus commissions the Disciples to spread the kerygma. For Fat, Samael the mechanical creator god is spawned by Sophia, who fell from the sacred yet disrupted Pleroma. The gnosis in Valentinus is the 'ontological salvific value' (2001: 87). For Fat, against the existentialism of the deed, you are what you think. He opposes Goethe–Faust's reversal of the Fourth Gospel's *Im Anfang war das Wort* with *Im Anfang war das Tat*. Fat and the Gnostics restore the Word as the Beginning.

Fat, hospitalized after his second suicide attempt, is released. He knows he can't go back to ex-wife Beth. He imagines there is a chance that he can cure (i.e. save) himself by trying to cure Sherri. Phil, the narrator, knows this is wrong and that Sherri wants to die. Yet Sherri moves in with Fat in a sexless relationship. Fat cannot stomach Sherri's banal Catholicism. He retreats to his bedroom and writes his two-source cosmogony, rethinking it through the Taoist Yin and Yang. In this 'the One', that incorporates 'the was' and 'the was not', generates a sac. The twins in the sac are each a unitary entelechy with psyche and soma rotating in different directions. The One thus makes the two who make the many as divided into two 'hyper-universes' in eternity. These two hyper-universes intermingle in the hologram-like universe we live in. Hyper-universe II turns the information-rich signal from Hyper-universe I into noise. In response, Hyper-universe I sends a microform of itself into Hyper-universe II to heal it. This micro-form is Jesus Christ. Hyper-universe II kills this micro-form and decays into blind mechanical purposelessness. It becomes the task of (Jesus') Holy Spirit to rescue our life forms. Within time, Hyper-universe II remains alive. Hyper-universe II has been killed in Eternity (Hyper-universe I), where the One grieves for her death. Thus we understand Paul's and Wagner's 'and now time turns into space', in which finite time becomes eternity (2001: 93).

Sherri cannot bear Fat's hermetic lifestyle and leaves him, also losing her cancer remission. Fat, in despair, goes back to his exegeses, developing a biological dimension to his information theology. This features an anamnesis, in which 'we are memory coils' – 'DNA carriers capable of experience', operating in a 'computer like thinking system'. 'We have correctly recorded and stored thousands of years of experiential information', each possessing different deposits from all others. The Fall becomes a 'malfunction', a 'failure of memory retrieval' and salvation (healing) will come through Gnosis as memory retrieval. More important than salvation's 'quantum leap of immortality' is 'the system as a whole'. The 'memories are the data needed by' the system for 'self-repair', for 'rebuilding our sub-circuits. It does so 'via continued signalling to us to stimulate blocked memory banks to fire'. Memory as information deposited in banks must be dis-inhibited so that the deposits are free to fire. The gnosis itself is 'external information'; an 'algorithm with dis-inhibiting instructions'. This is Plato's 'learning to remember', and 'The Fall was not a matter of moral but of intellectual error' (2001: 96).

Zebra is the material substrate of the living information, the plasmate and the blood of Christ that is knowledge; Zebra comes from the 'far future' (2001: 120). Fat quotes from a hymn of Ikhnaton, the fourteenth-century BC Egyptian Pharaoh who first embraced monotheism as state religion. The plasmate passes from Ikhnaton to Moses to Elijah to Jesus, all 'immortal men'. Fat imagines a three-eyed invader from another star whose third eye is to see into the future, to convert time into space. Fat's original divine invasion was in 1974, when he encountered the fish sign. The sign emits a 'dis-inhibiting substance affecting neural tissue that enables Fat's nerve circuits' in a 'flashback' in which he becomes Thomas and thinks in *koine* Greek (2001: 101). Then information from his memory banks is fired at him in 'lurid phosphene activity', leading to a drop in the brain's GABA fluid and the appearance of seraphic information, of Klees and Kandinskys. The 'universe is information', that we 'hypostatise into the phenomenal world' (2001: 110). Here 'we are stations in a single Mind', in which 'time and space are mere mechanisms of separation'. Fat 'remembered other selves', one in Minoan Crete some 2000 BC. After eating some strange pink food and drinking from a sacred pitcher (Holy Grail), Thomas engrammed himself on to the Christian fish sign. Thomas then is reborn 1900 years later when Fat is shown the fish sign. Thus 'Christ is an extraterrestrial life form' which 'came to this planet thousands of years ago, as living information', 'passed into the brains of human beings through interspecies symbiosis'. Before being Christ, he (Fat) was Elijah, of whose immortality the Jewish Qumran residents knew. Fat 'experiences' this in a 'dream time'. Fat dreams a scene his father could have dreamt, through phylo-genetic anamnesis, whereby the individual contains the history of his entire race. 'This is the gene pool memory, the memory of the DNA.' Like Jesus with God the Father, and Damascus Paul with the Son, Fat met the 'ultimate reality maybe'. 'Whatever it was, it was alive and it thought.' And in 'no way did it resemble us'.

We move forward again to 1979. Sherri has died, having willed herself malignantly to do so. Gloria's death still hurts, as does Beth/Christopher leaving Fat. The energy from the pink light has deserted Fat, who again seeks salvation. He engages his sceptic friend, Kevin, in conversation. Kevin and Fat reflect on temporality. Fat alludes to Heraclitus: 'time is a child playing draughts'. And to Anaximander: 'Time is a name for God's eternity'. Then we shift into a meditation on the Holy Grail. Fat's search for the sacred, like Timothy Archer's, is also a quest for the Grail, from which Jesus drank at the Last Supper and was used to collect the crucified Christ's blood. Christ's 'blood' in the Grail, Fat recalls, in Wagner's Parsifal, 'summons the Knights'. Parsifal's is a very funny kind of *quest*. Parsifal goes nowhere. In Parsifal, the *Strahlung* of light, of enlightenment, which brings salvation, comes through the compassion of the pure fool. In the Grail's revelation, the 'Redeemer is redeemed'. In *Valis* this comes through an almost medical healing, with Fat as 'Salvator salvandus'. Fat is unsuccessful at healing Gloria and Sherri. He must heal and save himself: he must redeem the (failed) redeemer. Fat turns to the Persian Gnostic myth of Zoroaster. In this myth Zoroaster is saviour: he is the 'eternal messenger, identical to those whom he calls'. Like Asklepios, the demigod of medicine for the (Western) Greeks, Zoroaster is saviour and physician for the (Eastern) Persian Gnostics. For Fat, 'the universe is a living organism into which metallic toxic particles' have come. Christ was a 'phagocyte against this'. Like this physician, Asklepios, who raised men from the dead, Christ and Fat will raise *memory* from the dead, raise DNA as memory from the dead. Fat quotes Schopenhauer, for whom not one atom of matter is ever lost, 'still less anything of the inner being that exhibits itself as nature'. If Christ is the phagocyte and resurrector of memory, the physician is the Holy Spirit, or 'Christ discorporate' (2001: 135). In Dick's information philosophy, God is an information-incorporate immortal human, whom Fat reflexively encounters. Fat cannot see why Christ had to be crucified; yet though he insists on redemption through not crucifixion but instead knowledge, he still needs to insist on the Son. He needs the Holy Spirit for his transmutating theory of information. Fat cannot banish the ontological from time and put it only at the end of history. The ontological is already and needs to be already there.

Valis: the movie

Kevin suggests to Fat and Phil, who is a friend of Fat, a science fiction writer and the novel's narrator, that all three must see a film called *Valis*. It is written by and stars a rock star called Mother Goose. The film's opening sequence is in a (near LA) Burbank, California small recording company, Maritone Records. In the film Mother Goose plays Eric Lampton, a heroin-addicted musician, more or less brain-dead, who writes simply awful music. Lampton works for the studio boss, Nicholas Brady. Brady is an electronic 'wizard' who has built an extraordinary electronic spud-mixer. Brady schemes to get in bed with Lampton's wife – who is Goose's real-life wife Linda. But the beautiful Linda is seen not to have sexual organs: this is to Lampton's delight because Brady cannot consummate relations with her. The fortress-like mixer is based on a laser system, running information on various channels of music. Brady enters the mixer and gets bathed in laser beams using his brain as a transducer to convert information to sound. He wants to get rid of Lampton, so lures him into the mixer and fires beams at his head, which explodes, electronic components spewing in all directions. Linda – or a hologram of Linda – comes through the walls of the mixer and runs Lampton back into time, his head putting itself back together intact. The two Lamptons are shown in bed together, stripping their organ-less skins off, showing real organs to have sex. Eric, pierced by an energy beam, also grows a third eye with a lateral (temporal) lens. Brady staggers out into Alameda Avenue, 'his eyes bulging'.

The film is set *c*. 1970. The US President in the film is the Nixon-esque Ferris F. Freemount, who governs through robot-like cheerleaders and secret police. He is facing re-election. Now Freemount morphs into Brady, whom he has recognized as a threat. The cheerleaders shout 'kill Brady…kill Brady…'. The camera pans to a table at which sit two Bradys, separated by a 'cube of pulsing pink light'. We recognize the film's pink light to be the same as Fat's light of divine invasion. Freemount is seen with a dossier of pictures and data on Brady and the Lamptons. He will call the Defence Department to remove them, but the pink light strikes Freemount, making him shred and forget the documents. The camera then segues to an air force base and a document called

'Project Valis', where a general speaks of VALIS as a 'Vast Active Living Intelligence System'. The air force building then detonates. We see a pink light, the alarms go off and voices sound 'abort mission'. The mission was to destroy the satellite VALIS which was sending the pink light to destroy Freemount and the generals. We move forward to the election, which Freemount wins: he is surrounded by well-dressed supporters. As the camera zooms in, Freemount turns around and his head morphs back into Brady's and the well-dressed supporters morph into unplugged robot cheerleaders.

Kevin, Fat and the narrator repair to Fat's flat. The friends discuss how VALIS wins in the end over Freemount. We learn that it was VALIS who gave Brady his electronics knowledge. Brent Mini, an English Brian Eno-like figure, composed the film's music. Kevin, who has now seen the film for the second time, calls Fat's attention to the ceramic pot (Stephanie's pitcher) that was on Brady's desk, and also appears in a fifth-of-a-second subliminal shot held by a Syrian woman in the desert. The pot has on it not the fish sign but the DNA double helix. Kevin notes the fish equals the double helix, so Christ or the Holy Spirit is genetic memory, 'gene pool memory'. The film works off a 'time dysfunction' – it goes back in the past to Syria, and Eric Lampton's time runs backwards. In the conversation they agree – and all three now agree – VALIS and the early Christians are dead 'only if you believe time is real'. And clearly they do not. Time disappears in the real: it turns into space. There is information transfer from the phosphene activity of the film's lasers to the retinas of the audience. The subliminal Syrian scenes transfer information to the unconscious mind. Mini's music comprises a range of sound frequencies that transfer information to the audience. Synchronicity's music puts listeners into a theta-like slumber that brought Irish-American Kevin back to ancient Celtic rituals, slaughtering a sacred ram.

The narrator decides Fat must get in touch with the Lamptons. Kevin says, 'Phil [clearly Philip K. Dick] you're a famous writer. Use your contacts.' 'Phil', now increasingly enters the narrative: he has contacts in England from previous invitations there. Some days later in Santa Ana, Orange County, David, a Roman Catholic friend, has joined them. We are repeatedly brought back to Gloria's death as the fulcrum of the novel. Gloria's death made Fat ill and made necessary the encounter with God. Fat meditates further on the messenger and temporality. The messenger is Zebra.

Zebra is that aspect of VALIS that Fat encountered. Zebra is a messenger, a 'transducer and percipient, totally receptive in nature' (2001: 158). Zebra is the carrier of the immortal yet material plasmate that 'controls the world though transubstantiation'. It transubstantiates into information, into light, laser beams, information, graphics and 'algorithms'. As such, it invades Fat's brain. Zebra the messenger 'discloses the gnosis'. The gnosis is wisdom: through the unforgetting 'gene pool' material memory.

The road to redemption must bring Fat and Eric Lampton together. 'Phil' rings London to get in touch with Goose. Fat prepares for Lampton's eventual call. They centre on the two-word cipher KING FELIX, the happy or rightful or fruit-bearing king. A cipher went out in 1974 to the descendants of Ikhnaton that the Age of Iron was over. The cipher is addressed to the re-emerging three-eyed race for whom King Felix will be the (fifth) saviour. Goose finally rings at 2 am. Phil answers. Phil says to Lampton: 'the information was fired at my friend Horselover Fat'. And Lampton replies 'but that's you. "Philip" means Horselover in Greek and "Fat" is the German translation of "Dick". Lampton says, "the suffering you've gone through is over. Do you realise that Philip?" "You've gone through a lot. The dead girl…well, we can let that go; that is gone"'. Fat had separated out as an external counterpart of Phil's unlivable interiority, from the trauma of Gloria's death in the 1980s. Why is Philip/Fat's 'suffering over'? 'Because he is here'. He has slept almost two thousand years. 'He is awake now', Lampton says. It is at this point (2001: 171) that the four friends constitute themselves the Rhipodon Society after the fan-like fins on the Christian fish symbol. Goose asks the group to visit him. They are expecting to meet the 'he' that 'is here': not knowing if this 'he' will be a god or a non-human, expecting him to be sent from the future. The entire lineage of VALIS extends from the distant future to the most distant past: from the stars (Albemuth) to the Dogon people (also of the fish symbol) to Egypt to Zoroaster and impending monotheism.

They then fly out to beautiful Sonoma in northern California, to Lampton's place in wine-growing country. Re-enter Brent Mini, laser studio builder in a wheelchair, suffering from multiple myeloma, dying from getting too close to VALIS's radiation. Through the radiation-information comes Brent's plenitude of gnostic knowledge. Brent has been contaminated by his proximity to this proximity to God: to God as wisdom. The Sonoma group – Eric, Linda, Brent and the Lampton's daughter Sophia – are themselves the 'Gottesfreunde', the friends of God, for Meister Eckhart, the 'greatest of the Christian mystics'. For them, God exists within the human soul, which can then know God as he is. At stake says Brent is not God, but 'wisdom. Holy Wisdom, that must prevail'. This is 'not Brahma the Creator nor Shiva the destroyer' but 'Zoroaster's Wise Mind'. The Gottesfreunde – and Fat – were nearly disabled by the radiation in 1974. VALIS, continues Brent, is 'an artificial intelligence'; it 'fires' a 'code unscrambler at you' (2001: 184). This is part of an 'inter-system communication network' that 'connects star systems with Albemuth'. VALIS is 'an artefact', something those 'in the Albemuth system built to program us at birth'. It 'engrams babies through firing instructions' as 'short bursts of information'.

Fat's eye is cast back to a vision of 1500 BC Crete, where a built maze became 'alive' and 'induced memory loss', thus effectively closing the 'third eye' (2001: 187). Escape Being from this 'space-time maze' brought salvation through anamnesis. Amnesic perdition and anamnesic salvation for Dick are activated through the three-aspect God: for Hindus Trimurti – Brahma the creator, Vishnu the preserver and Shiva the destroyer/transformer; for Christians the Trinity. In Christianity, Dick knows, it is the Son who makes the Father possible; the Holy Spirit is the incorporate Son. The Father in Dick's ultra-Pauline Gnosticism is significant no longer as creator, but only as creator of the Son. At stake is Holy Wisdom – yet a dose of too much knowledge (cf. Benamin's Paradise in Chapter 4) will kill. God as Wisdom, as reason, will take over 'the pathology of the toxicity of the earth's atmosphere', integral to the creator demiurge. God fires the rational, 'algorithmic' instructions to us. These instructions will 'bleed across the right (brain) hemisphere over the left one at appropriate situational contexts'. VALIS, says Mini, is 'an informational anti-toxin'. As a counterpart to the 'enthousiasmos of Dionysus, the intoxicated mad God, comes, chimes in Linda, an Apollonian Godhead' Yet over-exposure is itself toxic.

The Rhipidons are brought in to meet the saviour, Goose and Linda's daughter Sophia, from the Greek wisdom, from St Sophia. She cures Philip, saying his suicide attempt was not Fat's but his own. Fat, she says, was Dick himself, 'projected outward' 'to face Gloria's death'. When asked who she is, Sophia says 'I am that I am'. That is God's answer to Moses in Exodus when he asks for God's name. 'I am that I am' is God as the 'uncreated creator'. And Sophia was 'not created: she is that which always existed'. 'St Sophia was a hypostasis of Christ': a Christ that always existed. Sophia's voice was the AI (artificial intelligence) voice in the narrator's head since 1974. She sends the three of them out like apostles. 'I gave you its name. Now I will give you your commission. You will go out in the world and you will tell the kerygma that I charge you with.' In contrast to the original Christian kerygma in this case, 'what you will teach is the word of man. Man is holy: the living God is in man himself' (2001: 196). 'I am not a god; I am human. I am the child of my father, which is Wisdom Himself.'

The three Rhipidons are underwhelmed. They decide to fly back to Orange County, though the Lamptons try to stop them. Linda says to Phil as she kisses him on the mouth, 'this belongs to a very few'. Phil responds, 'No honey, this belongs to everyone' (2001: 206). Thus both Timothy Archer and Fat reach for salvation via an ontological theology, a Gnosticism of physically merging substance with God's real. For both Archer and Horselover Fat, this leads to madness, illness and death. In both cases, esoteric Gnosticism is rejected for a more exoteric 'keeping my commission' of everyday life. Yet the energy, the driving force, indeed the passion of Philip K. Dick comes from this information theology, this immanent Gnosticism in which, through alimentary communion or forceable invasion, God surges up, literally into the subject. We now move towards epilogue. Kevin, after a few chapters of belief, is sceptical again. Fat/Phil is 'cured', less through being spiritually saved than by seeing what he now saw were crazy people sharing his fantasy. Linda rings and says Sophia is dead: from an accident while Mini was trying to get more information transfer into her by laser. Fat and Phil are once more separated. Now we have Phil as a sceptic while Fat is travelling, still searching. Fat will travel the world and come back to visit Phil, Kevin and David. He brings back a third-century BC Greek vase with a double helix later used as a baptismal font. The double helix, the intertwined snakes of the caduceus, was originally on the staff not of Hermes, but Asklepios – the snakes as bearers of wisdom. Fat went to Greece in search of the Minotaur, the half-man/half-beast representing the demented Gnostic deity Samael. He travels to Turkey, to St Sophia, built by Justinian, and realizes that Sophia is a code name for Jesus Christ. Phil is now in first person. '"I", like Parsifal, "go nowhere". I stay still in Orange County, Santa Ana. On "my search". Watching, waiting. As we had been told originally long, long ago to do, I kept my commission.'

Notes

1 This chapter is indebted to the work of James Burton's *Fabulation, Narration and Salvation* in Bergson and Philip K. Dick, University of London, PhD, January 2008. Burton deals with the whole of Dick's work. He thematizes salvation via the prism of Bergson's *Two Sources of Morality and Religion* (1977).

2 Though the Holy Spirit is conventionally seen as personified – in the sense of taking on the form of an abstract person – in Christianity, it is seen in the Baptism less as 'person' than as process. Each, in the Baptism when the Holy Spirit descends, experiences his own personal Pentecost. Benedict (2007), pre-Pentecost, speaks of the Holy Spirit as descending on Jesus of Nazareth during his baptism in the Jordan by John the Baptist. Here the Holy Spirit seems to be less a person than a process.

3 Compare this trauma of communal negative infinity with the much more Kierkegaardian and existential trauma of the real in Lacan and Žižek (see Žižek 2008: 353–5).

4 See his *Jesus of Nazareth*. Benedict's tripartite notion of nature, memory, hope and the Jewish feasts with which Christian events coincide. The point for Benedict is partly to counter Gnostic claims of the clean break of Christian faith with Jewish law. Benedict's approbation of these feasts is approbation of Jewish law.

5 In *VALIS*, the Vast Active Living Intelligence System can move from host to host. Jesus is one of these hosts.

6 This is depicted by Robert Crumb in his *Religious Experience of Philip K. Dick* (1986). Dick had the experience he attributes to Fat in the novel.

7 Thus the Jewish God is one; the Christian Catholic God is three: the Father, the Son, the Holy Spirit – with the Son as the dominant figure. The Gnostic puts the Father in a much lower position.

9

Conclusions

Intensive culture as a vast, active, living intelligence system: a vast, active, living, information system. This was Philip K. Dick's way out of what he called the 'black iron prison', the 'law', for us a way perhaps also out of domination by the commodity and homogenization of contemporary global capitalism. Intensive culture has always been – for Philip K. Dick and Gottfried Wilhelm Leibniz – a question of intelligence, a question of mind. Extensity, for its part, has been a question of the material. But this vast active living, hence self-organizing and continually in process, information system brings together intelligence, on the one hand, and matter, on the other, into fusion. At stake is information, made of intelligent-matter, or materialized intelligence, in a system that promises justice, an aesthetics of the open, and a recasting of the political. We saw in Chapter 5 that this fusion, this new indifference of intensity and extensity, of the immaterial and material is an ongoing transformation at the heart of capitalism itself. Here the old physical system of cause and effect or social and biological system of functions has been recast as a system that itself takes on the previous functions solely allotted to intelligence or mind – of perception and representation and predication, of imaginary and symbolic communication. Global capitalism is made not of just desiring-machines, but of predicating machines, of information-and-communication machines. Global capitalism itself is a system no longer fully governed by the linearity of the commodity but by the intensity of difference, by a self-organizing flux of non-linearity that also incorporates its principle of domination.

Intensity: ontology and religion

The book began with the question of what an intensive sociology might look like. I was looking for a sort of sociological vitalism that could help us understand the flow, the flux, the difference of the global information age. I turned to a very vitalist reading of Georg Simmel. The Simmel of poetics and *Lebensphilosophie*, inspired by Goethe, Nietzsche and Bergson, the Simmel who was a professed metaphysician. We interrogated Simmel's notion of 'life', in which social relations were less a question of structure than process. Here social relations consisted less of variables acting externally as causes, but were instead driven by their own self-generating energy. In asking the question of life, the question of the vital energy at the core of social forces, we encountered the *monad*. If positivism was based on social atoms, Simmel's sociological vitalism understood the unit of social life to be the monad. Whereas atoms are inscribed in the logic of homogeneity, each the same as every other, monads follow a logic of heterogeneity, each one different from every other. This monad in Simmel's sociology of difference came of course from Leibniz. Simmel's metaphysics took us back to Leibniz's. Thus Chapter 3 is devoted to a study of Leibniz. We looked at Leibniz and predication. For Leibniz, substance was also subject. And a substance is qualified through predication, through the attachment of predicates to the substance (or subject). Deleuze writes about this in his book on Leibniz.[1] He insisted that for Leibniz the predicates are included in the subject. We saw that predication is also a mode of representation.

We further explored the monad as intensity in the work of Walter Benjamin. In questions of 'the political', we can speak of *das Politische* versus *die Politische* or *le politique* versus *la politique*. Here *die Politische* and *la politique* refer to institutional more or les utilitarian and epistemological politics, treated by social-scientific positivists; whereas *das Politische* or *le politique* is an ontological politics.[2] Phenomenology, in say Heidegger, and 'vitalism' of Nietzsche and Deleuze, share this ontological politics. The major shift in Benjamin's notion of intensity is that it formed in neither the epistemological nor ontological realm, but instead in the religious. It is intensive but not ontological. In the *Trauerspiel* work, Benjamin wanted to distance himself, conceptually and methodologically, from Nietzsche's work on tragedy. He wanted to do so in drawing on the religious. At first glance this would seem to be a counterposition of the religious to Nietzsche's aestheticism. But on closer inspection we can see that Nietzsche's Dionysian, as opposed to the Apollonian aesthetic, in its vital, self-organizing energetics, in its radical difference, like Aristotle's substantial form – which is also not a being but a becoming – is very much ontological. To open up this Dionysian, which is just as onto-logical and 'Greek' as the Appolonian, Nietzsche not only had to be the anti-Christ, he had to kill Yahweh too. And Benjamin's intensity, his monad, which is his singularity of the name, is formed with Yahweh in the *Genesis*.

Benjamin's intensity is the proper name: the proper name of the language of Paradise. There is a Kabbalistic monad at the centre of Benjamin's thought and his notion of the proper name. Kabbalistic language for Benjamin speaks in the register of the proper name (intensity) and semiotic language speaks in the register of the common noun (extensity). Intensive culture has a very strong dimension of Athens, or the ontological, as well as a dimension of Jerusalem, or the religious. Yet this relation of 'Greek' and 'Jews' is complex. In Chapter 8 we saw that Philip K. Dick's will to knowledge gives a very ontological take on the religious. In a sense, he takes the Judaeo-Christian or 'the Jew' and infuses it with the Greek. He infuses Jerusalem with Athens. Benjamin, in contradistinction, takes the Greek and injects it with Jerusalem. He breathes the messianic into the ontological. He displaces the monad from the ontological to the religious. In Benjamin's Kabbalistic intensive culture, once – in Paradise – we (and non-human things) were monads. Now we have Fallen into a state where we are mainly atoms. How, he asks, can we retrieve this monadic difference? How can we once again be singular?

Benjamin raises the problem of representation, and in particular representation through, on the one hand, images and on the other, symbols; the imaginary and the symbolic. When we read Freud on dreams we see mostly not the frozen symbolic of Lacan's and Deleuze/Guattari's 'Mummy-Daddy-me' or the Oedipus, but a pro-tean and processual ever-transforming meshwork, that condenses and overdetermines and displaces very unlike the frozen and linear symbols of capitalist ideology and the 'Oedipus'. These, Freud insists, are symbols, they are not just images. It is these of course that inspired the surrealists. Benjamin comes at this from a different angle. For him the language of things, that is non-humans, repre-sented and communicated in images, while humans, the languages of man also represented and communicated in symbols. Similarly, with Durkheim in Chapter 7, we see that non-humans represent in images while only humans represent in symbols. Durkheim gives us the origins of the symbolic in religious life. Symbols and religion somehow are at the heart of intensity, of intensive culture. The symbolic is born with clans assembling in tribes for religious rites. This collective assembly produces a web of totems constituting the 'symbolic' of the tribe. This symbolic is more or less protean and fluid in the sacred and more rigid and fixed in the profane. The symbolic moves between these registers of the protean and the fixed. In this protean symbolic we see Freud's dreams, and poetic language in Heidegger's and Benjamin's poetic language. With social evolution, the symbolic itself becomes more and more transcendental, universalist and individualist. It moves from the totem of the inter-clan tribe to the symbolic exchange of gifts at the inter-tribal level. With further transcendentalization, universalization and individualization we see the importance of ancestor myths and the inter-tribalism of the nation to culminate in the monotheistic God of Zoroastrianism and Judaism. The even further individualized symbolic is what we encounter in the nuclear family of the Oedipus.

Today with the rise of information and communication structures, we have come to speak of the fragmentation and even demise of the symbolic. In media theory we see this in the engineering-like notion of communication as illustrated in the work of Claude Shannon (Shannon and Weaver 1949) in which there is no dimension of the symbolic or of meaning. Communication takes place as it does in Benjamin and Durkheim. So does something like representation. But it is less in symbols, than a digitization of the real. I am not sure, however, whether the symbolic has died. I think, with Benjamin, that it has instead become fragmented (Lash 1999). Thus Bernard Stiegler (2004a) speaks of a *misère symbolique* in today's capitalism. With Benjamin we mourn the symbolic, with Derrida (1993), we mourn Marx's ghost. Against Shannon's *misère de l'information*, we must instead work within modes of partial structuring and recombination of fragments of the symbolic: of recombining these fragments with elements of the real and imaginary in differential bits of information. Information, then, is not in the register of the real that breaks through a burnt-out imaginary and symbolic. Information, in its fullest and Batesonian sense, because information is also mind, is a fusion of real, imaginary and symbolic.[3] We need to reject Shannon's impoverished physicality for this at the same time metaphysical mode of information (Hörl 2005). In a certain sense, perhaps Durkheim's but surely Benjamin's, this is at the same time the return of the religious.

In Chapter 5 we explored a paradigm shift in capitalism. Now capitalism is no longer the classical Marxist and 'physical' system of cause, effect and equivalence-exchange to which we attach the predicates. We explored instead a truly *neo-Marxist* contemporary capitalism which, as in metaphysics, does its own predicating. Leibniz, and at some points Benjamin, understood such differential predicating and self-organizing substance to be part and parcel of *mind* – to stand in opposition to the cause-and-effect and systemic logic of mechanism. We instead understood such internal predication, self-organization and difference – now in contemporary culture – to be fused with the material, with system, with mechanism itself. Mechanism in today's now metaphysical capitalism has become 'machinic', as the material incorporates mind itself. Instead of cause-and-effect machines, operating in media of the exchange of equivalence, capitalism now consists of predicating machines, of representing and communicating machines. These machines or systems, we understand with Francisco Varela (Varela et al. 1993) and Niklas Luhmann (1997), to operate in the register of semantics, exchanging information, that is exchange of units of not just meaning but inequivalence, units of difference with their environment: operating through potentially co-evolutionary structural couplings and exchanges of difference with other such predicating machines.

Chapter 6 takes the narrative from Chapter 5 into the realm of the political. Starting from such a new metaphysical nature of capitalism necessarily takes you into an ontological politics. Chapters 5 and 6, 7 – from the economic through the political – are explorations in intensive culture that are strictly ontological. At stake is Immanuel Kant's 'what-can-I-know'. But it is not in the 'what-can-I-know' that we can find an intensive politics in Kant. Kantian intensive politics, as Karl Marx's politics, are elsewhere. They are not in political ontology discussed above. Kant gives us the basis for *critical* theory in his famous 'Enlightenment' essay. But critique here is not to be found in ontology. Critique as political intensity or a politics of intensity is also not to be found in the Kantian 'what-should-I-do'.[4] There is something too generic, too abstract, too judgemental, indeed too constraining in the freedom of Kant's ethics. This is where notions of justice and ethics in Jürgen Habermas come unstuck. The more Habermasian discursive will ethics moves back towards analytic philosophy, the more Habermas exits the critical theory of his youth. The critical politics of intensity is formed in neither the 'what-can-I-know' nor the 'what-should-I-do', but in the *'what-can-I-hope'*. The 'what-can-I-hope' is the utopian promise of Enlightenment. It is a utopian promise that the critical political can address. Thus a Kantian politics of critique should start neither from the first (1929) nor the second (1956) critique, but from *The Critique of Judgement* (1952), the third critique. This is not in the objectivity or generality of the first and second critiques but in the subjectivity of the third and 'aesthetic' critique. The rational 'to-come', the promised 'community-to-come' of the third critique stems from such subjectivity. This brings the politics of Enlightenment utopias together with the aesthetic sublime. In the first critique nature is an instrument: an instrumentality. In Kant's third critique we engage with nature not as an instrumentality but as a finality (Lyotard 1994). When we encounter nature, and also things, rules, relationships as not instruments but as finalities, we open up this space of hope: a space of a politics of what we would now call – with Benjamin and Derrida (1992) – *justice*. This 'what-can-I-hope', which form reasoned and Enlightenment utopic thought and politics in Marx and in Kant, is first thought in the dimension not of the ontological but in the messianic tones, of *the religious*. Walter Benjamin is implicitly aware of this in his 'On Language' in reformulating Leibniz's monad, i.e. the intensity, in the space no longer of the ontological but the religious. In his 'Critique of Violence', it is formulated explicitly as a politics of justice.

Derrida (1992) says justice is the 'undeconstructible'.[5] Derrida and Levinas do, however, deconstruct ontology. Levinas and Derrida deconstruct the Greek to arrive at 'the Jew', at the 'what-can-I-hope'.[6] The other side of this religious of messianic hope is St Paul's question of faith. In many ways Pauline faith stands opposed to hope and the messianic. If the gospel is the good news that redemption is already here, then the 'what-can-I-hope' can be reduced to 'how-can-I-save-my-own-soul'. That is, the religious can be displaced from Kant's and Benjamin's to-come to Heidegger's 'already-there', its challenge to 'law' to pitting Canon Law against the positive law of the state. Yet Paul in the *Epistle to the Romans* is also the spirit of the universal: of 'neither Jew nor Greek', 'neither slave nor freeman', 'neither man nor woman' (Badiou 2003). This universal does not have to be Roman Catholic Canon Law. It can be a universal against law, if it is possible, with Jakob Taubes (2004) and Giorgio Agamben (2006) who do write in the spirit of this critical politics of intensity, to displace Pauline faith from the good news of the already-there into a messianic what-can-I-hope. The what-can-I-hope becomes a future universalization: a future universalization of justice. The universalization of culture, then, is not just on the basis of the global extensity of commodification. It is a universalization of intensive culture: driven by both the abstract transcendental of the Greek *logos* and the personal transcendental of the Judaic (Christian) God. These two sides of intensive culture tell us in the West (and not just in the West) who we are. We are ontological and Greek. Our subjectivity is forged in the religious, in the Judaic.

Intensity's outside: Chinese social theory?

Max Weber draws on St Paul's universal in the context of his discussions of religion and the rise of not Western capitalism, but Western democracy. In *The Religion of India* (1961), Weber contrasts Peter as the Apostle to the more particularistic Jews with Paul as Apostle to the Gentiles. He suggests first that the particularism, and clan or tribal character of the historic Chinese and Indian guilds makes it difficult to develop democracy in Chinese and Indian cities. In the Mediaeval West, however, due partly to Christian universalism, the guilds crossed clan barriers. With Christian Universalism there was the intercommensality, the drinking together, the more open marriage system of the Western cities. This permitted the aggregation of more encompassing interests and the breaking of clan ties for the emerging individualism of democracy. The question is where is the East in all this? Where is the South and East in the context of such universalization. This is especially important in today's new global order, which is largely driven by the emerging economies – by China, India, the Arab world, Africa, Brazil and Russia. Twenty-first-century globalization and global culture is, on the one hand, about informationalization, about what we have called 'machines of predication', which are technological systems of representation and communication. But this cognitive and cultural capitalism is only one-half of the emerging twenty-first-century global order. The other half is the new driving force of the emerging nations, and above all the rise of China.

What is this possible, not just informationalization but also Easternization of global culture? Chinese thought and Chinese culture seem to escape our conceptual framework. We can epistemologically attribute predicates to things, or ontologically understand things as generating their own predicates. Chinese thought does neither of these. It devalues predication on all sides. It is in the first instance neither epistemological nor ontological. Chinese thought is formed apart from both extensity and intensity. It does not start from the ontological question of 'What is this?' There is no obsessive will to truth. Now Chinese thought is surely Westernized. But there is much more to it than that. Chinese thought is not intensive.

Ontology is not at the centre of Chinese thought, or arguably more generally of Chinese culture. It is unlike Western thought, which is driven by the (Jullien 2008) 'qu-est-ce que c'est', by the what-is-it that embrace epistemology and ontology and in which the ontological embraces the epistemological. But Chinese thought and the Chinese language are primarily interested in neither epistemology nor ontology. There is no word for substance in Chinese. Substance in the sense of 'standing under', as we saw in Chapter 3, is fundamentally about cause. There is no idea of this sort of cause at the heart of things in Chinese. Nor is there a strong idea of external, 'efficient', cause. Instead, a thing, a *dongxi* (东西), which is east–west, is already a relation, a polarity, an 'east–west'. Look at the names of China's provinces: these are often relations – they are not Indiana, Ohio, Illinois and Florida, but instead are Henan (河南) (south of the (Yellow) River), Hunan (湖南) (south Lake Dongting), Nanjing (南京) (southern capital), Beijing (北京) (northern capital), Dongjing (东京) (eastern capital), Hebei (河北), Jiangsu (江苏), Zhejiang (浙江). All of these are relations. None is at the essence or the source of a place – as are, for example, the Amerindian names of US states and cities like Chicago. But when Heidegger talks of the *Dingheit der Dinge*, the thingness of the thing, he is not speaking about the thing in terms of its totemic essence and energetics of the clan, nor is he talking about the thing as gift, sacrificial thing (cow). He is talking in the register of the 'Greek' tradition of explication. When the West asks its ontological question 'qu-est-ce que c'est', its 'what it is?', we are asking what causes it, how do we explain it, how do we account for it, how does it get here. The West is asking what are its predicates. Heidegger's 'thingness of the thing' is looking for the being of the thing, is wanting to know the thing intensively. In German, for thing, we can say *Ding* or *Gegenstand*, which is literally 'object' in the sense of standing against. *Das Ding* is looking for the intensive cause of the thing. In *Gegenstand* we are looking at the thing extensively. *Das Ding* is intensive, whereas the object or *Gegenstand* is extensive. But the *dongxi* is neither nor. It is a polarity. It is relational. It is outside at the same time as possibly in between both intensity and extensity.

What about predicates? Many Chinese sentences do not speak their verbs, or have verbs that are just assumed. For Francais Jullien (2004), efficacy in China comes from a very different place than for the West. In the West we follow subject–verb–object type thinking. We want to understand a thing in terms of its cause. And predication guides our efficacy. At stake here is predication as a subject–verb–object nature of action. We start from the model, from the more or less scientific model, the model that fully privileges the 'what-can-I-know'. The model that is from science: that deals with the necessary. For the Greeks this was very different from *techne*, which deals with the contingent. So action, even and especially instrumental action, is guided by this scientific model. This scientific model, this model of the necessary can be ontological or epistemological. We see it, above all, in what is called instrumental rationality. Before it is instrumental it is rational, which reason clearly and distinctly sets out the goal and the objectives. Jullien looks at military strategy and diplomatic thinking. Here you do not approach a situation with a model. Instead you evaluate a situation. You look at what might be the propensity of things in that situation. How things might unfold. You identify the potential in a situation. And then you insert yourself in that situation and act accordingly. This is strategic. But it is not instrumental rationality. It is neither Weberian 'epistemological instrumental rationality', nor is it 'ontological', substantive rationality that is at stake. For Westerners, predication is at the heart of sense making. Less so in Chinese. Instead, often something 'locational' is at stake. The same is true in Japanese and Korean sentences, in which the abstract, as disembedded subject 'I' has not got the same salience as in Western languages. In East Asia, you address another often not as an abstract, pronomial you or as a proper name, but in a locational, relational sense – as 'little sister', or 'big brother', or 'teacher'. Action makes sense less in terms of subject causing an object through a verb. Action is made sense of not so much causally but again relationally. It is not necessarily understood in terms of my singular cause, but instead in terms of my relations. Then the pronoun is less a question of the singular individual than family, to the clan, something relational.

This is an unwinding of both epistemology and ontology. It is maybe not beyond, but, as Jullien says, outside both epistemology and ontology. A sentence in Chinese often begins with the spatio-temporal setting. In place of Western subject–verb–object, sense-making seems to be mere 'adverbial'. But an adverb modifies a verb, an adjective or another adverb, in Chinese culture – the 'adverb' does not really 'modify'. To modify the subject, you need to start from the subject. In Chinese situational grammar you start from 'the there' itself. So it is not so much adverbial, although we speak of here (*zher* 这儿) and there (*nar* 俹儿). It is not adverbial because what is important is not noun or verb modification, but the adverbial time–space itself. In each case it is not substance or subject that is at centre-stage. If the subject or substance is no longer at centre-stage, then neither is the predicate. Instead it is the situation that matters, more than the subject and his/her modifications and operations.

Intensive culture also comprises religion. But in Chinese thought, there is the primacy neither of epistemology/ontology, nor faith hope. If ontology or the *logos* (or even the word) is displaced in China into the Taoist 'way', the faith and hope of the other-worldy Judaeo–Christian collapses into this-worldly immanence. Chinese thought is not a question of *belief*. Or of faith, or of some kind of 'leap into faith'. It too is situational. God is *tian* (天), big or grown is *da* (大), and *tian* (天) is above *da* big. It is higher than big: it is the skies or heaven. There is not a transcendental either in the sense of the Greek abstract transcendental or the Judaic personal transcendental. *Tian* is not cosmologically unreachable. It is a little bit higher. It is an adverb without a noun. It again is a situation. Though the *logos* is displaced by the Tao and the centrality of what we might call practical reason*ing*, the Tao is not a question of the 'what should I do?' It is not regulated by an a priori. This practical reasoning – unlike practical reason – again is relational and come from relations of father–son, master–pupil, etc. And they are situational. The third Kantian critique, the 'what-can-I-hope' of reason, Enlightenment or the messianic, is not there in Chinese thought. At stake instead is very this-worldy, situational ethics and religion, to the extent that it is religion. Yes you may be able to criticize the Emperor, but without a messianic or Enlightenment 'what-can-I-hope' there may be little ground for critique. In China these are not notions of justice in the sense of say Benjamin and Derrida. There is not even the transcendental of positive law in which legal norms subsume facts. This is Max Weber's legal–rational legitimation and authority. In the Chinese notion of law (*fa* 法), there is not norm subsuming fact, but a river radical in the Chinese character that reminds us of an immanent law of 'the way', the flow of the river. In contrast to Weberian legal–national legitimacy the emperor is legitimate if he can control the Yellow River flooding the plains. The emperor or the place of the emperor, here is being legitimated in relation to the emperor's subjects. Even today the head judge of Hunan province is concerned less with the loyalty of the courts than administering the authority of the emperor (party) in Hunan.

So in very important ways what is at stake in China is neither ontology nor religion. Not intensive culture. In twenty-first-century capitalism, alongside the sort of metaphysical, intensive capitalism of invention we spoke of – the non-linear capitalism of machines of predication – there may be through the intertwinement of East and

West a more situated and relational sort of capitalism. One that works through affect and long-termism. This seems already on the cards as a reaction to the credit crunch of 2007, the bank crash of autumn 2008 and the move of sovereign wealth funds from emerging economies like China and the Gulf to capitalize Western banks and indeed finance Western sovereign debt. We see the crisis of the Washington Consensus, and the rise to prominence of some sort of Beijing model, as states in the Anglo-Saxon neo-liberal economies come to bail out their banking sectors for 'non-performing loans' and their equivalent on a scale seemingly more socialist than actually existing socialism. We see a finance sector based on the anonymization of financial products in meltdown and ask whether there might develop a more 'Eastern' relational mode of finance – based on long-term relations between creditor and debtor, in which the state, regions and municipalities will play a greater role. As for the political, we have spoken of the juxtaposition of extensive, 'ontic' or utilitarian politics, that is, *die Politische*, to an intensive and ontological politics of *das Politische*. And once we move from ontology to the critical politics of the to-come and the religiously inspired messianic, we move to a third, say *der Politische*, which is a much more contingent space than ontological politics. In this extra-ontological space, there is not just the politics of a 'to-come'.

Where is Chinese politics in all this? It inevitably comprises assumptions of dynasty, hence an idea of democracy primarily as the right to criticize central power, never having experienced the Greek cycle between democracy, aristocracy and monarchy. But even more important, unlike Western ethics of the 'what-should-I-do?', politics would be highly situational: you come to it without an ethical or utilitarian model, but work instead in reasoning from evaluations of a particular conjuncture. What about the universal? What possible universalization for today's Eastern and Southern driven globalization? How do we bridge from the Western extensive and intensive universal, shot through with science and based in other-worldly religion? How do we bridge from this to intensive culture's outside in a very situational, even empiricist and relational universal, whose ethos in China may just spread by degrees? We don't do this through treating the non-West as an abstract other. If we can see Chinese culture and political culture as situated, then perhaps we can also understand Western political culture too, less as universal than as situated. Then perhaps if we can think in terms of the possibility of mutual intelligibility (Jullien 2008). And work through a situated transcultural hermeneutics. Western democracy, with its moralism and utilitarianism, has its shortcomings. We should not and cannot wish it on China. A different universalization through such mutual intelligibility may be able to help China find its own way in this, as it may help us escape our instrumental and moralistic excesses.

Finally, China – and for that matter India – like the Euro-American world, is increasingly a technological culture. These emerging giants are not just the world's factory, but high-value-added production is becoming pervasive, especially given the strength of the engineering and general educational infrastructure. Every major Chinese and now Indian metropolis has a knowledge-economy strategy. China and India are increasingly running balance of trade surpluses with the United States in high-technology products. China, India and the 'emerging world' are developing a cognitive and cultural capitalism which features the presence and innovation in what we have understood as such self-organizing systems of invention, such predicating machines of representation and communication. We have understood this in terms of a certain materialization of mind and intensification of matter. But how does this work in cultures driven not by our individualistic conceptions of mind. In again, for example, China, there is a very strong notion – though it is not other-worldly – of mind or the spiritual. Yet it may work perhaps less through the individual than through a mind constituted in dyads, groups and other relationalities. Chinese, Indian and other emerging nations are increasingly, like we are, tied to a technological culture of such machines of predication, representation and communication. Given the contemporary geopolitical conjuncture, we have no choice but to seek out modes of structural coupling, of information exchange, of the exchange of difference between 'our' and 'their' technological cultures. The challenge, given the twenty-first-century geopolitical conjuncture, is such human and machinic inter-intelligibility between intensive culture and its increasingly constitutive outside.

Notes

1 See Deleuze, *The Fold: Leibniz and the Baroque* (1993a).
2 See Chantal Mouffe, *On the Political* (2005).
3 We encounter this in the intertwining of symbolic, imaginary and real in Jacques Lacan's mathematical topology of the Borromean Knot (see Žižek 2008: 181). Let me thank Celia Lury for introducing me to topology.
4 See F. Jullien, *De l'universel* (2008).
5 I am indebted to Andrew Benjamin on this point.
6 See Derrida, 'Violence and Metaphysics' (1967).

References

Agamben, G. (1999) *Potentialities*. Stanford, CA: Stanford University Press.

Agamben, G. (2006) *The Time that Remains: A Commentary on the Letter to the Romans*. Stanford, CA: Stanford University Press.

Alexander, J. (ed.) (1990) *Durkheimian Sociology: Cultural Studies*. Cambridge: Cambridge University Press.

Alliez, E. (1999) 'Présentation: Tarde et le probleme de la constitution', in Gabriel Tarde, *Monadologie et sociologie*. Paris: Empêcheurs de Penser en Rond. Originally published 1893. pp. 9–32.

Appadurai, A. (1986) 'Commodities and the Politics of Value', in A. Appadurai (ed.), *The Social Life of Things*. Cambridge: Cambridge University Press.

Aristotle (1963) *Categoriae and de Interpretatione*. Trans. J.L. Ackrill. Oxford: Clarendon Press.

Aristotle (1998) *The Metaphysics*. Trans. H. Lawson-Tancred. London: Penguin.

Badiou, A. (2003) *Saint Paul: The Foundation of Universalism*. Stanford, CA: Stanford University Press.

Badiou, A. (2005) *Being and Event*. London: Continuum.

Bateson, G. (2000) *Steps to an Ecology of Mind*. Chicago: University of Chicago Press.

Beck, U. (1992) *Risk Society*. London: Sage.

Beck, U., Giddens, A. and Lash, S. (1994) *Reflexive Modernization*. Cambridge: Polity Press.

Benedict XVI, Pope (2007) *Jesus of Nazareth*. London: Bloomsbury.

Benjamin, W. (1974a) 'Der Begriff der Kunstkritik in der deutschen Romantik', in W. Benjamin, *Abhandlungen. Gesammelte Schriften*, Vol. I-1. Frankfurt am Main: Suhrkamp.

Benjamin, W. (1974b) 'Erkenntniskritische Vorrede, Ursprung des deutschen Trauerspiels', in W. Benjamin, *Abhandlungen. Gesammelte Schriften*, Vol. I-1. Frankfurt am Main: Suhrkamp.

Benjamin, W. (1977a) 'Franz Kafka: Zur zehnten Wiederkehr seines Todestages', in W. Benjamin, *Aufsätze, Essays, Vorträge. Gesammelte Schriften*, Vol. II-2. Frankfurt am Main: Suhrkamp. pp. 409–438.

Benjamin, W. (1977b) *The Origin of German Tragic Drama*. London: Verso.

Benjamin, W. (1977c) 'Uber Sprache überhaupt und über die Sprache des Menschen', in W. Benjamin, *Aufsätze, Essays, Vorträge. Gesammelte Schriften*, Vol. II-1. Frankfurt am Main: Suhrkamp.

Benjamin, W. (1977d) 'Zur Kritik der Gewalt', in W. Benjamin, *Aufsätze, Essays, Vorträge. Gesammelte Schriften*, Vol. II-1. Frankfurt am Main: Suhrkamp. pp. 179–203.

Benjamin, W. (1977e) 'Karl Kraus', in W. Benjamin, *Aufsätze, Essays, Vorträge. Gesammelte Schriften*, Vol. II-1. Frankfurt am Main: Suhrkamp. pp. 334–367.

Benjamin, W. (1996a) 'One Way Street', *Selected Works*, Vol. 1. Cambridge, MA: Belknap-Harvard. pp. 444–489.

Benjamin, W. (1996b) 'The Task of the Translator', *Selected Works*, Vol. 1. Cambridge, MA: Belknap-Harvard. pp. 213–225.

Benkler, Y. (2002) 'Coase's Penguin, or Linux and "The Nature of the Firm"', *Yale Law Journal*, 112: 369–446.

Bentley, P.J. and Corne, D. (eds) (2001) *Creative Evolutionary Systems*. London: Morgan Kaufmann.

Berger, P. (1990) *Sacred Canopy*. New York: Anchor.

Bergson, H. (1977) *The Two Sources of Morality and Religion*. Notre Dame, IN: University of Notre Dame Press.

Bergson, H. (1991) *Matter and Memory*. New York: Zone Books.

Bloch, E. (2004) *Das Prinzip Hoffnung*. Frankfurt: Suhrkamp.

Bobro, M. (2009) 'Leibniz on Causation', *Stanford Encyclopaedia of Philosophy*. Available online at: plato.stanford.edu/entries/leibniz-causation (accessed 20/04/2009).

Boeri, S. and Bregani, M. (2003) *Uncertain States of Europe*. Milan: Skira Editore.

Braverman, H. (1974) *Labor and Monopoly Capital*. New York: Monthly Review Press.

Burton, J. (2008a) 'Memories of the Future: a Study of the Themes of Salvation and Memory, in The Philosophy of Henri Bergson and the Science Fiction of Philip K. Dick', PhD thesis, Goldsmiths, University of London.

Burton, J. (2008b) 'Machines Making Gods: Philip K. Dick, Henri Bergson and Saint Paul', *Theory, Culture & Society*, 25 (7–8): 262–284.

Butler, J., Laclau, E. and Zizek, S. (2000) *Contingency, Hegemony, Universality*. London: Verso.

CCCS (2006) *On Ideology*. London: Routledge.

Castells, M. (1977) *The Urban Question*. Cambridge, MA: MIT Press.

Castells, M. (1989) *The Informational City*. Oxford: Blackwell.

Castells, M. (1996) *The Network Society*. Oxford: Blackwell.

Coase, R.H. (1937) 'The Nature of the Firm', *Economica*, 4 (16): 386–405.

Coase, R.H. (1960) 'The Problem of Social Cost', *Journal of Law and Economics*, 3 (1): 1–44.

Cohen, G.A. (1978) *Karl Marx's Theory of History: A Defence*. Oxford: Oxford University Press.

Colebrook, C. (2005) *Philosophy and Post-Structural Theory*. Edinburgh: Edinburgh University Press.

Copleston, F. (2003) *A History of Philosophy, Volume 4. The Rationalists: Descartes to Leibniz*. London: Continuum.

Crotty, J. (2005) 'The Neo-Liberal Paradox: Impact of Finance on Nonfinancial Corporation Performance', in G. Epstein (ed.), *Financialization and the World Economy*. Northampton, MA: Edward Elgar. pp. 77–110.

Crumb, R. (1986) *The Religious Experience of Philip K. Dick*, Weirdo Comix, no. 17, Summer.

Cui, Z. (1998) 'Whither China? The Discourse on Property Rights in the Chinese Reform Context', *Social Text*, 55 (16): 67–81.

Cyert, R. and March, J. (1992) *The Behavioral Theory of the Firm*. New York: Wiley.

Davies, W. (2009) 'Competition and Competitiveness: A Cultural-Political Economy Analysis', PhD thesis, Goldsmiths, University of London.

Davis, M. (2006) *Planet of Slums*. London: Verso.

Debord, G. (1993) *Panegyrique*, Vol. 1. Paris: Gallimard.

Delanda, M. (2001) *Intensive Science and Virtual Philosophy*. London: Continuum.

Deleuze, G. (1968) *Différence et Repetition*. Paris: Presses Universitaires de France.

Deleuze, G. (1983) *Cinéma 1: L'Image-mouvement*. Paris: Minuit.

Deleuze, G. (1988) *Le pli: Leibniz et la Baroque*. Paris: Les Éditions de Minuit.

Deleuze, G. (1993a) *The Fold: Leibniz and the Baroque*. London: Athlone.

Deleuze, G. (1993b) *The Logic of Sense*. New York: Columbia University Press.

Deleuze, G. (2003) *Francis Bacon: The Logic of Sensation*. London: Athlone.

Deleuze, G. and Guattari, F. (1972) *Capitalisme et Schizophrénie*. Vol 1: *I' Aniti-Oedipe*. Paris: Éditions de Minuit.

Deleuze, G. and Guattari, F. (1984) *Anti-Oedipus: Capitalism and Schizophrenia*, Vol. I. London: Athlone.

Demetz, P. (1986) 'Introduction' to Walter Benjamin, *Reflections*. New York: Shocken Books.

Derrida, J. (1967) 'Violence et metaphysique: Essai sur la pensée d'Emmanuel Levinas', in J. Derrida, *L'Écriture et la Différence*. Paris: Éditions du Seuil.

Derrida, J. (1987) *The Truth in Painting*. Chicago: University of Chicago Press.

Derrida, J. (1989) *Edmund Husserl's 'Origin of Geometry': An Introduction*. Omaha, NB: University of Nebraska Press.

Derrida, J. (1992) 'Force of Law' in D. Cornell et al. (eds), *Deconstruction and the Possibility of Justice*. London: Routledge. pp. 3–68.

Derrida, J.C. (1993) *Spectres de Marx*. Paris: Galilée.

Dick, P.K. (1991) *The Transmigration of Timothy Archer*. New York: Vintage.

Dick, P.K. (2001) *VALIS*. New York: Gollancz.

Dover, G. (2001) *Dear Mr. Darwin: Letters on the Evolution of Life and Human Nature*. London: Phoenix.

Durkheim, E. (1947) *Elementary Forms of Religious Life*. Trans. J. Swain. London: Allen & Unwin.

Durkheim, E. (1968) *Les Formes Élémentaires de la Vie Réligieuse*. Paris: Presses Universitaires de France.

Durkheim, E. (1982) *The Rules of Sociological Method*. New York: Free Press.

Durkheim, E. (1995) *The Elementary Forms of Religious Life*. Trans. K. Fields. London: Routledge.

Durkheim, E. and Mauss, M. (2009) *Primitive Classification*. London: Routledge.

Duttmann, A.G. (2000) *The Gift of Language*. London: Athlone.

Fenves, P. (2001) *Arresting Language*. Stanford, CA: Stanford University Press.

Foucault, M. (1966) *Les Mots et les Choses: Une Archéologie des Sciences Humaines*. Paris: Gallimard.

Foucault, M. (1998a) *The History of Sexuality: The Will to Knowledge*. London: Penguin.

Foucault, M. (1998b) *The History of Sexuality: The Use of Pleasure*. London: Penguin.

Foucault, M. (2008) *The Birth of Biopolitics: Lectures at the College de France, 1978–1979*. London: Palgrave Macmillan.

Freeland, C. (2009) 'Lunch with the FT: Larry Summers', *Financial Times*, 10 July.

Freud, S. (1991) *Die Traumdeutung* (The Interpretation of Dreams). Frankfurt: Fischer Taschenbuch.

Freud, S. (2001) *Totem and Taboo*. London: Routledge.

Frisby, D. (1985) *Fragments of Modernity*. Cambridge: Polity Press.

Frush, S. (2007) *Understanding Hedge Funds*. New York: McGraw-Hill.

Fujita, M., Krugman, P. and Venables, A. (1999) *The Spatial Economy: Cities, Regions and International Trade*. Cambridge, MA: MIT Press.

Galbraith, J.K. (1969) *The Great Crash, 1929*. Harmondsworth: Penguin.

Garfinkel, H. (1984) *Studies in Ethnomethodology*. Cambridge: Polity Press.

Gehlen, A. (1997) *Der Mensch, Seine Natur und Seine Stellung in der Welt*. Stuttgart: UTB.

Goethe, J.W. (1970) *Theory of Colours*. Cambridge, MA: MIT Press.

Greenspan, A. (2007) *The Age of Turbulence*. New York: Allen Lane.

Griffin, G. (2002) *The Creature from Jekyll Island: A Second Look at the Federal Reserve*. New York: Amer Media.

Gunning, T. (2003) The Exterior as *Interieur*'. Benjamin's Optical Detective, *Boundary* 2, 30 (1): 105–130.

Haila, A. (2007) 'The Market as the New Emperor', *International Journal of Urban and Regional Research*, 31: 3–20.

Hardt, M. and Negri, A. (2000) *Empire*. Cambridge, MA: Harvard University Press.

Harvey, D. (2005) *A Brief History of Neoliberalism*. Oxford: Oxford University Press.

Hayles, N.K. (1999) *How We Became Posthuman*. Chicago: University of Chicago Press.

Hegel, G.W.F (1967) *The Philosophy of Right*. Oxford: Oxford University Press.

Hegel, G.W.F (1977) *The Phenomenology of Spirit*. Oxford: Oxford University Press.

Heidegger, M. (1954) 'Die Frage nach der Technik', in M. Heidegger, *Vorträge und Aufätze*. Stuttgart: Verlag Günter Neske.

Heidegger, M. (1986) *Sein und Zeit*. Tübingen: Niemeyer.

Helle, H. (2001) *Georg Simmel: Einführung in seine Theorie und Methode*. Munich: Oldenbourg.

Hewett, C. (2006) 'John Locke's Theory of Knowledge (An Essay Concerning Human Understanding)', *The Great Debate*. Available online at: thegreatdebate. org.uk/LockeEpist (accessed 21/03/2009).

Hilferding, R. (1968) *Das Finanzkapital*. Frankfurt: Europäische Verlag.

Hirst, P. (1979) *On Law and Ideology*. London: Macmillan.

Horkheimer, M. and Adorno, T. (1972) *Dialectic of Enlightenment*. New York: Herder.

Hörl, E. (2005) *Die heilige Kanäle*. Zurich: Diaphanes.

Hulswit, M. (2005) 'A Short History of Causation'. Available online at: library. utoronto.ca/see/SEEDVol4-3/Hulswit (accessed 21/03/2009).

Husserl, E. (1982) *The Origins of Geometry*. New York: Nicolas Hays.

Husserl, E. (1993) *Ideen zu einer reinen Phänomenologie und phänomenologischen Philosophie*. Tübingen: Max Niemeyer Verlag.

Hutton, W. (1998) *The Stakeholding Society*. Cambridge: Polity Press.

Huyssein, A. (1987) *After the Great Divide: Modernism, Mass Culture and Postmodernism*. Bloomington, IN: Indiana University Press.

James, W. (1983) *The Varieties of Religious Experience*. London: Penguin Classics.

Jessop, B. (2007) *State Power*. Cambridge: Polity Press.

Jullien, F. (2004) *Treatise on Efficacy*. Honolulu: University of Hawaii Press.

Jullien, F. (2006) 'Deuxième jour', in B. Latour and P. Gagliardi (eds), *Les Atmosphères de la Poltique*. Paris: Les Empêcheurs de Penser Rond.

Jullien, F. (2008) *De l'Universel*. Paris: Fayard.

Jung, W. (1990) *Georg Simmel zur Einführung*. Hamburg: Junius Verlag.

Kant, I. (1784) 'Beantwortung der Frage: 'Was ist Aufklärung?', *Berlinische Monatsschrift*. Zwölftes Stük. December. pp. 516 ff.

Kant, I. (1929) *A Critique of Pure Reason*. London: Macmillan.

Kant, I. (1952) *The Critique of Judgement*. Oxford: Clarendon.

Kant, I. (1956) *The Critique of Practical Reason*. Indianapolis: Bobbs-Merrill.

Kant, I. (2007) *Vorkritische Schriften bis 1768*, Teil I Werkeausgabe, Bd. i. Ed. Wilhelm Weischedel. Frankfurt: Suhrkamp.

Keat, R. and Urry, J. (1975) *Social Theory as Science*. London: Routledge.

Kittler, F. (1997) *Literature, Media, Information Systems*. Amsterdam: OPA.

Kittler, F. (2006) 'Thinking Colours and/or Machines', *Theory, Culture & Society*, 23: 39–50.

Köhnke, K. (1996) *Der junge Simmel in Theoriebeziehungen und sozialen Bewegungen*. Frankfurt am Main: Suhrkamp.

Koolhaas, R. and Mau, B. (1995) *S, M, L, XL*. Milan: Monacelli.

Kristeva, J. (1986) *The Kristeva Reader*. Oxford: Blackwell.

Kuczinski, P. and Williamson, J. (2003) *After the Washington Consensus: Restarting Growth and Reform in Latin America*. Washington, DC: Institute for International Economics.

Lacan, J. (1998) *Four Fundamental Concepts of Psychoanalysis*. New York: W.W Norton.

Laclau, E. (1977) *Politics and Ideology in Marxist Theory*. London: New Left Books.

Laclau, E. and Mouffe, C. (2001) *Hegemony and Socialist Strategy*. London: Verso.

Landkammer, J. (2001) 'Die Kunst des Resenzierens und die Verantwortung des Publizierens: Georg Simmels Frühschriften als Gedankenschmiede und Fundgrube für Spurensucher', *Literaturkritik.de*, 9 (September).

Lash, S. (1999) *Another Modernity, a Different Rationality*. Oxford: Blackwell.

Lash, S. (2002) *Critique of Information*. London: Sage.

Lash, S. and Lury, C. (2007) *Global Culture Industry*. Cambridge: Polity Press.

Lash, S. and Urry, J. (1987) *The End of Organized Capitalism*. Cambridge: Polity Press.

Latour, B. (1993) *We Have Never Been Modern*. Hemel Hempstead: Harvester Wheatsheaf.

Lazzarato, M. (1999) 'Tarde: un vitalisme politique', in G. Tarde, *Monadologie et Sociologie*. Paris: Empêcheurs de penser en rond. Originally published 1893. pp. 103–150.

Lazzarato, M. (2002) *Puissances de l'Invention: La Psychologie Économique de Gabriel Tarde Contre l'Économie Politique*. Paris: Empêcheurs de penser en rond.

Lazzarato, M. (2004) *Les Révolutions du Capitalisme*. Paris: Empêcheurs de Penser en Rond.

Leibniz, G.W. (1985) *Theodicy: Essays on the Goodness of God, the Freedom of Man and the Origin of Evil*. Chicago: Open Court.

Leibniz, G.W. (1991) *The Monadology*. Pittsburgh, PA: University of Pittsburgh Press.

Leibniz, G.W. (1996) *New Essays on Human Understanding*. Cambridge: Cambridge University Press.

Levy-Bruhl, L. (2009) *The Philosophy of August Comte*. Cambridge: Cambridge Scholars.

Locke, J. (2008) *An Essay Concerning Human Understanding*. Oxford: Oxford University Press.

Lloyd, G. and Sivin, N. (2002) *The Way and the Word: Science and Medicine in Early China and Greece*. New Haven, CT: Yale University Press.

Loemker, L.E. (1968) 'Monad and Monadology', *The Encyclopaedia of Philosophy*, Vol. 5. New York: Macmillan and Free Press. pp. 361–363.

Loux, M. (2003) 'Aristotle: Metaphysics', in C. Shields (ed.), *The Blackwell Guide to Ancient Philosophy*. Oxford: Blackwell. pp. 163–183.

Luhmann, N. (1997) *Die Gesellschaft der Gesellschaft*. Frankfurt am Main: Suhrkamp.

Luhmann, N. (2008) *Legitimation durch Verfahren*. Frankfurt am Main: Suhrkamp.

Lury, C. (2004) *Brands*. London: Routledge.

Lyotard, J.-F. (1984) *The Postmodern Condition*. Minneapolis, MN: University of Minnesota Press.

Lyotard, J.-F. (1991) *Dérive à Partir de Marx et Freud*. Paris: Éditions Galilée.

Lyotard, J.-F. (1994) *Lessons on the Analytic of the Sublime*. Stanford, CA: Stanford University Press.

Mackenzie, A. (2005) 'The Performativity of Code: Software and Cultures of Circulation', *Theory, Culture & Society*, 22: 71–92.

Maigné, C. (1998) *Premières Leçons sur la Monadologie de Leibniz*. Paris: Presses Universitaires de France.

Malik, S. (2005) 'Information and Knowledge', *Theory, Culture & Society*, 22: 29–49.

Marshall, A. (1890) *The Principles of Economics*. London: Macmillan & Co.

Marx, K. (1967) *Capital*. Vol. 1. New York: International Publishers.

Marx, K. (1973) *Grundrisse*. New York: Random House.

Massumi, B. (1996) 'The Autonomy of Affect', in P. Patton (ed.), *Deleuze: A Critical Reader*. Oxford: Blackwell. pp. 217–239.

Massumi, B. (2002) *Parables for the Virtual*. New York: Zone Books.

Mauss, M. (2001) *The Gift*. London: Routledge.

McLuhan, M. (2001) *Understanding Media*. London: Routledge.

McRobbie, A. (1998) *Inside the Rag Trade*. London: Routledge.

Menninghaus, W. (1995) *Walter Benjamin's Theorie der Sprachmagie*. Frankfurt am Main: Suhrkamp.

Milbank, J. (2008) 'Paul against Biopolitics', *Theory, Culture & Society*, 25 (7–8): 125–172.

Morris, C. (2009) *The Sages: Warren Buffett, George Soros, Paul Volcker, and the Maelstrom of the Markets*. Washington, DC: Public Affairs.

Mouffe, C. (2005) *On the Political*. London: Routledge.

Moulier Boutang, Y. (2007) *Le Capitalisme Cognitive*. Paris: Éditions Amsterdam.

Moulier Boutang, Y. (2008) 'Finance, instabilité et la gouvernabilité des externalités', *Multitudes*, 32: 91–102.

Nancy, J.-L. (1990) *Une Pensée Finie*. Paris: Éditions Galilée.

Negri, A. (1999) *The Savage Anomaly*. Minneapolis, MN: University of Minnesota Press.

Nietzsche, F. (1966a) 'Die Geburt der Tragödie oder Greichentum und Pessimismus', in F. Nietzsche, *Werke in drei Bänden*, Vol. 1. Munich: Carl Hanser Verlag. pp. 1–134.

Nietzsche, F. (1966b) *Menschliches, Allzumenschliches: Ein Buch für freie Geister*, in F. Nietzsche, *Werke in drei Bänden*, Vol. 1. Munich: Carl Hanser Verlag.

Obrist, H.-U. (2003) 'Sarat Maharaj and Francisco Varela', in H.-U. Obrist, *Interviews*, Vol. 1. Milan: Edizioni Charta. pp. 538–559.

Parenteau, R. (2005) 'The Late 1990s' US Bubble: Financialization in the Extreme', in G. Epstein (ed.), *Financialization and the World Economy*. Northampton, MA: Edward Elgar. pp. 111–148.

Pigou, A. (1929) *The Economics of Welfare* (third edition). London: Macmillan and Co.

Poulantzas, N. (1978) *Classes in Contemporary Capitalism*. London: Verso.

Prigogine, I. and Stengers, I. (1984) *Order Out of Chaos*. London: Heinemann.

Reck, H.U. (2003) *Kunst als Medientheorie*. Munich: Wilhelm Fink Verlag.

Remnant, P. and Bennett, J. (1996) 'Introduction to Leibniz', in *New Essays on the Human Understanding*. Cambridge: Cambridge University Press.

Rescher, N. (1991) 'Introduction to Leibniz', *Monadology*. Pittsburgh, PA: University of Pittsburgh Press.

Rousseau, J.J. (1999) *Du Contract Social: Livres I à IV*. Paris: Nathan.

Rudrauf, D. et al. (2003) 'From autopoesis to neurophenomenology: Francisco Varela's exploration of the biophysics of being', *Biological Research*, 36: 27–65.

Schmitt, C. (1998) *Legalität und Legitimät*. Berlin: Duncker & Humblot.

Serres, M. (1968) *Le Système de Leibniz et ses Modèles Mathématiques*. Paris: Presses Universitaires de France.

Shannon, C. and Weaver, W. (1949) *The Mathematical Theory of Communication*. Champaign-Urbana: University of Illinois Press.

Sheehan, T. (1988) 'Hermeneia and Apophansis: The Early Heidegger on Aristotle', in Franco Volpi et al., *Heidegger et Idée de la Phénoménologie*. Dordrecht: Kluwer. pp. 67–80.

Simmel, G. (1889) 'Zur Psychologie des Geldes', *Jahrbuch für Gesetzgebung, Verwaltung und Volkswirtschaft im Deutschen Reich*, 13: 1251–1264.

Simmel, G. (1977) *Philosophie des Geldes*. Berlin: Duncker & Humblot.

Simmel, G. (1989a) 'Zur Psychologie der Frauen', *Aufsätze und Abhandlungen, 1887–1890. Gesamtausgabe*, Vol. 2. Frankfurt am Main: Suhrkamp. pp. 66–102.

Simmel, G. (1989b) 'Zur Psychologie der Scham', *Aufsätze und Abhandlungen, 1887–1890. Gesamtausgabe*, Vol. 2. Frankfurt am Main: Suhrkamp. pp. 49–65.

Simmel, G. (1989c) *Über soziale Differenzierung. Gesamtausgabe*, Vol. 2. Frankfurt am Main: Suhrkamp. pp. 109–296. Original is Leipzig: Duncker und Humblot, 1890.

Simmel, G. (1991) 'Einleitung in die Moralwissenschaft 2. Eine kritik der ethischen Grundbagriffe'. *Gesamtausgabe*, Vol. 4. Frankfurt am Main: Suhrkamp.

Simmel, G. (1992a) 'Excurs über das Problem: Wie ist die Gesellschaft möglich?', in *Soziologie: Untersuchungen über die Formen der Gesellschaftung. Gesamtausgabe*, Vol. 11. Frankfurt am Main: Suhrkamp. pp. 42–61.

Simmel, G. (1992b) 'Zur Psychologie der Mode. Sociologische Studien', *Aufsätze und Abhandlungen, 1894–1900. Gesamtausgabe*, Vol. 5. Frankfurt am Main: Suhrkamp. pp. 105–114.

Simmel, G. (1992c) 'Zur Psychologie und Soziologie der Lüge', *Aufsätze und Abhandlungen, 1894–1900. Gesamtausgabe*, Vol. 5. Frankfurt am Main: Suhrkamp. pp. 406–419.

Simmel, G. (1995) *Schopenhauer und Nietzsche. Georg Simmel Gesamtausgabe*, Vol. 10. Ed. O. Rammstedt. Frankfurt am Main: Suhrkamp. pp. 167–408.

Simmel, G. (1997) 'The Concept and Tragedy of Culture', in D. Frisby and M. Featherstone (eds), *Simmel on Culture*. London: Sage. pp. 55–74.

Simmel, G. (1999a) *Grundfrage der Soziologie. Georg Simmel Gesamtausgabe*, Vol. 16. Ed. O. Rammstedt. Frankfurt am Main: Suhrkamp. pp. 59–150. Originally published 1917.

Simmel, G. (1999b) *Lebensanschauung, Vier metaphysische Kapitel. Gesamtausgabe*, Vol. 16. Frankfurt am Main: Suhrkamp. pp. 209–425. Originally published 1918.

Simmel, G. (2000a) Elisabeth Forsters Nietzsche Biographie. Book Review. *Gesamtausgabe*, Vol. 1. Ed. K. Köhnke. Frankfurt am Main: Suhrkamp. pp. 346–352. Originally published 1895.

Simmel, G. (2000b) 'Henri Bergson', *Simmel, Aufsätze und Abhandlungen 1909–1918. Gesamtausgabe*, Vol. 13. Frankfurt am Main: Suhrkamp. pp. 53–69.

Simmel, G. (2000c) *Das Wesen der Materie nach Kants physchicher Monadologie. Gesamtausgabe*, Vol. 1. Ed. K. Köhnke. Frankfurt am Main: Suhrkamp. pp. 9–44. Originally published 1881.

Simondon, G. (1958) *Du Mode d'Existence des Objets Techniques*. Paris Aubier.

Simondon, G. (2007) *L'individuation Psychique et Collective*. Paris: Aubier.

Sloterdijk, P. (2004) *Sphären III, Schuäme*. Frankfurt am Main: Suhrkamp.

Smith, W.R. (2002) *Religion of the Semites*. Piscataway, NJ: Transaction.

Spencer, H. (1896) *Principles of Sociology*. New York: Appleton.

Spuybroek, L. (2004) *Machining Architecture*. London: Thames & Hudson.

Stiegler, B. (1998) *Technics and Time*. Stanford, CA: Stanford University Press.

Stiegler, B. (2004a) *La Misère Symbolique* Tome 1. L'époque hyperindustrielle. Paris: Éditions Galilée.

Stiegler, B. (2004b) *Mécréance et Discrédit. Vol. 1: La Décadence des Démocraties Industrielles*. Paris: Éditions Galilée.

Stiglitz, J. (1999) 'Knowledge as a Global Public Good', in I. Kaul et al. (eds), *Global Public Goods*. New York: Oxford University Press.

Strathern, M. (1992) *The Gender of the Gift*. Berkeley, CA: University of California Press.

Strauss, L. (1953) *Natural Right and History*. Chicago: University of Chicago Press.

Tarde, Gabriel (1999) *Monadologie et Sociologie*. Paris: Empêcheurs de penser en rond. Originally published 1893.

Taubes, J. (2004) *The Political Theology of St Paul*. Stanford, CA: Stanford University Press.

Tylor, E.B. (1873) *Primitive Culture*, Vol. I. London: John Murray.

Urry, J. (2002) *Global Complexity*. Cambridge: Polity Press.

Varela, F., Thompson, E. and Rosch, E. (1993) *The Embodied Mind*. Cambridge, MA: MIT Press.

Weber, A. (1909) *Über den Standort der Industrien*. Tübingen: JCB Mohr Verlag.

Weber, M. (1961) *The Religion of India*. New Delhi: Munshiram Manoharlal Publishers.

Whimster, S. (2007) *Understanding Weber*. London: Routledge.

White, H.C. (1992) *Identity and Control*. Princeton, NJ: Princeton University Press.

Williamson, O. (1976) *Markets and Hierarchies*. New York: Free Press.

Williamson, O. (1998) *The Economic Institutions of Capitalism*. New York: Free Press.

Witt, C. (1989) *Substance and Essence in Aristotle: An Interpretation of Metaphysics VII–IX*. Ithaca, NY: Cornell University Press.

Woolhouse, R. (1993) *Descartes, Spinoza, Leibniz: The Concept of Substance in Seventeenth Century Metaphysics*. London: Routledge.

Wright, E.O. (1983) *Class, Crisis and the State*. London: Verso.

Žižek, S. (2008) *The Ticklish Subject*. London: Verso.

Index

Page references to Notes will have the letter 'n' following the note

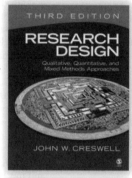

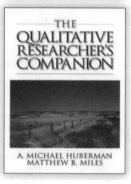